MW00899517

Power BI

For Beginners

Unlock the Full Potential of Data Analytics - Master Advanced
Techniques and Visualizations for Transforming Your Data into
Actionable Intelligence with Cutting-Edge Strategies

Copyright © 2024 **Alec Carter**

All Rights Reserved

This book or parts thereof may not be reproduced in any form, stored in any retrieval system, or transmitted in any form by any means—electronic, mechanical, photocopy, recording, or otherwise—without prior written permission of the publisher, except as provided by United States of America copyright law and fair use.

Disclaimer and Terms of Use

The author and publisher of this book and the accompanying materials have used their best efforts in preparing this book. The author and publisher make no representation or warranties with respect to the accuracy, applicability, fitness, or completeness of the contents of this book. The information contained in this book is strictly for informational purposes. Therefore, if you wish to apply the ideas contained in this book, you are taking full responsibility for your actions.

Printed in the United States of America

TABLE OF CONTENTS

INTRODUCTION

What's New in Power BI 2024?

Visual calculations

There's a new method for performing computations now! Visual calculations, which are DAX calculations written and performed directly on a visual, allow you to add calculations to your visual. Any data in the visual, such as columns, measurements, or other visual computations, can be referred to by a calculation. This method streamlines the DAX writing process and gets rid of the semantic model's complexity. Common business computations like running sums and moving averages can be finished visually. Calculations that were formerly extremely difficult or nearly impossible to complete are now simple to do with visual aids. You must activate the option to use visual calculations while in preview by going to Options and **Settings >Options > Preview features**. After choosing Visual Calculations, click **OK**. Restarting the Desktop will enable visual computations. You have to choose a visual before you can add a visual calculation.

Next, click the **ribbon's "New calculation" button:** In the visual calculations edit mode that appears, enter the term in the formula bar to add a visual calculation. One way to add a visual calculation to a visual that shows Sales Amount and Total Product Cost by Fiscal Year is to type Profit = [Sales Amount] - [Total Product Cost]. This will compute the profit for each year. Numerous DAX functions are currently available for use in visual computations. There are other functions available that are specialized in visual computations, like RUNNINGSUM, PREVIOUS, and MOVINGAVERAGE. Visual computations are far simpler to comprehend, create, and maintain with the help of these and other functions than they are with the existing DAX requirements.

Dynamic subscriptions for Power BI reports

For Power BI reports, dynamic per-recipient subscriptions are now available in Preview! You may now provide each receiver of an email subscription with a customized copy of a Power BI report, similar to dynamic subscriptions for paginated reports. Assume you have access to a report that details every team member's sales information. You wish to set up an email subscription to deliver a weekly PDF copy of this report, filtered to just display the sales results for each salesperson, to each of them. Connecting to a semantic model (formerly a Power BI dataset) that specifies the mapping between receivers and corresponding filter values is now possible to accomplish this. When it comes time to distribute the report, the most recent information in your semantic model will decide which employees should receive it via email and under what filter settings.

On-object Interaction Updates

Support for multi-visual container formats has been added! In the past, the format pane did not offer any formatting options when multiple selections were made across distinct types of graphics. We've now included formatting support for container formatting, so you can adjust the size, and background color, add a shadow, or switch on/off titles in bulk while you're multi-selecting different visuals. There has also been the addition of the ability to format the visual's container size and position even when it is not filled.

Power BI Home in Desktop is enabled by Default

Power BI Home is now available as the default experience! All of your Power BI operations within the desktop program now have a centralized, comfortable location thanks to the redesign of Power BI Home. The goal is to increase efficiency and simplify the process of finding and consuming material. You may now access your files and reports without having to go through several menus or tabs while using Power BI Home. Like other well-known office tools, this user-friendly interface acts as a hub where you can conveniently manage your reports from one place. Regardless of your level of experience with Power BI, Power BI Home guarantees a smooth and uniform experience for all your Power BI endeavors.

Enhanced Reference Layer in Power BI Azure Maps Visual

There is also a major update to the visual reference layer capability of Power BI Azure Maps. We have enhanced the reference layer's capabilities in response to insightful user input and under-changing industry requirements. Now users can use KML (Keyhole Markup Language) and WKT (Well-Known Text) formats in addition to the supported GeoJSON format. Along with file upload, there is also an integration URL as a data source. With this update, users may import spatial data into Power BI with even more ease and flexibility. The Power BI Azure Maps visual integrates data in several forms, including GeoJSON, KML, WKT, and URL links, to provide a comprehensive and adaptable geospatial analytical experience.

Storytelling in PowerPoint

You can paste a link to a specific report or select one that is offered to you when you add the Power BI add-in to a presentation. If the URL you copied from the browser address bar is a normal report link, and if your company allows shareable links and you have re-share access for this report, the Power BI add-in can replace the pasted link with a shareable link. In that instance, you will notice that a checkbox offering you automatic access to this report has been added underneath the report URL. Simply tick this option to have the Power BI add-in generate a shareable link for you. It is ensured that other users who are seeing the presentation have the necessary authorization to read the report by using a sharable link, eliminating the need for them to request access.

OVERVIEW OF THIS BOOK

This book about Power BI has been strategically and carefully written to ensure that readers are well informed and are also provided with the latest information as regards the major upgrades provided to Power BI.

This book has 10 chapters containing all you will need to get started with the use of Power BI. Below is an overview of all you will get to learn when you purchase this book. It is worth noting also that at the end of each chapter are activities designed to test your knowledge based on all you have read.

Chapter 1: Intro to Power BI

This is the first chapter of the book where you will be introduced to what Power BI is all about which includes its components, service, platform, and a host of other very important things needed to know. In this chapter, you will also learn about the SQL server which includes analysis service multidimensional and also server reporting services. Furthermore, in this chapter, you will learn about Vertipaq and DAX and you will also get to know about the various things that distinguish Power BI from all other competitors.

Chapter 2: The Report and Data Views

In this chapter, you will get to know more about the report view; the home section where you will learn about the clipboard subsection, and the data subsection and you will also learn about the queries subsection which involves the insert section and the calculation subsection. The insert tab is another part of the report view where you will learn about the pages' subsection, the visuals subsection, the AI visuals subsection, the power platform subsection as well as the elements subsection. The modeling tab is another aspect of the report view where you will learn about the relationships subsection, page refresh subsection, security subsection as well as the Q&A subsection. The help section, the external tools section, the pane interface of the report view, the visualizations pane, the fields, and filters pane, and the data view are some of the other things that you will get to learn about in this chapter.

Chapter 3: Importing and Modeling Our Data

In this chapter, you will learn how to get your data, and import data, and you will also learn about the power query ribbon. Also, you will learn about the transform tab, the add column tab, and the model view, and you will also be adequately informed about what a relationship is; here you will get to know about the various types of relationships in Power BI, how to create and manage various relationships in Power BI and you will also gain first-hand information about the various benefits and applications of relationships in Power BI.

Chapter 4: Let's Make Some Pictures

Visualizing data and the visualization pane are the features that will be made bare to you in this chapter. You will learn how to alter the interaction behavior, the use of the column and bar chart, stacked bar and column charts, and you will also learn about the use of clustered bar and column charts. Furthermore in this chapter, you will learn about waterfall charts which includes having a perfect understanding of the benefits of making use of waterfall charts in Power BI and also building a waterfall chart in Power BI. The line and area charts are also another very interesting chart you will learn about in this chapter; you will get to know how to create a line chart, area chart, stacked area chart, and also the line and stacked column chart. Other charts you will learn about in this chapter include the ribbon chart, the funnel chart, the scatter chart, and the pie and donut chart. Lastly in this chapter, you will learn about the treemap; you will learn about the map visuals, the flat visuals, gauge, card/multi-row card, table/matrix, and also the slicer.

Chapter 5: Aggregations, Measures, and DAX

In this chapter, you will learn about measures, calculated columns, calculated tables, the various types of functions, sum, average, minimum, and maximum, and you will also learn about standard deviation, variance, and median. Furthermore, you will get to learn about the implicit and explicit measures which include their characteristics and applications, and you will also learn about the interaction between rows and filter context.

Chapter 6: Putting the Puzzle Pieces Together: From Raw Data to Report

In this chapter, you will learn about your first data import, you will learn how to choose and transform the data when you import, you will learn how to get tables consolidated with append and you will also get to learn how to make use of merge to get columns from other tables. Furthermore in this chapter, you will learn how to auto-detect during load, get to configure other options, have a perfect understanding of additional options and you will also have access to automatic relationship updates.

Chapter 7: Advanced Reporting Topics in Power BI

In this chapter, you will learn about AI-powered visuals, and key influencers, and you will also learn how to make use of the key influencer's visuals in Power BI. Furthermore in this chapter, you will learn about the decomposition tree; which includes important benefits of the decomposition tree and also making use of the decomposition tree visuals in Power BI. Also, you will get more information about smart narrative, what-if-analysis which includes benefits, techniques, and also the best practices.

Chapter 8: Introduction to Power BI Service

In this chapter, you will learn about the basics of the service; you will get familiar with the navigation menu, home and browse feature, data hub, settings, metrics, and deployment pipelines, and you will also get to know what workspace is all about.

Chapter 9: Licensing and Deployment Tips

Licensing and all of the very important tips that are needed when it comes to deployment are the things discussed in this chapter. You will also learn about the common issues that may arise with licensing and tips for optimizing Power BI license costs.

Chapter 10: Third-Party Tools

In this concluding chapter, you will learn about the various third-party tools that you can also consult when making use of your Power BI.

CHAPTER 1
INTRO TO POWER BI

What Is Power BI?

For a brief period, picture yourself as a data analyst employed by a huge firm in a busy environment. Finding important insights from the data and presenting them clearly and concisely can be challenging since you are constantly inundated with a huge amount of data from a variety of sources. That being said, Power BI is a product that can change the way you analyze data. With the assistance of the advanced technology known as Power BI, you will be able to convert raw data into visually appealing reports and interactive dashboards. Thanks to its user-friendly interface, you can effortlessly establish connections with numerous data sources, be they databases, spreadsheets, or cloud services storing data. Popular tools that are simple to combine with Power BI include SQL Server, SharePoint, and Excel. Data retrieval and aggregation are made simple by this connection. Once your data is connected, Power BI allows you to work with it and model it the way you need it to.

You may quickly merge tables, define associations between different datasets, and perform calculations to create a well-organized and structured foundation for your study. Because of its adaptable data modeling features, which let you investigate the buried relationships and patterns in your data, you can gain deeper insights. However, Power BI's true strength lies in the data visualization tools it provides. The days of employing static graphics and dull spreadsheets are long gone. A vast array of dynamic visualizations, such as bar charts, line graphs, maps, and gauges, are available to users of Power BI. Drag and drop data fields onto a canvas to quickly and simply create stunning visualizations that make your data come to life. Your ability to communicate effectively is enhanced and stakeholders can grasp insights quickly thanks to these visually stunning and interactive reports that make complex information easy to understand. Beyond only its appearance, Power BI is supported by a strong and effective engine that manages large datasets with unexpected speed and agility. Your reports will always be up to date thanks to real-time updates and the ability to refresh data, which will also provide you with the most recent information to help you make decisions promptly.

Using Power BI's sophisticated analytics features, you may gain fresh insights and a deeper understanding of your data. You may perform intricate computations, find patterns in the data, and identify anomalies thanks to these functionalities. To enable colleagues to review the data, pose inquiries, and provide their perspectives, you may easily share your dashboards and reports with others. One additional aspect of Power BI is collaboration. Power BI's collaboration capabilities facilitate smooth interaction, which in turn fosters a culture of data-driven decision-making across your company. Finally, when it comes to data analysis, Power BI is the most dependable companion you could hope for. It enables you to exchange, link, model, and show your data in ways that were previously unthinkable. With Power BI, you can transform unprocessed data into actionable insights that can help your company make better decisions and move closer to success. Therefore, you should make use of Power BI's capabilities if you want to get the most out of your data analysis efforts.

Power BI Components

Users are now able to produce and use reports based on your data with the help of a wide selection of products that together make up Power BI today. **The following is a list of all the components that are included in the Microsoft Power BI family of products, as provided by Microsoft:**

- Power BI Desktop
- Power BI service
- Power BI Mobile
- Power BI Report Builder
- Power BI Report Server on-premises
- Power BI Embedded

- **Power BI Desktop:** This Windows program serves as the main development tool for designing and creating interactive dashboards and reports. Microsoft is the company behind Power BI Desktop. Among its many features is a wide range of data linking possibilities, data transformation capabilities, modeling tools, and visualization capabilities. In addition to creating intricate data models and implementing custom calculations using DAX (Data Analysis Expressions), Power BI Desktop users may produce visually appealing reports and dashboards. This tool is used by anyone while generating and editing Power BI content before submitting it to the Power BI Service.
- **Power BI Service:** Also referred to as Power BI Online and Power BI Cloud, Microsoft's Power BI Service is a web-based platform. Microsoft makes it available. With the usage of this capability, users may publish, share, and collaborate on Power BI dashboards and reports. With Power BI Service, users can safely store and manage their data on the cloud. Additionally, users may use a web browser or the Power BI mobile app to access reports and dashboards from any place, schedule data refreshes, and create data-driven alerts. It has strong analytics capabilities along with additional features like collaboration and content sharing.
- **Power BI Mobile**: These are a selection of mobile apps that are available for download on mobile devices made by Apple and Google, respectively. It enables users to access and engage

with Power BI reports and dashboards when they are on the go. Users may access and explore data, receive notifications based on data, and stay connected to their company's data insights even when they are not at their desks thanks to the responsive and optimized experience provided by the mobile apps. With Power BI Mobile, users can consume data more conveniently and adaptably by guaranteeing they will always have access to their most critical information, no matter where they are.

- **Power BI Report Builder**: Users can create paginated reports in Power BI with this stand-alone application. Examples of the typical, fixed-layout reporting requirements that frequently necessitate the use of these reports are statements, invoices, and operational reports. The broad feature set of Power BI Report Builder includes features that may be utilized to build and author pixel-perfect reports, including table-based layouts, flexible formatting options, and complex parameters. Businesses that need precise control over the format and content of their structured reports—which are primarily printed out—will find it very useful.

- **Power BI Report Server (on-premises)**: Businesses may host, manage, and distribute Power BI reports inside their infrastructure with the help of Power BI Report Server, a reporting solution. It is the Power BI Report Server version that is hosted on-premises. By offering a mechanism to keep sensitive data and reports on local servers, it guarantees compliance with regulatory standards and our data governance principles. Similar capability to the Power BI Service is offered by the Power BI Report Server. These features include secure information exchange within an organization's network, data updating, and interactive reports.

- **Power BI Embedded**: Developers can directly incorporate Power BI dashboards and results into other websites or applications with the help of this service. Thanks to this innovation, which enables developers to seamlessly incorporate Power BI's vast data visualization capabilities into their apps, end users will be able to view interactive reports and real-time analytics without ever leaving the primary application. Software developers, SaaS providers, and companies looking to offer embedded analytics to their clients outside of the company or to their staff often use Power BI Embedded.

These Power BI components cater to various areas of data analysis, reporting, and visualization. As a result, Power BI offers a comprehensive array of tools and services to address a wide variety of business objectives and scenarios.

Power BI Desktop

In the data-driven world of today, companies in a wide variety of fields are struggling to make sense of massive amounts of data. The ability to draw meaningful conclusions from this data has become necessary to make intelligent business decisions. Users are given the ability to connect, transform, and efficiently visualize data through the utilization of Microsoft's Power BI Desktop, which is a highly effective business intelligence application. With Power BI Desktop, a multitude of data sources, including databases, spreadsheets, websites, and cloud services, can be seamlessly integrated. Customers may extract data from a wide range of platforms, including SQL Server, Excel, SharePoint, Salesforce, Azure, and many more, thanks to its robust data integration. The ability to combine data from multiple sources simplifies the data integration process. Users can see their company's information from a wider angle as a result. Power BI Desktop provides you with a wealth of options for data transformation and modeling after it's linked. Users can clean, reformat, and modify their data using the more sophisticated Power Query Editor, or they can use the simpler user interface. Power Query users can use the program to do data cleaning tasks like eliminating duplicates, filtering records, and merging databases. Another function that Power BI Desktop supports is data modeling. With the use of this tool, users may create associations between tables, produce calculated measures and columns, and employ business rules to enhance data analysis.

One of Power BI Desktop's most prominent features is its ability to produce visually appealing and interactive data displays. The application may generate a variety of data visualization options, including tables, charts, graphs, maps, and customizable visualizations. With only a few clicks on the canvas, users can easily create visually appealing reports and dashboards by dragging and dropping fields and altering the corresponding visual elements. Power BI Desktop offers a wide range of formatting options, animations, and interactive capabilities, enabling users to present data in a way that is both engaging and relevant. Power BI Desktop offers capabilities for more sophisticated analysis, going beyond conventional approaches to data visualization. It works with Microsoft's modeling and data analysis tools, including the R scripting language and DAX (Data Analysis Expressions) data analysis tools. These features allow users to construct advanced measurements, carry out intricate computations, and build prediction models. With Power BI Desktop's Q&A tool, customers can quickly gain insights by asking questions about their data. Power BI Desktop's ability to accept natural language queries makes this possible. Collaboration and sharing of data-driven insights among individuals, teams, and organizations are facilitated with Power BI Desktop. Stakeholders from throughout the organization can see reports and dashboards that users upload to SharePoint or the Power BI service. With cloud hosting, Power BI provides real-time data refreshing and sharing features. Users can collaborate and make decisions using the gathered data thanks to these features. It is also easy for other users to access and share Power BI Desktop files (.pbix), which guarantees that collaboration on analysis and reporting is seamless. In the mobile-first world of today, being able to get data insights while on the go is essential. Because of the seamless interaction between the Power BI desktop application and the Power BI mobile app, users can view and interact with reports and dashboards on their mobile devices, including smartphones and tablets. Because of this cross-platform adaptability, users may access critical data insights from any device or operating system at any time and from any location.

Its components

The extremely distinctive components that make up the Power BI Desktop application. Because they are so essential to someone who is just starting with Power BI, the Power BI canvas and Power Query will be the elements that we focus on the most. The Power BI canvas is where you build your visualizations with the program. Consider the canvas to be a PowerPoint slide containing all of your data. This section will walk you through the process of dragging and dropping data into different kinds of visualizations so you can examine your data and gain new insights. In addition, you can format the images, add text boxes and photographs, and carry out several other operations here. Data modeling is essentially importing data and using Power Query to manipulate it. Unlike

Microsoft Excel, for instance, you can modify entire columns of data with Power BI by utilizing the built-in functions, wizards, and formulas of the application rather than individual data cells. You can create customized columns using Power Query according to the rules of your choice. You may add values from one table to another and merge multiple data tables into a single one with its help. Getting data from your sources is the starting point for everything in Power Query, and Power Query supports a very large number of different sources of data. You'd like to establish a connection to a database, right? SQL? Oracle? Teradata? You have nothing to worry about using Power Query. You want to obtain a table by establishing a connection to an Excel worksheet, right? No issue. Comma-separated values (CSV)? Easy. Cloud sources? Also not an issue.

The Power BI Service

Microsoft created the cloud-based business intelligence platform known as Power BI Service, which is often referred to as Power BI Online and Power BI Cloud. It works in conjunction with Power BI Desktop to expand the sharing, collaboration, and data management features of that tool. Users are presented with a wide range of potential data connectivity methods via the Power BI Service. A vast range of data sources, including databases, cloud services, online services, and data sources housed on the user's property, are accessible to users through connections. Direct connections to widely used platforms such as SQL Server, Azure SQL Database, Excel, SharePoint, Salesforce, and Google Analytics, amongst many others, are supported by the Power BI Service. Users are granted the ability to build connections, import data, and construct datasets for analysis and visualization. Dashboards in Microsoft Power BI Service provide a consolidated view of important metrics and key performance indicators (KPIs) that are gathered from several datasets and reports. It is possible for users to "pin" visualizations from different reports to a dashboard, creating an interactive and personalized summary of relevant insights. With Power BI Dashboards, users can measure and monitor their corporate KPIs dynamically because real-time data updates are provided.

Power BI Service allows users to create and share interactive reports. With Power BI Desktop, users may create reports. These reports can then be published to the Power BI Service for sharing and usage. Reports can be read, explored, and interacted with by Service users via a web browser or a mobile application. Users can perform ad hoc analysis of the data, delve into the data, and add filters to the published reports. Another feature that can be used with Power BI Service is real-time dashboards, where the visuals are updated instantly whenever new data is received. Users have the option to change the data in their datasets and reports by using the Power BI Service. To guarantee that reports and dashboards always show the most recent data available, users can schedule automatic data refreshes. A variety of refresh options are available, such as scheduled, on-demand, and incremental refreshes. Power BI Service supports several distinct data refresh situations. These options include real-time connectivity to data sources, imported data, and direct inquiry. Among the most notable benefits of the Power BI Service are its collaborative and sharing capabilities. Users can share statistics, dashboards, and reports with colleagues both inside and outside of their business to facilitate collaboration. Sharing options include limiting access to viewing only, allowing users to interact with the data, and facilitating teamwork features like leaving comments and exchanging insights with other users. Role-based access control is a feature of the Power BI Service that allows users to have the rights required to see and interact with delivered content. Users of the Power BI Service can access pre-built templates, dashboards, and reports that have been customized for certain data sources or industries by utilizing the Content Packs and Apps. Through the use of Content Packs, users may import pre-built dashboards and reports from popular services like Salesforce, Dynamics 365, Google Analytics, and many more. Apps are groups of dashboards, reports, and information that have been bundled together to facilitate easier distribution and use. Users can create their apps to share with other users or download programs from AppSource.

Features that are beneficial for data governance and security are available through the Power BI Service. Organizations may manage user access and permissions, enforce data security standards, keep an eye on data usage, and manage user access through the Power BI Admin Portal. Power BI Service supports integration with Azure Active Directory (AAD). Centralized user management and single sign-on (SSO) are made feasible by this integration. Businesses can use row-level security, or RLS, to limit access to data based on user responsibilities or attributes. There are no issues with the Power BI Service's ability to integrate with the different Microsoft services and platforms. Because Power BI is integrated with Office 365, users can use it to include reports in Teams or SharePoint Online. Azure services like Azure Data Factory, Azure Machine Learning, and Azure Synapse Analytics are also integrated with Power BI Service. Users can benefit from strong analytical and data engineering skills thanks to this integration. Thanks to a recently released feature in the Power BI service, users can now define goals. Data from the Power BI service is used to track the objectives. Subsequently, pertinent users might be provided with information about the objectives to obtain prompt and useful insight.

The Power Platform

Users can construct custom business apps, automate processes, analyze data, and create chatbots with the help of Microsoft's Power Platform, which is a set of low-code and no-code technologies produced by the software giant. Power Apps, Power Automate, Power BI, and Power Virtual Agents are the four primary components that make up this offering. **These individual elements, when combined, constitute a complete answer to the problems of app development, automation, data visualization, and client interaction. Let's explore each component in more detail:**

1. **Power Apps:** With the Power Apps platform, users may create custom software for business use without knowing how to write traditional computer code. It enables users to create internet and mobile applications by giving them access to pre-built templates and a visual interface. Users can create interactive apps that connect to several data sources, including Dynamics 365, SharePoint, Excel, and SQL Server. These programs can collect data, automate tasks, and streamline procedures. Power Apps facilitate responsive design by allowing apps to adapt to different screen sizes and devices.

2. **Power Automate:** Previously known as Microsoft Flow, this is a process automation application. With its help, users can create automated workflows spanning several services and apps. Microsoft Flow was the original name of Power Automate. By connecting a range

of actions and triggers with a graphic designer, users may create their workflows. Thanks to Power Automate's connection with a wide range of apps and services, including those created by Microsoft and third parties, users may automate repetitive tasks, synchronize data, and trigger actions based on specific events or scenarios.

3. **Power Virtual Agents**: With the help of this chatbot development platform, users may create intelligent chatbots without the need for any coding skills or experience. It offers a graphical user interface (GUI) where users may design questions, responses, and conversation flows for the chatbots they are developing. Microsoft's artificial intelligence technologies, such as Azure Cognitive technologies, can be integrated with Power Virtual Agents to enhance the chatbot's natural language understanding and sentiment analysis capabilities. Power Virtual Agents can be used to construct chatbots that can be used on several platforms, such as Facebook Messenger, Microsoft Teams, and websites.

The parts of the Power Platform are designed to work together and can be assembled in several ways to create complete solutions. For example, Power Apps can be used to create custom applications; Power Automate can automate the processes and workflows found in those applications; Power BI can visualize and analyze the data the application collects; and Power Virtual Agents can offer a chatbot interface for customer support and engagement. The Power Platform's low-code/no-code methodology enables users without any programming skills to quickly and effectively create and implement custom solutions. It makes it possible for businesses to speed up the process of digital transformation, automate operations that were previously done manually, acquire insights from data, and provide customers with engaging experiences.

Discovering Power BI?

The first stage in Microsoft's development of Power BI was the company's recognition of the growing importance of data analytics and business intelligence in the modern information age. Thanks to an earlier product it produced called Microsoft SQL Server Reporting Services (SSRS), which could handle basic reporting duties; Microsoft already had a presence in the business intelligence sector. However, Microsoft realized that a more comprehensive and user-friendly business intelligence tool was needed due to the advent of new technologies, increased data volumes, and the necessity for more potent analytical and visualization capabilities. Microsoft decided to develop Power BI as part of their larger Power Platform strategy as a direct result of this. In 2011, the Power BI project was initially made available to the general public as Power BI for Office 365, a cloud-based service. It provided possibilities for Excel and SharePoint users to explore and visualize data on their own. Over time, Microsoft has expanded Power BI's capabilities beyond those of Excel and SharePoint, realizing the product's potential as a stand-alone solution. In 2015, Microsoft released a standalone program called Power BI Desktop. This program gave users the ability to connect to a variety of data sources, convert and model data, as well as create beautiful visuals and reports. Because it provides more complex capabilities and functionalities, Power BI Desktop has emerged as the key tool for data modeling and the development of reports. Microsoft has also introduced Power BI service, formerly known as Power BI Online or Power BI Cloud, in addition to Power BI Desktop. A cloud-based platform called Power BI service makes it possible to collaborate on and manage Power BI content in addition to sharing it. A multitude of features are available with the Power BI service, such as dashboards, content packs, sharing options, and data refreshes. Microsoft has kept enhancing and broadening the capabilities of Power BI while considering user feedback and industry advancements. Along with the inclusion of whole new features, there have also been continuous improvements. Support for natural language queries, advanced analytics using R and Python, paginated reports, and AI integration are a few of these enhancements. Microsoft has also created mobile apps to be used with Power BI. On their mobile devices, such as smartphones and tablets, users may view and interact with reports and dashboards thanks to these apps.

Power BI has become one of the most potent business intelligence products on the market today thanks to its intuitive interface, numerous data connectivity choices, extensive visualization features, and integration with the broader Microsoft ecosystem. Due to its widespread adoption across numerous industries, it has developed into a full platform for data analysis, visualization, and decision-making. Microsoft's dedication to giving customers efficient and accessible data analytics solutions is shown in the creation of Power BI. Given the increasing importance of data-driven insights in today's corporate environment, this pledge was made.

This section will provide you with valuable context; which will answer the following questions: why were Power BI developed, why is it important, and what products are interrelated? Having this information at the outset will be beneficial to you in the same way that it is beneficial to do research about a firm before going into a job interview. The enlightenment you attain will be beneficial to you in the years to come.

SQL Server: Microsoft's Relational Database

In 1989, SQL Server was initially made available by Microsoft as a relational database management system. Microsoft originally published SQL Server. When SQL Server was first published, its primary focus was on basic database management tasks, like processing and managing queries, as well as storing and managing data and transactions. As SQL Server grew over time, Microsoft added several new capabilities and enhancements to increase its overall performance, scalability, and security.

SQL Server Analysis Services Multidimensional: One Small Step into BI

As computer processing power expanded, new methods of processing data, such as data cubes, gained traction. Microsoft released OLAP Services, the original name of its online analytical processing (OLAP) engine, in 1998. SQL Server Analysis Services would eventually be the new name for this product. When we discuss OLAP Services, we mean an approach to data interaction that uses cubes to carry out the analysis. The cube model was the industry standard in many business intelligence (BI) settings used by large corporations for more than ten years.

SQL Server Reporting Services: Pixel-Perfect Reporting, Automated Reports, and More

The fact that Microsoft had to add a pixel-perfect reporting option to SQL Server ultimately resulted from the need to develop reusable assets that had to follow extremely strict guidelines—for example, you have to ensure that every invoice you print has the same format as the one before it. Microsoft first released SQL Server Reporting Services in 2004 as an add-on to SQL Server 2000, and then the company released the second version of the software concurrently with SQL Server 2005. SQL Server Reporting Services had several useful features in an enterprise deployment. These features included pixel-perfect report generation, automated report distribution, and, in many deployments, the ability for end users to generate queries to the backend SQL Server database through a user interface. These features were all included in SQL Server Reporting Services.

Excel: A Self-Service BI Tool

One core product, Microsoft Excel, which nearly everyone has used or encountered at some point, can be used to summarize the history of Microsoft's self-service business intelligence services. Microsoft first published the Macintosh version of Excel in 1985. At its most basic level, Excel is a tool that allows users to pull data into a "flat" extract, modify the data, and do ad hoc computations on it as needed. By enabling users to evaluate their data, Excel enables them to derive insights from it. This is the core notion underlying the self-service business intelligence concept. Microsoft Excel has long been a vital tool for professionals involved in data analysis and business intelligence across a broad range of industries. Because of its versatility, ease of use, and potent features, Excel has emerged as a go-to tool for tasks ranging from simple calculations to intricate data modeling. Because of its extensive feature set and range of functions, Excel has evolved into much more than just a spreadsheet creator. It has developed into a self-service business intelligence (BI) tool that gives users the ability to investigate and analyze data in an efficient and user-friendly manner.

Here are some key aspects of Excel as a self-service BI tool:

1. **Data Import and Transformation:** Excel users can import data from a wide variety of sources, such as databases, text files, web services, and more. Excel also enables users to transform the data after it has been imported. It simplifies the process of retrieving data by providing user-friendly wizards and connections to work with the data. Utilizing Excel's functions, formulae, and Power Query, users can conduct operations such as data purification, transformation, and shaping within the spreadsheet program.

2. **Data Modeling**: Excel is a helpful tool for data modeling because of its data modeling features, which let users arrange their data effectively. Users can build hierarchies, link tables together, and create calculated columns and metrics. Users of Excel's Power Pivot feature can create data models that can manage enormous volumes of data and do intricate computations by using the DAX (Data Analysis Expressions) programming language.

3. **Visualization and Analysis:** Excel provides users with a broad variety of options for visually representing data, and the program also includes an analysis module. Excel users can produce interactive dashboards, pivot tables, charts, and graphs. It offers a variety of formatting options, including conditional formatting and charting capabilities, to improve the data's overall aesthetic appeal. Excel's built-in formulae and functions make it possible for users to carry out complicated calculations, explore trends, and compile data.

4. **Advanced Analytics**: Excel has some different advanced analytics tools that make it possible for users to carry out statistical analysis, predictive modeling, and what-if scenario simulations. Excel's built-in functions and tools, such as Solver (for optimization issues), Data Analysis Toolpak (for statistical analysis), and Power View (for interactive data exploration), can be utilized by users. To take advantage of Excel's advanced analytics features, users can now interface Excel with programming languages such as R and Python.

5. **Sharing and Collaboration:** Excel has features that let users work together and exchange data and outcomes. The File tab provides access to these features. Users may simply exchange Excel files using cloud storage services, SharePoint, or email. Multiple users can collaborate simultaneously on a shared Excel worksheet and make real-time edits. Version management is included in Excel so users can track changes and go back to previous versions. Additionally, Excel has connections to Power BI and Microsoft Teams, enabling smooth teamwork and information sharing.

6. **Integration with External Data Sources:** Integration with other Data Sources Excel allows for the integration of a wide variety of other data sources, including SQL Server, Oracle, SharePoint lists, Azure services, and many others. Excel users can make connections to the aforementioned data sources, create live connections, or import data into Excel to do analysis and generate reports. Users can make use of Excel's well-known interface while simultaneously accessing and analyzing data from a variety of sources thanks to this integration feature.

7. **Extensibility with Add-Ins:** Add-ins and extensions can be used to increase Excel's functionality. Specialized add-ins, such as those for financial modeling, data mining, and data visualization, are available for users to download and install. Users can then make use of this add-ins. This add-ins not only increases the functionality of Excel but also provide users with additional tools and features to fulfill their self-service business intelligence requirements.

Because of its broad use and familiarity, Excel is frequently selected as a self-service business intelligence tool. Because of its large feature set, data manipulation capabilities, visualization options, and integration capabilities, it is a flexible tool that can be used by people and small teams to analyze data and generate insights from that data without the need for heavy programming or expert business intelligence skills.

Power Pivot

Microsoft released PowerPivot for the first time in 2010. The name PowerPivot was eventually updated to include a space between the two words, making it two words long and matching the other products in the new Power BI tool suite in terms of naming rules. At first, Power Pivot was created as an Excel add-on. It lets users gather information from multiple sources and store it in a worksheet's relational online analytical processing (ROLAP) paradigm. The Power Pivot installation came with Power Query. Power Pivot is a powerful data modeling and analysis feature that is available in Microsoft Excel and Power BI. It enables users to create advanced data models by importing and linking large volumes of data from a variety of sources. Users can also perform complex calculations and analyses by making use of the Data Analysis Expressions (DAX) language. Power Pivot is available in both of these applications.

The following are some of the most important characteristics of Power Pivot:

1. **Data Import and Linking:** Users can build links to different data sources and import large amounts of data into the Power Pivot data model. Power Pivot supports various data compression techniques to improve efficiency and be able to deal with massive data scenarios. Users can import data from a variety of sources, including relational databases, text files, Excel tables, SharePoint lists, and more.
2. **Data modeling and Relationships**: With the help of Power Pivot, users may create relationships between tables by utilizing shared fields. The foundation for building strong data models is laid by these relationships. One-to-one, one-to-many, or many-to-many relationships can be created by users, allowing for rapid data exploration and analysis. Furthermore, Power Pivot enables the creation of calculated measures, columns, and hierarchies that may be applied to data manipulation and aggregation.
3. **Data Analysis Expressions**: DAX is a formula language that is utilized in Power Pivot to develop individualized calculations and measures. Users can do advanced calculations, create custom aggregations, and generate calculated columns because of the comprehensive collection of functions and operators that are provided by this platform. Calculations that are based on connected tables, time intelligence, filtering, and other features can be created with the help of DAX formulae.
4. **Advanced-Data Analysis:** Power Pivot allows users to execute complex data analysis and modeling within Excel or Power BI. Users can design interactive dashboards, create pivot tables, and produce reports using the data model created in Power Pivot. Users of Power Pivot are given the capacity to explore and analyze data from various dimensions, discover trends, and acquire useful insights as a result of the software's efficient ability to manage enormous volumes of data.
5. **Integration with Power Query and Power View**: It is simple to integrate PowerPivot with the other Power BI components. The capacity to reformat and shape data before importing it

into Power Pivot is provided to users of Power Query, which greatly enhances the capabilities of data transformation and purification. With Power View, users can create interactive reports and data visualizations based directly on the Power Pivot data model.

6. **Collaboration & Sharing:** Power Pivot models can be shared and worked on within Excel workbooks, or they can be published to the Power BI service, where numerous people can collaborate on them. Some people can work on the same Power Pivot model at the same time, and they can make changes in real-time. Furthermore, Power Pivot models can be utilized as sources of data for further Excel workbooks or Power BI reports, allowing for the reuse of data and preservation of its integrity throughout a wide range of analyses.

7. **Scalability and Performance**: Power Pivot stores and processes data inside of an Excel or Power BI file by utilizing in-memory technology. Power Pivot can now handle and store massive volumes of data thanks to this. This allows for faster calculations and query response times, even when working with large datasets. Power Pivot's compression techniques optimize memory use, allowing users to deal with large datasets without experiencing a decrease in performance.

Important New Functionality That Brings About Power BI

A new feature that Microsoft unveiled as part of Analysis Services in SQL Server 2012 is called the tabular model. An arrangement of data that is more akin to a classic data warehouse may now be supported by Analysis Services, as opposed to a cube structure, which becomes harder to maintain over time and tends to be more confusing for end users. This differs from the prior approach, which was more akin to a data mart. The primary difference was that Microsoft developed its first columnar (column-based) data store technology to enhance performance in this tabular paradigm. The goal of doing this was to get performance advantages. In the end, this would evolve into what we know today as VertiPaq, which is an in-memory columnar data storage using the tabular architecture of Analysis Services. Consequently, as a result of these enhancements, the performance became extremely quick.

To enable these tabular models, DAX, a new formula language, was created concurrently with this procedure. This language made it possible to do computations across the data columns, which aided in transforming the information into something that could be used for action. The next version of Power Pivot, which was released concurrently with Excel 2013, was built on top of this engine.

Power BI Desktop is born

On July 24, 2015, the globe was given access to the initial version of Power BI Desktop that was open to everyone. The Power BI Desktop program came with a full enterprise-level semantic modeling tool that comprised the VertiPaq engine and the DAX formula language. A semantic model is intended for human comprehension. It pulled data into the engine from a variety of sources by utilizing Power Query. It also made modifications possible that may change the data for further study.

Power BI Desktop under the Hood

Power BI Desktop is successful because it hides not one, but two powerful engines. More technically speaking, these are the components that enable the entire system to function. The formula engine is in charge of receiving requests for data, processing them, and creating an execution plan for the query. The storage engine, on the other hand, is in charge of both keeping the data produced by the data model and retrieving the data needed by the formula engine to satisfy a query's needs. From an alternative perspective, you may think of the formula engine as the brain. It assesses the situation, decides on the best course of action, and then relays this information to the appropriate body parts so they can implement the plan. The storage engine is the part of the system that receives those commands and performs the tasks required to compile all of the data.

VertiPaq: The Storage Engine

In Power BI Desktop, the in-memory storage engine known as VertiPaq is responsible for optimizing data storage and retrieval to facilitate effective analysis. It is a columnar database engine that was developed especially for the demands associated with analytical work.

The following is a list of important aspects of the VertiPaq:

1. **Columnar Storage**: VertiPaq saves data in a format known as columnar, which stores each column of a table in its distinct location. This method of columnar storage offers some benefits to the analytical processing that can be utilized. It allows for faster data retrieval for particular columns, improves compression rates, and minimizes the amount of RAM that is used. In addition to this, it enables efficient processes such as aggregation and filtering, which are frequently used in analytical queries.

2. **In-Memory Technology:** When we say that VertiPaq "stores data in memory," we mean that it does so by keeping the data in Random Access Memory (RAM) as opposed to periodically fetching it from disk. One of the main benefits of storing data in memory is the speed at which it can be retrieved from RAM as opposed to disk. This allows for significant performance gains when using RAM for data storage. In-memory storage allows for interactive data exploration and visualization in addition to real-time data processing and faster query response times.

3. **Compression**: Strong compression methods are used by VertiPaq to maximize memory use. It uses several encoding and compression techniques, including dictionary encoding, run-length encoding, and high-performance compression methods, to reduce the size of the data. The compression techniques, which take advantage of the repetition that takes place inside a column as well as the values' similarity to one another, were created specifically

for columnar storage. As a result, VertiPaq can efficiently employ memory while managing enormous volumes of data.

4. **Query Execution**: VertiPaq's in-memory architecture and columnar storage allow for efficient and fast query execution. While a query is running, VertiPaq will only access the columns required for the calculation. This contributes to minimizing the amount of disk I/O and data migration. To handle data as efficiently as possible, it uses the columnar structure to conduct tasks like filtering, aggregating, and joining at the column level. These modifications enable significantly faster interactive analysis as well as a notable increase in query speed.

5. **Data Compression and Encoding**: To further enhance performance and minimize the necessary memory footprint, VertiPaq combines encoding and compression techniques. To do this, the data values are encoded so that they occupy less space in the representation that is provided. Another technique VertiPaq uses is dictionary encoding. Using this technique, unique values are first stored in a dictionary and then those values are replaced in the data with corresponding dictionary IDs. This technique can significantly speed up data retrieval while also achieving even higher compression ratios.

6. **Advanced Calculations**: VertiPaq is capable of storing data as well as carrying out sophisticated computations thanks to the Data Analysis Expressions (DAX) language. Using the DAX formula language, which functions similarly to a programming language, users can define calculated columns, measures, and complex calculations within the data model. VertiPaq performs these calculations quickly and effectively, allowing for real-time insights and interactive analysis.

The columnar storage, in-memory technology, and powerful compression techniques that VertiPaq possesses make it an essential component of Power BI Desktop's ability to operate efficiently and scale effectively. Users are given the ability to successfully explore and display their data by utilizing Power BI Desktop's quick data retrieval, interactive analysis, and efficient memory use, all of which are made possible through the exploitation of these features.

DAX: The Formula Engine

Power BI Desktop uses a formula language and calculation engine to define calculations, create custom measures, and perform sophisticated data analysis. The acronym DAX represents "Data Analysis Expressions." It performs the function of the formula engine within the VertiPaq in-memory storage engine. A powerful tool designed especially for use in analytical and corporate intelligence situations is the DAX formula language. With the help of its extensive library of functions and operators, users can create expressions and computations that can be used to change and inspect data. Calculated columns, measures, tables, and more complicated calculations can all be produced with the use of DAX formulae, which take into account the relationships, present within the data model. Calculated columns can be defined by DAX users inside the tables they are working with. A calculated column uses the values of an expression or formula that the user has defined to generate the values of those columns. These created columns are added to the data model and can be utilized for further computations and analysis. While the data loading process is underway, calculated columns are created and stored in the VertiPaq engine. Measures are important because of the DAX. Measures are computations that combine data according to predetermined requirements; examples include sum, average, count, and more complex aggregations. Examples of measures include the sum, the average, and the count. Users can define measures by employing functions and expressions that work on the columns that make up the data model when working with DAX. The results of measures are computed dynamically at the time of a query, making use of the capabilities of the VertiPaq engine to perform calculations efficiently.

One powerful component of the DAX platform is called "contextual intelligence." It is this characteristic that allows DAX equations to automatically adapt their computations to the environment in which they are being evaluated. In this sense, the data model's structure and "filters" and "slicers" are included. Contextual intelligence makes it possible to do dynamic and adaptive computations based on user interactions and selections, producing accurate and situation-relevant results. The DAX platform can handle a great deal of intricate computation and analytical techniques. It offers capabilities for time intelligence, such as computing the year-to-date, comparing data across multiple periods, and managing rolling averages, among other things. The DAX language supports calculations based on text functions, logical functions, statistical functions, and hierarchies. This capability allows users to create complex analysis scenarios and perform challenging computations within Power BI Desktop. Using DAX, integrating Power BI Desktop's graphics is simple. Users can create calculations using DAX formulas, and those results can then be shown in tables, charts, and other visual components. When DAX is used, the computations can respond to how the user interacts with the report, filters, and slicers, enabling the creation of dynamic and interactive visualizations. This connection allows users to create interactive and relevant visualizations that represent the results of calculations. DAX is a crucial part of the data analysis and manipulation procedures because it is the formula engine available in Power BI Desktop. Thanks to this capacity, users may create complex calculations, create one-of-a-kind measurements, and do thorough analysis inside their data models. DAX uses the power of the VertiPaq engine to facilitate quick and effective computations, giving users precise insights and simplifying the interaction and exploration of data.

What Makes Power BI Different from Its Competitors?

Imagine yourself sifting through the vast array of available business intelligence tools in an attempt to locate the one that will completely transform the way you gather, analyze, and present data. Power BI is the most notable option among the others because it offers a distinct set of features and capabilities that set it apart from the competition. One of the first things you notice when using Power BI for the first time is how well connected it is to the rest of the Microsoft ecosystem. Because Power BI is made to integrate with apps like Excel, SQL Server, Azure, SharePoint, and Teams, you'll find that integrating it into your present workflow is simple. Because of this connectivity, you can make use of the Microsoft environment with which you are already familiar, which simplifies the data analysis process. Your attention is captured and held by Power BI's user interface's straightforward design as soon as you start experimenting. It follows Microsoft's design guidelines, which produce a natural and easy-to-use interface. With its drag-and-drop features, pre-built templates, and interactive visualizations, you'll discover that creating eye-catching reports and dashboards is simple and doesn't require specialized technical knowledge. What sets Power BI apart from other business intelligence solutions is its remarkable connectivity to a vast array of data sources. Power BI provides you with an abundance of alternatives to connect and integrate your data, regardless of the location of that data. Your data could be stored in databases, cloud-based platforms, files, or internet services. Because of this versatility, you can compile information from a variety of sources, giving you a full perspective of your data and allowing you to make more informed decisions.

You have complete control over how your data is created and shaped thanks to Power BI's data transformation tools. Using Power Query will make it simpler for you to clean, transform, and enrich your data. The user-friendly interface of Power BI enables you to connect to a wide range of data sources, perform the required transformations, and import the enhanced data. In addition to saving you a ton of time and effort, this will guarantee that your data is prepared correctly for reporting and analysis. As you move in your data analysis journey, you'll discover that Power BI's advanced data modeling and analysis features fulfill their full potential as an effective tool. Power Pivot is an in-memory data modeling engine that helps you create sophisticated data models. These models may involve defining measurements, calculations, hierarchies, and correlations. Combining it with the VertiPaq engine allows for the effective processing of large datasets, allowing you to do complex computations and gain a deeper understanding of your data. The integration makes this feasible. Working together is a breeze thanks to Power BI's many sharing and collaboration features. You can publish your reports and dashboards to the Power BI service, where they can be safely shared with coworkers both inside and outside of your organization. Your team will be able to make decisions that are data-driven jointly, which will increase your overall analytical capabilities. This will also create collaboration, stimulate the sharing of knowledge, and empower team members. Your road toward better data analysis will be made easier by the fact that Power BI is dedicated to providing enterprise-level security and governance. Your data is always kept safe and secure thanks to features like robust encryption, access limits, and data loss prevention. To ensure compliance with regulatory requirements and peace of mind, you can create security standards, restrict user access, and control data sharing. The enterprise-grade security and governance, seamless integration, user-friendly interface, connectivity to a wide range of data sources, advanced modeling and analysis features, advanced data transformation capabilities, collaboration, and sharing capabilities, and all of these features combined make Power BI an outstanding business intelligence tool when you reflect on your time spent using it. You and your team will be able to make decisions that are based on data with confidence and clarity if you use Power BI because it gives you the power to unleash the full potential of your data.

Conclusion

The exploration of Power BI and its associated technologies has shown the exceptional features and functionalities that set Power BI apart in the field of data visualization and business intelligence. Power BI gives consumers a smooth and comfortable experience with its user-friendly design and seamless connection with the Microsoft ecosystem. Its broad connectivity options enable users to bring data from diverse sources, empowering comprehensive analysis and reporting. When considering the evolution of Power BI, it is evident that it has been shaped by Microsoft's commitment to providing powerful tools for data analysis and visualization. From its origins in SQL Server and Excel to the development of Power Pivot and Power Query, Microsoft has continually refined and expanded the capabilities of Power BI to meet the evolving needs of users. All things considered, Power BI provides a strong and all-encompassing solution for businesses looking to maximize the value of their data. It offers a distinctive and alluring solution in the business intelligence space thanks to its connection with the Microsoft ecosystem, user-friendly interface, wide range of connectivity choices, sophisticated modeling and analytical capabilities, collaborative features, and enterprise-grade security. In today's data-driven world, organizations can use Power BI to gain valuable insights, make wise decisions, and propel success.

Activity

1. What is Power BI?
2. Briefly describe Power BI components and desktop.
3. What are the important new functionality that leads to Power BI?
4. What is DAX?
5. What makes Power BI different from its various competitors?

CHAPTER 2

THE REPORT AND DATA VIEWS

You already know how easy it is to create reports with several perspectives and insights into your data if you have any experience with Power BI. Another option is Power BI Desktop, which offers a more comprehensive feature set. You can create complex queries with Power BI Desktop, integrate data from several sources, create relationships between tables, and do a lot more. Power BI Desktop includes a *Report view*," in which users can generate an unlimited number of report pages that include visuals. The report editing view in the Power BI desktop program and the report editing view on the Power BI service are fairly comparable. Visualizations can be moved, copied, pasted, combined, and many other actions can be performed on them. With Power BI Desktop, you will be able to work with your queries and model your data. By doing this, you'll be able to guarantee that your data will provide the most insightful reports available. Following that, you can choose to store your Power BI Desktop file in the cloud or on your local drive, based on your preferences. When you load data for the first time in Power BI Desktop, the Report view will appear before you. It will include a blank canvas and links that will assist you in adding data to your report.

Make Use of the ribbon in Power BI Desktop

The advantages of using the ribbon are designed to make the experience of using Power BI Desktop as well as other Microsoft applications simple.

These benefits can be grouped into the following categories:

- **Search bar** - The search experience available on the ribbon is similar to that seen in other Microsoft programs. Every time you select the search box in Power BI, it will suggest actions to perform based on the state of your report at that moment. The search results will automatically update as you type, and buttons offering help or directing you to the next step will show up.

- **Improved look, feel, and organization** - Icons and functionality in the updated Power BI Desktop ribbon are aligned to the look, feel, and organization of ribbon items found in Office applications.

- **An intuitive Themes gallery**: Both the look and feel of the Themes gallery in PowerPoint and the gallery that is visible on the View ribbon are comparable. The images on the ribbon will help you visualize the changes you make to the theme, including the typefaces and color schemes when you apply them to your report.

- **Dynamic ribbon content based on your view**: In the previous version of Power BI Desktop's ribbon, icons or actions that were unavailable were grayed out, which resulted in a less-than-ideal user experience. You will always be aware of the options that are accessible to you based on the context thanks to the new ribbon, which displays icons in a manner that is both dynamic and ordered in a certain order.
- **A single-line ribbon, when collapsed, saves you space**. This is one of the many advantages of the updated ribbon. Another advantage of the updated ribbon is the option to collapse the ribbon itself into a single line, dynamically displaying ribbon components depending on your context.

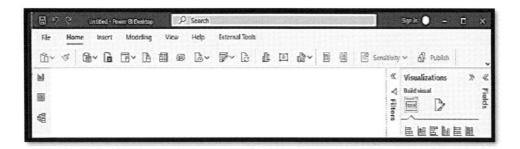

- **Keytips to traverse and choose buttons**: Using the Alt key, you can activate keytips. You'll find it easier to navigate the ribbon this way. You can navigate by pressing the keys that appear on your keyboard once the mode has been activated.

- **Custom format strings** - Not only is the Properties pane where you may set custom format strings, but the ribbon also has this feature. You can also set custom format strings there, in addition to this. Selecting the appropriate element will bring up a contextual tab titled Measure tools or Column tools, depending on whether you want to alter the measure or the column. To create your unique format, just enter your format string into the selection box on that tab.

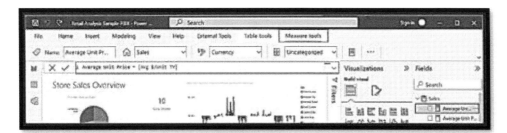

- **Accessibility** - The ribbon, the file menu, and the title bar are all easily accessible. Use the keyboard shortcuts Ctrl and F6 to access the ribbon area. The Tab key switches between the top and bottom bars and the arrow keys are used to move between the objects.

In addition to those visible changes, an updated ribbon also allows for future updates to Power BI Desktop, and its ribbon, such as the following:

- The creation of more flexible and intuitive controls in the ribbon, such as the visual gallery
- The addition of *black* and *dark gray* Office themes to the Power BI Desktop

- An improved accessibility

Report View: Home Section of the Ribbon

Power BI will automatically take you to the Report view when you first open it. There is a classic ribbon interface at the top that allows you to search for various things you can perform. The user interface's pane part is located on the right. This portion of the interface strongly reminds me of the work Microsoft did on the first Xbox 360 UI. You can see multiple panes at once by using the View section of the ribbon. You can also minimize panes that are presently visible, such as the Filters and Fields panes in the picture below, which shows the **Visualizations window** open. This is shown by the fact that the **Filters and Fields panes** are minimized.

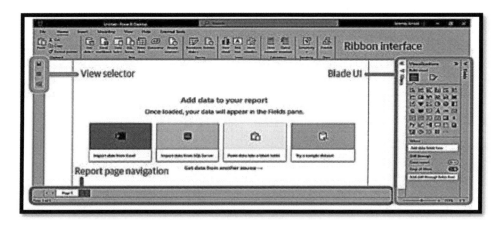

The Report Page Navigation choices are located near the bottom of the page. If your report is lengthy, you can use the arrows to browse through the list of pages or click on individual report pages to move between the worksheets in Excel in a way very similar to how you would navigate through worksheets in a report. Now, on the left side of the screen, is the view selector, which is made up of three icons. The views are arranged from top to bottom on the website in increasing order: Report, Data, and Model. The ribbon menu appears differently in each of the views. The Home tab is the starting point for the default view when using the ribbon interface, as can be seen in the figure below. There are some different names for the Home tab, some of which include Home view, Home ribbon, and Home section. From this point on, I'll call its components (Home, Insert, and Modeling) as tabs.

Every one of the tabs, or primary parts of the ribbon, is broken up into subsections that are denoted by a slender vertical line. On the row that is located at the bottom of the ribbon, you will find the names of the subsections. The following are the subsections that can be found in the picture above **Clipboard, Data, Queries, Insert, Calculations, Sensitivity, and Share**.

The Clipboard Subsection

One useful feature of Power BI is the Clipboard, which lets users manage and arrange visualizations, measurements, and queries that they have copied when working within the Power BI Desktop application. The items can be dropped into the relevant directories by dragging and dropping them. You can store items there and utilize them as temporary storage for a range of reports and pages. An object in Power BI, such as a measure, query, or graphic, is copied and saved to the Clipboard. To access the Clipboard, select the **"Clipboard" button** from the "Home" tab on the Power BI Desktop ribbon. You will be able to use the Clipboard as a result. The copied content will be displayed in a window known as the Clipboard that opens on the right side of the screen.

The Clipboard provides several helpful functions:

1. **Cutting and Pasting**: The Clipboard's principal function is to provide users with the ability to cut objects from one report or page in Power BI and then paste them elsewhere inside the application. This eliminates the need to start from scratch when recreating visualizations, metrics, or queries, which allows effective reuse of these elements.

2. **Organizing Copied Items**: You can arrange the things you have copied in a hierarchical structure by using the Clipboard to create folders and subfolders. Sorting your items based on what kind of item they are or any other pertinent criteria will make it easier for you to find and manage them later.

3. **Removing and Clearing Items:** If there are objects in the Clipboard that you no longer need, you can either delete them one by one or clear out the whole Clipboard to start again with a clean slate. This contributes to the Clipboard being less cluttered and more structured overall.

4. **Exporting and Importing**: The buttons on the clipboard can also be used to import and export its contents. By letting you export the items on the Clipboard to a file, which can then be imported into another instance of Power BI Desktop or shared with colleagues; this tool facilitates teamwork and simplifies the sharing of reusable components.

The Clipboard is a highly helpful feature for users who frequently work on numerous reports or who need to reuse components across a range of projects. It simplifies the process of copying and pasting objects, helps manage and organize copied content, and promotes teamwork by making it easier for people to share copied content to the clipboard.

The Data Subsection

In the next section, which is titled **"Data**," you will find multiple fast connection options that will allow you to rapidly connect to various data sources.

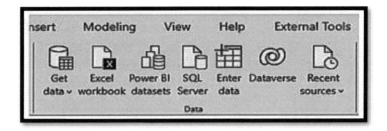

You will see a button labeled **"Get data"** on the left side of the screen. This button consists of an icon and an arrow that point down. If you choose the icon, Power BI will provide you with a new menu that has the whole catalog of data connections that are available to use.

If you choose the **"drop-down"** option, you will be presented with a shortened and more concise list of the data sources that are most often used. When you don't need access to the whole list of connections, this can be a very useful feature.

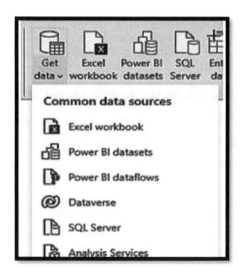

You can navigate to your Excel file immediately by clicking the "Excel workbook" button, which will cause an Explorer window to open. Selecting "Power BI datasets" will bring up a window where you can select a dataset that is already published in the Power BI service and establish a "live connection" with it.

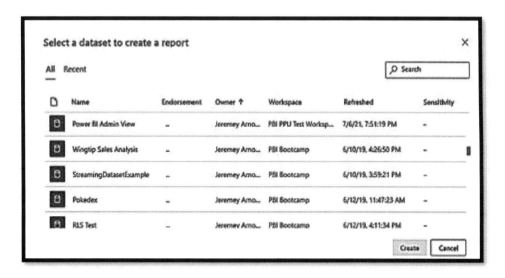

A pop-up box allowing you to enter the name or location of the server and, optionally, the name of the database appears when you select the SQL Server button from the toolbar. It will ask for your credentials when you try to log in to the server. When you are on this page, you will also have the choice of selecting Import or DirectQuery. You can download the data into your local data model by selecting the Import mode. If you pick the DirectQuery option in Power BI, Power BI will create queries to run against the database. Once the queries' results are in, Power BI will process the data as needed. There is also a button labeled "**Advanced options**". This button gives you the ability to specify a command timeout in minutes, pass a custom SQL statement, include relationship columns, browse using complete hierarchies, and enable SQL Server failover support. All of these features can be accessed by clicking the button.

The interface that appears when you click the "Enter Data" button should look very familiar to you if you are familiar with Excel. This is so that you may insert columns, give them names, and enter data into cells within the structure that the button produces, which looks like a table. It is imperative to note that there is no formula feature in this user interface. It is limited to entering simple data into systems. Additionally, you can copy and paste data into this window, but before you go crazy, make sure to use caution. You can use this window to create a lookup table for your model or testing purposes. Here, you can achieve any of those goals. Nevertheless, it is not a good idea to place large amounts of data in this type of table structure because it can only hold 3,000 cells' worth of data and needs manual management. I very much advise against it.

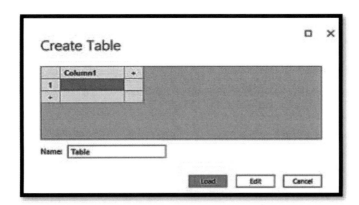

When you click the Dataverse button, a pop-up box with an instruction will appear so you may enter the details required for your environment domain. If you are familiar with Microsoft Dynamics, you have undoubtedly previously encountered references to this idea under the name

Common Data Model. Your most recent sources will be listed in a drop-down menu that appears when you select the "Recent sources" option. This ensures that the data source will be available and ready for you if you ever need to connect to it again. To obtain an even more extensive compilation of current data sources, choose "**More**" from the drop-down option.

The Queries Subsection

You can manage and alter your data using the Power Query Editor in the Queries Subsection of the Power BI Desktop application. This portion is referred to as the Queries Subsection. Before putting it into your Power BI model, you will be able to connect to a variety of data sources, apply data transformations, and shape your data using this feature.

The following actions need to be taken to access the Queries Subsection in Power BI Desktop:

1. Open Power BI Desktop.
2. Simply navigate your mouse to the "**Home**" option on the ribbon that is located at the very top of the window.
3. You will locate the "**Transform data**" button in the "**External Data**" group under the "**Home**" tab of the ribbon. Click on it.

Depending on whether you choose the drop-down arrow or the icon, you can use the "Transform data" option for two different purposes. You can access the Power Query interface immediately by clicking on the icon. Here, you may perform several data manipulation tasks, such as filtering, sorting, merging, appending, and changing data, using an easy-to-use user interface. A menu with a wide variety of options will appear when you click on the downward-pointing arrow. If you select "Data source settings," a pop-up box will show up where you may change several factors, including file locations and credentials. If you have parameters and variables, you can also change them in this section.

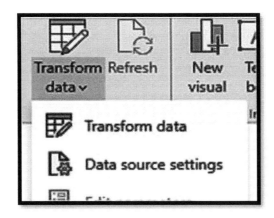

The Insert Subsection

There are three options available when you select the Insert tab. You can add a text box, add visualization to your collection of visualizations, or add a new visualization to your report page using the Visualizations pane. In case you select **"New visual**," the canvas you are working on will receive an additional image. When the document is saved, the default image that appears on the canvas is a stacked column chart. A text box will be added to your canvas in the same way as it would appear in PowerPoint when you click the **"Text box" button.** Selecting "More visuals" will cause the page to look like the one in the following image. If you select "From my files," an Explorer window will open and you can select a visual to add from a file that is already on your local system. Should you select "From a URL," a box allowing you to enter a URL will appear. Though Microsoft has been emphasizing AppSource as the preferred method for obtaining custom graphics in recent years, PBVIZ remains the official format for these files.

The Calculation Subsection

You can choose between **"Quick measure" and "New measure" under Calculations.** Measures are DAX calculations that are carried out across all of your data. After selecting "New measure," you'll notice that the ribbon has been replaced by a formula bar. You can input the DAX for your measure at this point. This works in a manner akin to that of the Excel formula bar. A pop-up window that walks you through the process of constructing a measure using a wizard with multiple prepared calculations will display when you click the **"Quick measure" button.** Microsoft introduces new fast measures in specific versions, which is a helpful tip. Therefore, it's always worth checking back after an update to see if any new quick measures have been added. This is a result of Microsoft adding fresh fast fixes in some versions.

Report View: The Insert Tab

The Pages Subsection

The **"New page" button** will always respond to your click by displaying a drop-down menu wherever you click inside the Pages area. This menu offers you the choice between "Duplicate page" and "Blank page." A newly created page that appears in your report to the right of every other page is referred to as a "blank page". Clicking the "Duplicate page" button will make a copy of the report page you are currently viewing. All of the currently displayed images will be included in this copy, which will be to the right of every other page in the report.

The Visuals Subsection

The Home tab's toolbar's Visuals section also has the **"New visual" and "More visuals"** buttons. You can also find these buttons under the subsection called Visuals. All of them operate in the same way. For your convenience, they are repeated here in case you are looking for any other specific objects in this section of the ribbon, which is about placing objects onto the canvas. You can also look for them from this location. This section of the ribbon explains how to arrange objects on the canvas.

The AI Visuals Subsection

Visualizations of artificial intelligence are covered in the next subsection under the Insert tab. Public access is provided for four of these AI-generated photos. Selecting one of them will add a blank version of that image to the canvas in the upper left corner and as high as it can go. What is important to highlight here is that this particular visualization offers unique functionality in terms of analytical capabilities. Power BI is no different from the other Power Platform products in that Microsoft is very keen to showcase its artificial intelligence (AI) capabilities.

The Power Platform Subsection

The contents covered in the next part, "Power Platform," are essentially different from all the other visuals featured in the platform, even though they are formally classified as visuals. The other Power Platform components that we previously discussed can be interacted with and engaged with when you incorporate Power Platform visuals into your Power BI report. They aid in showcasing the Power Platform's value to a company in a comprehensive manner and are highly effective.

The Elements Subsection

The final area under the Insert tab is called Elements, and it covers the report's elements. While these may not be as interactive as Power BI visualizations, they can nevertheless help to increase the usefulness and clarity of your report. Text boxes, button groups, shape libraries, and image libraries are examples of control possibilities for elements. The "Text box" tool in Power BI serves the same purpose as its equivalent in PowerPoint. It gives you basic formatting options for your content and adds an editable text box on the canvas. Using this tool, you will be able to alter the font, font size, text color, bolding, italicizing, and underlining, as well as the alignment of the text, and you will also be able to add hyperlinks to websites that are not part of your report. Other elements on the "**Text box**" can be edited in the "**Format text box**" pane that appears when a text box is selected.

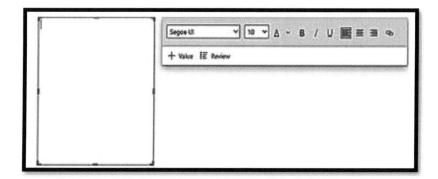

When you click the Buttons element, a variety of alternatives that can assist with navigating the report or give further information will appear before you. There are a good many of them. The whole list is included in the picture that follows; thus, you can immediately begin considering how you can incorporate them into any future reports that you write.

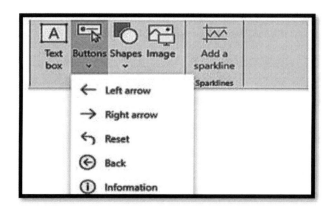

It is important to remember that placing the button on your canvas has no bearing on any of these buttons, except the Q&A, Bookmark, and Navigator options. This is because placing the button on your canvas has no bearing unless you give Power BI instructions on how to use it. One of these buttons will cause a "Format button" window to pop up on the right when you place it on your canvas. When you place one of these buttons on your canvas, it will show up and offer visual formatting options that underline the action that the button should take. The Q&A and Bookmark buttons are already set up with their default behaviors corresponding to their respective functionalities. However, if you believe that your report may employ that button in a different context, you can still adjust the tasks that it does. You can choose from a wide variety of shapes that can be utilized in reports when you select the Shapes option. The shape you choose will show up on your canvas prefilled with a color that comes from the default settings of your theme. After that, all you have to do to update it is change the graphic's size on the canvas. When the formatting option is selected, the shape can also be altered because it has a window. To include an image in your Power BI report, click the Image button. This will open an Explorer window where you may choose the photo to include. Pictures can be imported into Power BI in a variety of formats. (As a side note, there is a proper way to say GIF; make sure you're not pronouncing it incorrectly.)

```
BMP (*.bmp;*.dib;*.rle)
JPEG (*.jpg;*.jpeg;*.jpe;*.jfif)
GIF (*.gif)
TIFF (*.tif;*.tiff)
PNG (*.png)
```

After your photo has been uploaded and added to the report page, you will notice that it has its formatting window that opens on the right side of the page when selected, just like every other item in the Elements section of the ribbon. As with any other Power BI feature, you can adjust the shape's size in the report by clicking and dragging the box to the desired size. This applies to every Power BI component.

Report View: The Modeling Tab

The third part of the ribbon in the Report view is the Modeling tab. Here you have more data management options from the Report view.

The Relationships Subsection

On the left side is a button that says "Manage relationships." You can view all of the relationships that already exist in your model by clicking this button, which will open a window. Additionally, you can modify existing relationships or add new ones from this box. Naturally, Power BI will try to automatically identify associations based on column names by default. Though it's conceivable that this won't always be how the model is constructed the way you want it to be, this can assist in establishing an initial set of associations for your data model. You must take into account the fact that this button will be disabled if your data model has less than two tables.

The Calculations Subsection

The region of calculations is the next. There are functional buttons labeled "New measure" and "Quick measure." The other two items are prompts that open the inline DAX editor, allowing you to use it to create DAX-calculated tables from the "New table" button or DAX-calculated columns from the "New column" button. The "Inline DAX editor" will open when you click on any of the other two items. Please be aware that there is a strange quirk with the "New measure" button that can occasionally be bothersome. Power BI will assume that the measure will go into the first table it sees in the Fields pane and assign it as the destination for the measure if you pick this option before having a table selected in that pane. These elements can be moved to another table by dragging and dropping them from the Fields pane. But you should watch out for the behavior that goes along with this activity.

The Page Refresh Subsection

A "**Change detection**" button can be found in the "**Page refresh**" area, although it is only applicable in DirectQuery circumstances. You have the option of setting a specific refresh frequency for your pages, or you can have them automatically update whenever there is a change detected in the data. Using this functionality, you can create a simulation of this function inside Power BI Desktop.

The Security Subsection

There are two buttons in the Security area, and they are both quite important. The "Manage roles" and "View as" buttons in Power BI are used to provide row-level security or RLS. RLS is a feature that allows us to control how users in our model view the data it contains based on roles that are created algorithmically with DAX. Think of this as a way to make sure that people can only view the data in a format that has been filtered following the particular context and security restrictions that apply to them. For example, if we had a report that was published for different college courses, we could make simple DAX statements that described how we wanted the data filtered, and then we could assign users to those roles so that the data would be filtered in the manner that we desired for each of those users.

The Q&A Subsection

Lastly, the Q&A portion is presented. A large wizard explaining how to adjust the Q&A engine to better respond to the more natural language used by your clients will emerge when you click the "Q&A setup" button. This can be used to teach the engine synonyms so that the Power BI engine knows what a word means in the context of your data model when you ask a query including that term.

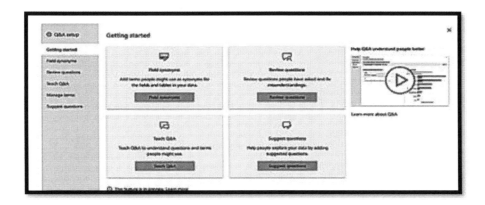

- Click the **Language** button to get a list of languages that are supported for the Question and Answer section.
- Lastly, the "**Linguistic schema**" button includes a drop-down menu that gives you the option to either import or export a file containing a linguistic schema.

Report View: The View Tab

The View tab is the next major section of the ribbon that you'll find. This option is crucial because it gives you the ability to choose themes, configure multiple page views to test how different people could read your report, and do other things. Do you want PowerPoint included in your Power BI report? This is where some things should start to take place.

The Themes Subsection

The Themes section functions in the same way as it does in PowerPoint. You can work with the pre-installed themes or modify your current theme and save any modifications you make by clicking the drop-down box on the right. You can also search for other themes, check the theme gallery, and select different themes from which to choose. Feel free to try out different themes—there are plenty!

The Scale to Fit Subsection

Upon selecting "**Scale to fit," the "Page view" button** will present you with an option to align your canvas with the page, adjust its width, or show its actual dimensions. You may also decide to make its true size visible. This complements the "Mobile layout" option in the Mobile section. Your report canvas will resize and take on a new shape when you click that button, making it suitable for reports that will be shown on a mobile device. Since there is less room for display on mobile devices, there are different considerations that must be made when creating mobile reports than when creating standard reports.

The Page Options Subsection

In this part's "**Page options" section**, you have three buttons to select from. It is possible to visualize the grid lines, to have objects snap to the grid, and to lock objects. Because they give you a reference point for where your things are concerning other items, gridlines are quite helpful. Only when the layout is set to Mobile is the "Snap to grid" option accessible, which will force all graphics to neatly adhere to the chosen pixel density. No changes can be made to the arrangement of items on a page when "Lock objects" is selected.

The Show Panes Subsection

The "Show panes" section is the last one to be found on the View tab. This paragraph discusses the several panes that are available for addition or deletion from the user interface (UI) in connection with this specific location. The Filters pane allows you to modify the filters at the visual, page, and report levels. You can "bookmark" a report page to have it open to a specific series of events and then revert to that state at a later time, just like you may bookmark a page in your browser. A focused selection of a single element can be made using the Selection pane, which offers a visual depiction of every element on the canvas of every report page. This can also be used to organize items into groups and create a hierarchy of importance amongst them, which is helpful when there may be overlap between the objects. The Performance Analyzer, which also displays the variables influencing the performance of your report page, allows you to extract machine-generated DAX. The "Sync slicers" panel allows you to select which slicers, if any, should be synchronized between report pages. This provides a means of maintaining consistency in comparisons despite the presence of many report pages.

Report View: Help Section

You will be able to determine the version of Power BI Desktop you are working with by clicking the Help button, which is located on the ribbon. This tab will also include connections to guided learning, training videos, documentation, and support links.

Within the Community section of the Power BI website, you will find links to frequently used external tools, access to the Power BI blog, and opportunities to connect with the larger Power Platform community. Additionally, there is documentation specifically for developers, dubbed "Power BI for developers." Finally, there is an option for developers to submit ideas for Power BI Desktop. Since this is something that will benefit you, you can vote on suggestions made by others and contribute your ideas. The Microsoft Power BI development team has stated numerous times that it considers user suggestions and votes. The program is updated around once every month or two, and after each release, the team reviews how popular a particular suggestion was on the **Power BI Ideas** platform. Therefore, if you have a suggestion, you should post it in this particular thread.

Report View: External Tools Section

The Report View's Pane Interface

Each component of the user interface has its own distinct set of panes, which enables that segment to perform a variety of functions. You can access seven panes in the report view.

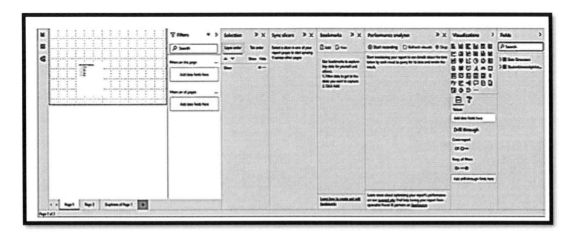

As you can see, there is not much room left for you to work with when all of the panes are displayed to their full extent. But only the Visualization and Fields windows are always visible at once. The Filters pane differs from the other panes in another way as well—it is not as separated from the canvas as the other panes. This is so because the behavior of objects on the canvas is set by the Filters pane.

Visualizations Pane

You can choose visualizations to add to a report, add columns and measures to show in those visualizations in the Values tab and do other tasks in the Visualizations pane. **First, let's look over the list of visuals. The visuals are listed in order from left to right, top to bottom:**

- Stacked bar chart
- Stacked column chart
- Clustered bar chart
- Clustered column chart
- 100% stacked bar chart
- 100% stacked column chart
- Line chart
- Area chart
- Stacked area chart
- Line and stacked column chart
- Line and clustered column chart
- Ribbon chart
- Waterfall chart
- Funnel chart
- Scatter chart
- Pie chart
- Donut chart
- Treemap
- Map
- Filled map
- Shape map
- Azure map
- Gauge
- Card
- Multi-row card
- KPI
- Slicer
- Table
- Matrix
- R script visual
- Python script visual

- Key influencers
- Decomposition tree
- Q&A
- Smart narrative
- Paginated report
- ArcGIS Maps for Power BI
- Power Apps for Power BI
- Power Automate for Power BI

That can be overwhelming because there are so many images displayed at once. It's not as bad as it sounds, though, because you might never utilize some of those items anyhow. You should be aware that any imported or custom graphics you have in your Power BI report will appear in this list, above the buttons for Fields and Format. The area between the Values section and the visualization list has two buttons. On the left side is the Fields portion; while on the right side is the Formatting part. They accept a wide range of criteria; therefore each visual's subsections will appear to be slightly different from one another. There is a possibility that a column chart and a line chart may seem comparable to one another; nonetheless, both types of charts are going to have different regions in which fields can be placed. Likewise, based on the look, the Format pane will have a different set of choices. This is because each visual needs to have something uniquely formatted. Some things don't change despite this.

Additionally, you'll see that a third option appears in this section once you've selected a visual. You must remember this. That is the Analytics button. You must comprehend that this capability is limited to the visualizations that come pre-installed with Power BI and that not all visualizations can utilize it. You can, however, do things like establish trend lines, constant lines, averages, and so forth. The most essential thing to remember about this part is that you should not be afraid to experiment with the plethora of different options that are at your disposal. If you aren't sure what to do, you can always let Power BI handle everything for you by using its default settings. The Format and Analytics subsections provide you with the capabilities you'll need when you're ready to take a little bit more control over your report. The final area of the visualization window that can be viewed is the "Drill through" section. This powerful feature allows you to drill down from one subsection of your report to another while maintaining all of the data elements filtered as you had them previously, so you can quickly develop a story with data that allows users to find specific examples that are relevant to their analysis.

Fields and Filters Panes

In the Fields pane, you can see a list of all the tables, columns, and measures that are included in your report. It will also contain any folders that you create and any hierarchies or groups that you may create within your data model of choice. To incorporate the column and measure into your current visualizations, just click and drag them to the desired spot in the Visualizations pane or onto the canvas itself. Ticking this option will also direct Power BI to click on the item and move it into the visualization of your choosing. Alternatively, Power BI will create visualization for you if you don't already have one and add it to the canvas along with the selected data piece. A context list will appear when you right-click on a table in your model. This list contains choices to add new measures, calculated columns, and fast measures, as well as to refresh the data and change the query in Power Query. In this area, when you right-click on a column, a context list will appear with options to add the column to your canvas, add a new measure or column, add the column to your filters list, or add it to the drill-through option. You will also be able to hide that specific data point from the display if you do not want it to be used at that time. The Filters pane is divided into three subsections. Most likely, you've used filters before, but just in case, let me explain. A filter is a function that sets a requirement for the data that is displayed. This condition must be met for the data to be displayed. For instance, if I have a filter for an age bracket and pick the grouping from 12 to 18 years old, then all of the data that I see will be related to that age range. Every other piece of data would be disregarded. **When you have a certain visual chosen, the Filters pane will provide you the option to apply filters to that particular visual when you make that selection.**

- **"Filters on this page"** filters all visuals on that specific report page.
- **"Filters on all pages"** sets a filter condition for the entire report.

By default, any fields that are part of a visual will also be displayed and interactable in the Filters pane, located under the "Filters on this visual" section. You can set up three different types of common filters, each with a particular purpose, in the Filters pane. The basic filtering shows you every value that might be entered for the given column and lets you select as many values as you want to have their status changed to "true." It's not at all difficult to grasp. **The sophisticated filtering provides you with the ability to combine two distinct and one-of-a-kind criteria, each of which has logic associated with it depending on the kind of data that the column represents:**

- Contains (text)
- Does not contain (text)
- Starts with (text)
- Does not start with (text)
- Is (all)
- Is not (all)
- Is blank (all)
- Is not blank (all)
- Is empty (text)
- Is not empty (text)
- Is after (date)
- Is on or after (date)
- Is before (date)
- Is on or before (date)
- Is less than (number)
- Is less than or equal to (number)
- Is greater than (number)
- Is greater than or equal to (number)

It is important to remember that you are the one who needs to enter the value into the subheading, even though most of these criteria are self-explanatory. This is not the case with the usual filtering option, which gives you a list of potential values. Next, by clicking the button, you can create a "and/or" condition and create a second logic set. Setting a second logic condition is not required to benefit from complex filtering. The third type of popular filter that is utilized is a Top N-type filter. With a specific value in your model that might or might not be in that graphic, you can indicate how many top or bottom values you want to show. Clicking the "Settings" button will allow you to accomplish this. You can choose how many of the field's values to show and whether the visual should show the highest or lowest values for that specific field by looking at your top 10 sales clients, ranked by state, country, revenue, or volume. This is a great example of how to do this. You will notice that the Top N option is not available when filtering for an entire page or report. The Top N filtering algorithm works best when applied at the visual level. Two additional types of filters can be applied to dates: relative date and relative time. The relative time will only be displayed when there is a time component in the date field. With the use of these filter options; you may specify exact time frames for a report or a visual, such as the last year, the next week, or the last 10 days. You can go into this degree of depth by using hours and minutes in conjunction with relative time.

A Quick Rundown of the Other Panes

You will not see the first four panes by default; however, you can make them visible by selecting the View tab, and they will display in the order that you add them. These panels are the Bookmarks pane, the **Selection pane, the Performance Analyzer pane, and the Sync Slicers** pane.

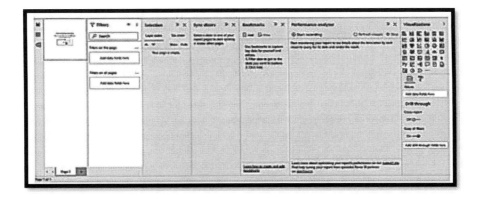

The Bookmarks box allows you to save filters, drills, and any other criteria you may have selected for a certain report page. This stores the page so you can view it at a later time. Suppose, for illustration purposes, that we have a sample report page that shows every piece of information. Ideally, though, end users should be able to quickly switch the report to a specific filtered view. Bookmarks can be used to switch between different states of the page. The Selection pane makes it simple to change the report's item visibility as well as the elements' stacking order. But when you add images to the canvas, even when the part of the box covering the logo is blank, the box related to the image covers up the logo. To fix it, you will need to bring the logo front and center. From within this panel, you may adjust the document's layering order as well as move the logo to the front. Moreover, grouping items makes them easier to handle and move together. When you're ready, the Performance Analyzer will walk you through the process of debugging any issues that may be causing a report to load more slowly than it did in the past or appear later than you think it should. Using the Performance analyzer, you can find out how long it takes to create the DAX query, display the results, and create additional items in milliseconds. This also applies to the DAX that Power BI used to produce the image. Knowing the complete filter and row contexts might help you better understand how Power BI generates the appropriate code to drive the visualization once you have some experience with DAX. This is because machine-generated DAX isn't always the easiest for beginners to understand. In a similar vein, if your report is experiencing problems, you can try out various settings to see if they affect the report's performance and whether or not it improves.

The "**Sync slicers**" pane is the last pane. When you add slicer visuals to a report, the visuals will only work on that particular page of the report. You can, however, choose a slicer, add it to additional pages, and sync them using the "**Sync slicers**" window. This will guarantee that any modifications made to the slicer on one page will be mirrored across all other websites that utilize it. This can be quite beneficial for exploratory research when someone is searching through the data and they find, for example, a specific company that they want to focus on. The slicer selection made in one area of the report will be applied to all other pages in the report that also contain that slicer if that filter is selected there. You can even specify that, for example, the synchronization should occur on Page A and not Page B.

Data View

Using the Data view in your report, you will be able to see the data at the table level. The columns in your report will be shown in the order that they occur in the report, rather than in alphabetical order. Ordinal order is the sequence in which the columns appear in the data source. The columns' Power Query display order before their importation into our data model is referred to as the ordinal order in our case. First, you'll notice that the ribbon now has two additional places that you can interact with. When a certain column is chosen, and only then, will the "**Column tools**" tab become visible. These tabs consider the context in every way.

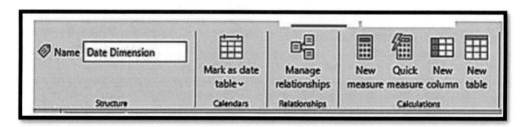

Here, you can change the name of the table, mark it as a date table, or view our relationships in the same way as we did from the ribbon. The Tools menu contains the Table Tools part. Furthermore, we offer several mathematical techniques for the construction of tables and metrics. Not much of this is new, and if you have selected a table or column, you can also find this view in the Report view. The sole unique feature of this platform that merits mention is the "Mark as date table" feature. Every time a date field appears in your data model, Power BI will automatically create a date table behind the scenes. This table will include all of the dates that fall between the first and final date associated with that field. It accomplishes this so that, behind the scenes, it can put together functionality for the date hierarchy as well as some other essential tasks. This is not a big problem at all in a model this size. However, the size of your model can grow very quickly if you start working with large models that contain dozens or even hundreds of hidden data tables. By creating your model to include a date table that will perform this function for all other dates, you may use Power BI to skip this step entirely. I can see the **"Column tools" tab** whenever I have a column selected for editing, as you can see in the image that follows.

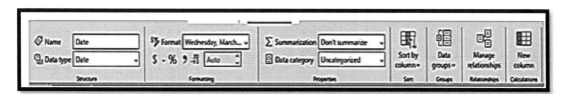

If I begin on the left, I can see the column name and the type of data it includes. The data type that this column uses, just called Date, is different from the Date/Time data type in this specific case. I'm looking at the Date column. I have a choice in the format of the data when it is shown visually. It's a date, therefore I may choose from a variety of options using a drop-down menu. You can display the value in several formats when you select a column containing numbers. These formats include money, decimal, whole, percentage, and scientific notation. The data model's default setting will be how the information is stored if you select the General option. The choices to select the currency, and percentage, display commas in numbers, and specify the number of decimal places for a value are all grayed-out and disabled since the data that was selected in the previously displayed picture is not of the numeric data type. Then, under "Properties," you'll discover a section where you can adjust that column's settings, including Power BI's default summary and the data classification scheme. Non-numeric columns are not summarized by default. Nonetheless, you can set up a default summary for any column, count, or count (distinct) that you like. For numerical columns, the sum operation is the default summary; however, this isn't always the best option. The default options for summarizing are the total, average, minimum, maximum, count, and count (distinct). If you want a certain column to not have any default summarizing, you can always set that column to "Don't summarize."

Under the Data category, you can find an overview of the events surrounding the specific data. Most columns have no data categories applied to them, so by default, they are left uncategorized. There aren't many options when it comes to numbers unless you want a certain number to be recognized as something else entirely, such as a postal code or barcode, for instance. For dates, there are no alternatives accessible in terms of data categories. Nonetheless, in certain visualizations, working with text-based data can be made much easier by selecting the appropriate options for the pertinent columns. The following categories are available for selection: **Address, Place, City, County, State or Province, Postal code, Country, Continent, Latitude, Longitude, Web URL, Image URL, and Barcode**. The next part is titled "**Sort by column**," and while it is tucked away, the environment it provides is very magnificent. When a column is included in a graphic, you will be able to provide a rule for it, allowing it to automatically sort itself per that rule. For analytical purposes, data groups allow you to swiftly assemble combinations of data, also called bins. There are many instances of this, but age groupings and anthropological classifications are among the most obvious. However, you can surely come up with a ton of other ways to divide them into groups. Possess an extensive and complex product list? Divide them into more manageable categories. Would you like to use a certain patient's condition as a control group and keep it apart from other patients' conditions? Please classify each of them specifically.

Conclusion

The Report and Data Views sections of Power BI are essential components that enable users to create visually appealing reports and gain deeper insights into their data. These components offer a wide range of features and capabilities that enable users to successfully analyze, display, and present their data. They give users access to a comprehensive set of tools that let them analyze findings, create insightful visualizations from data, and distribute reports to stakeholders. When users make use of these areas, they can fully utilize their data and make decisions based on facts, which is what propels the development of their organizations.

Activity

1. Configure the various aspects of the report view.
2. Configure the visualization pane and the field and filter panes.

CHAPTER 3
IMPORTING AND MODELING OUR DATA

Obtaining Data

One of the most important steps in importing and modeling data in Power BI is obtaining the right data for analysis. This is among the most crucial steps to take. This section focuses on the many methods and factors to be taken into account while gathering data from several sources and making it ready for Power BI modeling.

These techniques and concerns are discussed in further detail below.

1. **Identifying Data Sources**: Before importing data into Power BI, it is essential to first identify the data sources that are relevant to the data that will be imported. Databases, spreadsheets, online services, and storage in the cloud are all potential examples of these types of sources. It is of the utmost importance to have a crystal clear grasp of the location of the data as well as how it can be accessed.

2. **Extraction of Data**: Data extraction from the several sources that have been found is the next step. When it comes to the data extraction process, Power BI offers customers a variety of options. These alternatives include importing files from local storage, establishing direct connections to databases, and utilizing web connectors for web-based data sources. The selection of an extraction approach should be guided by two factors: the nature of the data and the accessibility of the data.

3. **Transformation of the Data**: To ensure that the data is appropriate for analysis, it is frequently necessary to alter it after it has been retrieved. Users of Power BI have access to a multitude of data transformation tools, including choices for cleaning, filtering, combining, separating, and aggregating data. These changes result in the data being improved and made ready for modeling.

4. **Integration of Data**: Data integration is required since it is common for the data required for analysis to come from multiple sources. With Power BI's assistance, users may combine data from several sources into a single dataset, making the integration of different datasets easier. To enhance the data quality, this process could involve merging tables, creating connections, or including computed columns.

5. **Refreshing the Data:** It is important to ensure that the data in Power BI is always brought up to date so that users may get accurate and pertinent insights. The imported data can be kept up to date with the help of Power BI's data refresh capabilities, which can be set to run on a predetermined basis. Users can specify refresh rates, and such frequencies can be based either on the update frequency of the data source or on the needs of the company.

6. **Data Security**: It is crucial to always keep data security and privacy concerns in mind when collecting data. A few of the unique security features of Power BI are encryption, row-level

security, and Azure Active Directory integration. These technologies are made to protect private information and restrict access to those who have been given permission.

7. **Data Governance**: It is very necessary to put in place appropriate data governance processes if one wants to maintain both the integrity and consistency of their data. Power BI makes it possible to put in place data governance measures inside an organization, such as defining data lineage, setting data refresh standards, and putting in place data access restrictions. These methods help to guarantee that data is used in a trustworthy manner across the business.

Importing the Data

These steps can be used to import data into a Power BI Desktop file:

1. **Launch Power BI Desktop**.
2. **Click on "Get Data":** The "**Get Data**" button is accessible on the Home ribbon on the Power BI Desktop home screen. Click it to start collecting data. A dialog window with numerous data source options will then be shown.
3. **Choose a Data Source**: From the list of options, choose the best data source. Many different sources are supported by Power BI, including databases, files, web services, and more. SQL Server, Excel, SharePoint, Azure services, Salesforce, and web connections are a few popular options for data sources.
4. **Connect to the Data Source**: After choosing the data source, a connection prompt will appear.

Depending on the source that is chosen, the connecting procedure differs. Here are a few illustrations:

- **Importing from Files**: To import data from a file-based data source, such as Excel or CSV, you can either explore your local file system or provide a file location.
- **Connecting to Databases**: The necessary connection details, such as the server address, database name, authentication type, and credentials, must be provided if you select a database source like SQL Server, Oracle, or MySQL.
- Power BI also provides web connectors for connecting to other internet services. You may have to provide API keys, URLs, or other authentication data for these sources.

Follow the prompts and provide the required information to establish the connection to your chosen data source.

5. **Specify Data Import Options**: After the connection has been made, you will be given the chance to choose how the data should be imported. Selecting the tables, views, or queries to import, defining import parameters, and carrying out any necessary conversions are all included in this.
6. **Transform and Shape the Data:** Data transformations can be used to clean and restructure the data once it has been imported. Power BI provides a range of tools and operations to filter, combine, divide, pivot, or aggregate the data to satisfy your analytical demands. The

Power Query Editor opens when the data is imported, and you can then access several transformation options from there.

7. **Load the Data**: Choose **"Close & Apply"** in the Power Query Editor to import the data into the Power BI data model after completing the necessary transformations. Power BI Desktop will then enable analysis and visualization of the imported data.

8. **Refresh Data**: If you expect that the data source may change over time, you can configure data refresh settings to maintain the currency of the imported data. With Power BI, you can plan when to update your data or create automated refreshes that happen in response to specific events.

9. **Explore and Visualize the Data**: Now that the data has been imported into Power BI Desktop, you can use the visualization tools and capabilities to explore and analyze it. To learn from your data, create reports, dashboards, and interactive visualizations.

The Power Query Ribbon

The Home Tab

In Power Query, the Home tab is mostly uncomplicated. We can see all the icons in their respective groups in the figure below. We'll go over each one and give you some ideas of how you can utilize it.

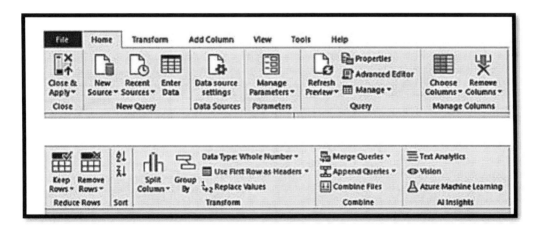

All of your previous edits are applied as soon as you click the Close & Apply button, which also refreshes any affected data components. Three options will display in a drop-down menu when you click the drop-down arrow: Close & Apply, Apply, which closes Power Query but implements changes, and Leave, which makes no changes, are the first three options. Power BI Desktop will alert you to any unapplied changes if you decide to exit. We can add new data by using the New Source button located in the New Query section. While clicking the drop-down arrow creates a drop-down menu with the most popular data, selecting its icon opens the whole data source selection menu. Using the Recent Sources button, you can quickly establish a connection to any data source you have previously used—not just the one that is included in your open Power BI Desktop file. This can be useful if you are constructing a new model and want to improve it with a feature from a previous project, or if you are testing and want to rapidly build a second file and link. A straightforward table structure where you may manually insert data and set column names will emerge when you enter data. Enter Data can be useful if you have multiple data sources and need to rapidly add a new dimension that might not be present elsewhere in your data, however, I wouldn't recommend using it frequently.

Enter Data's interface is similar to Excel, except it does not offer formulae or data validation criteria. There are merely rows and columns, and more human administration is needed the more data you add. Enter Data is available if needed, although I generally discourage utilizing it because of this. A window will open when you select the "Data source settings" button. After that, you can modify or remove rights, export a PBIDS file for that data source, and change sources. For that data source, a PBIDS file is effectively a Power BI Desktop shortcut that you may use in another Power BI file. Using Manage settings, you may add, check, and update each of your existing settings. Power Query parameters are settings that can be used in certain scenarios to alter how particular data is dealt with. There are many uses for parameters, including parameter rules in deployment pipelines, what-if analysis, and more. A query's meaning isn't always obvious, but you can manage it by checking its attributes, refreshing the preview, utilizing the Advanced Editor, or visiting the Query section of the Home page. You can obtain an updated preview of the data for the query that is currently highlighted and utilize it as a working reference by clicking on the Refresh Preview button. This can be helpful if you have datasets that are updated frequently and you want to ensure that your intended transformation behavior is still being obtained despite the data changes. By pressing the drop-down arrow, you can also select to update the preview of each active query in your model. When you click the Properties button, a dialog box appears with the query's name, description, and two checkboxes for "**Enable load to report**" and "**Include in report refresh**"—both of which are automatically chosen. Until it is added, there is nothing in the description box, thus explaining a query can be useful.

When "Enable load to report" is off, any graphics that rely on that table will stop functioning because the entire table will be treated as though it doesn't exist. Think of this as the equivalent of gently removing a table from your data model. It is still available in Power Query if you would like to re-enable it, but Power BI ignores it otherwise. A clearer indication of the "Include in report" refresh process would be preferable. If "Enable load" is turned off, then the table will not be included when the report refreshes. Deactivating this preserves the current state of the data in the model; however, data refreshes do not update that query. If you have a large table and would like to test some other changes in a data refresh without refreshing the largest table, use this method. People will sometimes keep specific data for a while to do things like audits. In the Advanced Editor, you can view the actual M that results from each adjustment you make. Seeing the code that is generated as you make a change is great, in my opinion, especially if you're interested in learning the language. I believe that M is a language that is easy to learn but difficult to master. Duplicate your working code in a text file or other backup before making changes if you want to attempt changing the M straight from the editor here. The reason is that, regardless of whether your code is usable or not, whatever modifications you make and then click **Done**, that's what you'll receive. As with everything programming, a good rule of thumb is to always keep a backup! And lastly, the Manage button. When you select this button, you have three options: Delete, Duplicate, and Reference. When a query is duplicated, it retains all of its original formatting. This is simple, but it does need you to store the information twice. The reference adopts a somewhat different strategy. It generates a new query that initially appears to be a duplicate but isn't. It allows you to pick up where the final version of the query it's referring to leaves off. Take care, as any changes you make to the parent query will also affect the referred query, perhaps causing problems with it. There are two options in the **Manage Columns** section: **Choose Columns and Remove Columns**. Both methods take you there, but they do it in different ways. Click the Choose Columns icon to select which columns to keep in the query and remove the others. Click the Choose Columns drop-down arrow to access the previously mentioned Choose Columns dialog box or to select a single column in the query. This second option can be useful if a query has a lot of columns and you are not sure which order to keep them in. The column is only removed when the Remove Columns button is clicked. No dialog box is displayed. Columns that are selected are removed. Clicking the Remove Columns drop-down arrow brings up a menu with another choice, to Remove Other Columns. By doing this, any column that you haven't selected is eliminated. The Reduce Rows portion is divided into two parts: Keep Rows and Remove Rows. Every has a unique use case that is focused on the rows between X and Y or the first X rows. One thing I do want to warn you about in this area is the ability to remove duplicate rows, as shown in the Remove Rows section. It's crucial to be aware that it eliminates duplicates depending on the columns you've chosen. Therefore, if you simply choose one column and eliminate duplicates, you risk losing information that you had planned to maintain. You can choose a column and then sort in either ascending or descending order using the Sort section. When more than one column is chosen, this is ineffective.

There are a few simple transformation choices in the Transform section that follow. With Split Columns, you may use any delimiter to split a given column into multiple columns. When you need to separate the first and last names in a single-name column, this is a popular use. Group By allows you to combine the outcomes of your current query. For instance, if you have a large amount of data and wish to pre-aggregate it to remove specific rows, this can be useful. Using the Data Type button, we may change the selected column's data type. When new data is added to Power Query, Power BI will try to identify the different types of data on its own. Although Power BI does an excellent job of identifying data types, there are instances when it makes a mistake and you will need to make a manual change. Coincidentally, by examining the icon in the column header, you may rapidly confirm the data type of a column. Use the First Row as headers is easily explained, and Power BI frequently makes an effort to ascertain if the first row contains column headers, based on the data source. Click the arrow next to the Use First Row as Headers button to see another option: making your headers the first row. Use the Replace data function to find and replace data in a certain column. Either treating zeros as nulls or nulls as zeros would be a typical use case, depending on your methodology. It is important to keep in mind that Power Query only comprehends columns; it does not understand cells, thus you cannot alter individual cells. With the help of the Combine section, we may add queries, merge queries, and merge files. Similar to a SQL **JOIN** statement, merge queries operate. A JOIN statement instructs the computer to provide the value for Column N and add it whenever the values in Columns A and A in Tables A and B are equivalent. Let's imagine you have Column A in Table A and Column A in Table B and you want to add Column N from Table B to Table A. The same thing is being done here.

Append Queries are designed to combine many inquiries with the same kind and structure of data into a single, lengthier query that resembles a UNION statement from SQL.. Combine Files helps you to avoid the issue in Append Queries by pre-combining many files into a single view. Make sure you are getting the intended outcome before adding any tables. This option will combine all of that to create a single result covering all the columns and values across the two tables, should you want to have any that are unique to each table. And lastly, there are resources in the AI Insights section that your business can use to connect to Azure AI services. Understand that you need to be using Power BI Premium for these capabilities to be updated. To find out more, find out whether your company uses **Azure Machine Learning Studio** or **Cognitive Services** by asking your **Azure administrator**.

Transform Tab

There are other options for converting your data on the Transform tab, beyond what we saw in the Transform section of the Home page. However, let's first have a look at the image below before examining the entire **Transform tab**. **Group By and Use First Row as Headers** are the first things we encounter in the Table section. Your columns become rows when you use transpose. Reverse Rows flip the row-by-row order of your data such that the last record appears before the first and vice versa. The command Count Rows will display the number of rows in the query.

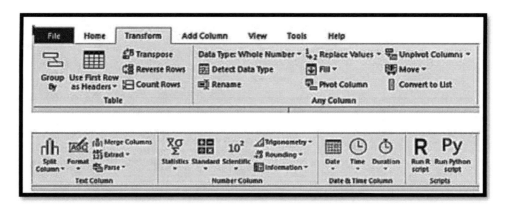

The **Any Column section** offers the option to alter a column's data type. Values can also be changed. With the help of **Unpivot Columns**, you can restructure the columns of data you've chosen into an "**attributes**" column and a "**values**" column. You may wish to reshape your data in this manner at times, such as when you want to combine many columns into a few columns with a larger number of entries. The Detect Data Type button will examine each column and attempt to assign the appropriate data type based on how the data is presented. Power BI will frequently do this function automatically when you first import data into Power Query. Nevertheless, you can tell Power BI to repeat this procedure if you make a lot of transformation changes that could change the data types of multiple columns. For any missing values, whether at the top or bottom of the column, you may use the Fill button to replace them with a value based on other values in the column. A column in a table can be moved by using the **Move** button. You can reposition it to the left, the right, the beginning, or the end. With many columns chosen, you can accomplish this. Rename lets you change the name of a selected column. The values of a column can be transformed into columns using Pivot Column, and the values can then be recalculated throughout the new combination. This can be useful when you wish to display the values and characteristics as columns, with the values in one column and the attributes in another. One unique function is Convert to List. It takes one column and uses Power Query to turn it into a list, a particular type of table. Lists can be passed to some custom functions in the same way as arguments are. Since you can use these functions on more than simply text columns, the Text Column section has an odd name. Thankfully, they are pretty straightforward for the most part.

Split Column enables you to choose a delimiter and divide a column into two columns. You cannot change the data type in format. You may make all the data lowercase, or uppercase, or add prefixes or suffixes, for example. By using this functionality, the column will change to a text-type column. With the option to choose a separator, **Merge Columns** mashes two or more columns together. With Extract, you can modify a column or columns while keeping certain characters within the column. Parse does something different from anything else here. Parse transforms semi-structured data from an XML or JSON file into a more structured format that is suitable for analysis. We don't utilize any JSON or XML files in our examples, but if you were working with NoSQL databases or getting results from API requests, you would have to parse the data before examining it. That's what this parse function does. In addition to doing conventional calculations against a column to change its values, the Number Column functions allow you to round a column, check if a number is even or odd, or ascertain its sign. You can also perform trig functions against a column. I advise duplicating a column before making any changes to the data, except the statistics function, so that you can have both the original clean value and the updated value. Similar to the **Number Column**, the **Date & Time Column** section performs a variety of date and time changes. The Scripts area, the last one in the Transform tab, allows you to execute R and Python scripts against your data. To use these functions, you must have installed R or Python, and Power BI must know where you have installed those language libraries. If you can work with data frames in R or Python more easily, you can do transformations there and use it as a single step. You can also use a script task, pre-prepare the job using Power Query, and then make additional modifications in Power Query. It is possible to combine these features, so you could use both.

The Add Column Tab

The first thing to note in the Add Column tab is that except for the General section, we have seen all the other functions in other places in the ribbon to this point. However, the General section contains so much that it still merits a section of its own.

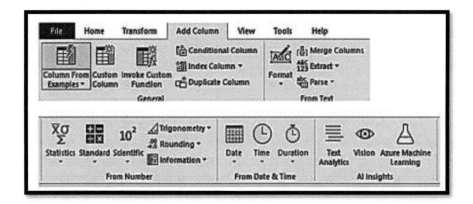

- You can create a custom column using M by choosing the "**Custom Column**" option, which will cause a dialog box to display. This method may be useful in situations when there are transformations that need to be carried out but are either not supported by the user interface or may be carried out more effectively by code. You will be notified of any syntactic mistakes in the code by the dialogue box. On the other hand, the mistakes might not necessarily be very instructive for people who are still learning M.
- One powerful tool that lets the user iterate over a function for a specified column is the Invoke Custom Function feature. In this process, a specific value is identified, and then a particular logic is applied to it. A simple example is the development of a function that produces a new column. The function then takes the value of one column and multiplies it by another to get a third value that is put into the newly made column. Have you understood the previously stated logic? This is a very powerful tool, but it could take some time to understand how to use it for the first time.
- The **Conditional Column** feature enables the creation of a column that follows the structure of an if-then-else statement. If **Column X** is smaller than **Column Y**, the answer is Yes; otherwise, it is No. It is also possible to include multiple clauses to create more complex or iterative if functions. If one is acquainted with SQL, it can be likened to a case-when statement.
  - By creating a column with a start value of 0 or 1, the Index Column function creates a unique array of values that are typically connected to the row number. An index column's most important feature is its complete uniqueness, which allows it to function as an impromptu key value. This value can then be combined with other columns to send the index or key value to other tables and create associations. Ideally, the keys to your data should already be there, thus an index becomes unnecessary. If an index is needed, though, the procedure is rather simple.
  - A copy of the current column is produced by the Duplicate Column function. That brings an end to the discussion. I have nothing insightful to say about that assertion. The task at hand merely involves duplicating and transferring information from one location to another.
- Lastly, the **View tab**. The options available on the View tab provide users with the ability to make minor adjustments to their Power Query interaction experience. To gain a more

comprehensive understanding of your data at the columnar level, highlight the **Column quality, Column distribution**, and **Column profile** checkboxes in the **Data Preview** section.

These choices offer more details on the particulars of your data. These include a percentage analysis of true, false, and null values in a column, a numerical breakdown of values in a column, and a data distribution covering the number of unique values in a column. Please click the **"Close & Apply"** option when you are ready to apply the changes to your data and have finished making all the necessary adjustments. You will be taken to the Power BI Desktop canvas after closing the Power Query window.

The Model-View

When you go back to Power BI, you should check out the Model view, which is the third view in Power BI Desktop. What purpose do connections serve? What have they accomplished? Is it possible to ignore relationships and produce a thorough table that solves the problem of world hunger? These ideas will be discussed in the section that follows.

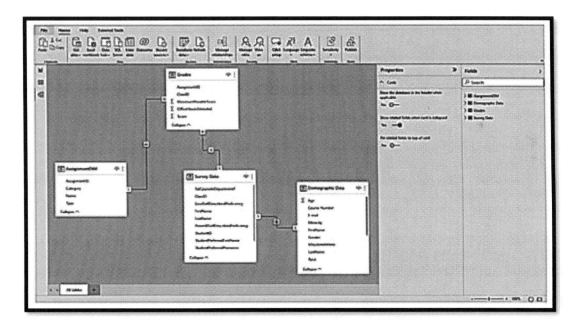

Power BI will automatically attempt to detect relationships during the data import process. This occurs when the data is arranged in a manner that allows Power BI to accurately identify the relationships between the various data elements. Regrettably, it does not consistently perform this task effectively. Consequently, it is advisable to verify your relationships post-importing data to ensure that your model is structured as per your intended design.

What Is a Relationship?

Relationships are intricate and multidimensional concepts. It describes the relationship or affiliation of two or more people, defined by a variety of social, emotional, and physical attributes. A relationship in Power BI is the connection created between two tables based on one or more common fields, or columns. A business intelligence and data visualization application called Power BI was created by Microsoft to let customers connect, transform, and analyze data from many sources. It is common to come across similar data that is scattered over several tables when using Power BI. A "Customers" table and an "Orders" table, each of which is associated with a unique customer, could be an example of this. By creating a relational connection between those tables, it is possible to combine and examine data from both sources with ease. By comparing the values of a column in one table—also referred to as the primary key—with the values of a column in another table—also referred to as the foreign key—a relationship is created in Power BI. Once the relationship has been established, Power BI may perform a variety of tasks, including filtering, aggregating, and creating visuals that combine data from several tables.

Types of Relationships in Power BI

Power BI facilitates three distinct relationship types, namely one-to-one, one-to-many, and many-to-many.

Each classification denotes a distinct form of correlation between tables and carries its ramifications for the analysis of data.

- **One-to-One Relationship:** Every entry in the primary table has a matching record in the associated table in a one-to-one relationship, but this relationship can only contain a single record. This association is useful for creating a hierarchical structure or establishing relationships between tables that share data. When each person is linked to a single address, this is an example of connecting a "Person" table to an "Address" table.
- **One-to-Many Relationship:** The most common kind of relationship in Power BI is one-to-many. With this specific relationship, every record in the main table may have several corresponding records in the related table. When a single entity has several linked entities, this kind of relationship is considered suitable. Creating a relationship between a "Customers" table and an "Orders" table, where each customer can have many orders, is one example of this.
- **Many-to-Many Relationship:** When every record in two tables can have several linked records in the other table, this is known as a many-to-many relationship. Nevertheless, many-to-many relationships are not directly supported by Power BI. To handle these kinds of circumstances, an intermediate table—also called a "bridge table" or "junction table"—must be employed. By creating two one-to-many linkages, the table referred to as the bridge table helps to resolve the many-to-many relationship. This approach avoids the problem of redundant data and enables effective data analysis.

Building and Controlling Relationships in Power BI

One of the most important parts of data modeling in Power BI is the process of establishing and maintaining relationships. Establishing connections between tables in a dataset is necessary to produce precise and perceptive reports. A detailed comprehension of the data sources and the connections among them is necessary for efficient relationship management in Power BI. Table relationship generation and administration are made easy with the help of the Power BI platform's intuitive interface. **The subsequent steps delineate the procedure:**

- **Identification of Common Fields**: To establish a relationship, it is imperative to identify the common fields (columns) that are present in both tables. The aforementioned fields ought to encompass analogous data that can be utilized to establish logical connections between the tables.
- **Defining Relationships:** Once common fields have been identified, users can go ahead and designate the primary key and foreign key columns to define associations. By examining the column names, Power BI can automatically find feasible relationships and suggest matches, which expedites the setup process.
- **Managing Relationships**: Once relationships have been established, users can further manage and customize them according to their preferences. Within Power BI, it is possible to modify the cardinality and cross-filtering direction for each relationship. Cardinality is a term used to specify the number of records from the primary table that can be linked to a single record from the related table. The process of cross-filtering is utilized to ascertain the impact of filtering in one table on the data exhibited in the associated table.
- **Handling Ambiguous Relationships:** Multiple relationships between tables may occur in scenarios where Power BI is faced with unclear relationships. It is required for users to define the active relationship explicitly in such cases. In doing so, it ensures that Power BI understands the precise relationship to use for analyzing data and producing reports.

Benefits and Applications of Relationships in Power BI

- **Comprehensive Analysis:** A thorough examination shows that relationships make it easier to combine data from different tables, producing a coherent and unified view of the data. This feature makes it easier to analyze the data in-depth, allowing for a careful investigation of its nuances and the acquisition of insightful viewpoints regarding different facets of the dataset.
- **Efficient reporting**: Relationship building is a means to this end since it allows users to create dynamic reports and visualizations that update automatically as they work with the data. One of Power BI's primary features is the use of relationships, which makes it possible to efficiently aggregate, filter, and summarize data. This feature makes creating educational dashboards and reporting easier.
- **Data Exploration and Discovery:** The utilization of relationships facilitates the process of data exploration and discovery, allowing users to uncover concealed patterns, correlations, and trends present within the data. Through the strategic utilization of relationships,

Power BI enables its users to seamlessly traverse the data model, discern interconnections, and execute impromptu analyses with ease.

- **Simplified Data Maintenance:** Relationships are used in data management to remove redundant data, which simplifies data maintenance procedures. Relationships allow users to store data in an organized way, which lowers the amount of data that has to be stored and makes changes and revisions easier. There is no longer any need to duplicate data across several tables with this method.

- **Scalability and Flexibility:** Power BI is capable of supporting interactions between large datasets, which makes it possible to scale complex data models. It also provides flexibility to accommodate various data sources and adjust to evolving business requirements. Relationships also let users integrate data from many sources more adaptable, which enables them to work with a variety of data formats and types.

The Properties Pane

The contextual nature of the Properties pane within the Model view is highly notable. The Properties pane can always be located on the right-hand side. The Properties pane will adjust according to the selected data object, displaying only the relevant information for the chosen data element. The Name, Description, Synonyms, Row label, Key column, Is hidden flag and Is featured table flag are displayed when a table is selected. This window will show the Storage mode under the Advanced section. There are three different storage modes: Import, DirectQuery, and Dual. It is crucial to remember that an item that is in import mode cannot be changed and is hence immutable. View the image below to see an example of the Properties pane in action. The "Name" field should go without saying. You can leave the Description field blank, but it's best to include a brief synopsis of the table's contents or its purpose in your data model. The Q&A feature has been made easier by the listing of synonyms. One way to designate a column to serve as the default column in Q&A sessions about a specific table is by using the Row label feature.

Finding a column that only contains unique values is made easier by the Key column. A unique icon will show up next to a column in the Fields pane if it has been determined to be the key column. The table won't show up in the Report view if the value for "Is hidden" is set to "Yes". As a result, objects from that table cannot be included in report items. Note that any pre-existing objects made with the previously specified table will still be viewable. However, it will no longer be possible to add data pieces from that table to new visualizations. When a single column is selected, the Name, Description, Synonyms, Display folder, and Is hidden flags are visible. The data type of the column and the format of the data it contains are visible in the Formatting portion of the pane. Users can select an additional column to be sorted for in the Advanced section. Additionally, they might recognize a pertinent data category, which acts as a unique identifier for particular kinds of data that Power BI would need in certain circumstances. Users also have the option to set a default summary. You may also choose whether or not to allow a column to include null values in this portion of the window. All the guidance provided in the preceding table section is applicable. Making use of display folders is a useful way to keep your data model structured. This entails organizing related data components within a table into a subdirectory. This procedure does not change or modify any factual facts; its only goal is to improve visual clarity. Alternatively, measures can be arranged into display folders. This is particularly useful when trying to group specific objects that aren't always easy to find in Power BI's more extensive alphabetical sorting mechanism in the Fields pane.

Conclusion

In conclusion, we have looked in-depth at a few key tools and functionalities that are built into Power BI. The Power Query Ribbon, Model View, Relationships, Add Column, Home, Transform, and Properties Pane are a few of these. Each of these elements is essential to the modeling, data analysis, and transformation processes. Together, the many capabilities and functionalities included in Power BI provide a stable and adaptable platform for reporting and data analysis. When these technologies are used effectively, people may create visually appealing reports and dashboards, build large data models, link meaningfully, and transform raw data into actionable insights. With Power BI, customers can make the most of their data to make wise decisions and propel their organizations to success.

Activity

1. Import your data.
2. Model your data as you would like to.
3. What is a relationship?
4. What are the various types of relationships in Power BI?

CHAPTER 4
LET'S MAKE SOME PICTURES (VISUALIZING DATA 101)

Why Visualize Data?

A group of devoted analysts were employed in a bustling business setting, where their task was to interpret complex data sets. They realized that one of their biggest challenges would be informing decision-makers and other stakeholders about their findings in an appropriate manner. At that point, they learned about the value of data visualization, specifically through the use of Power BI. The analysts soon realized that creating visually appealing charts and graphs was only one aspect of data visualization; another was converting unprocessed data into a compelling narrative. They began on a trip using the collection of visualization tools provided by Power BI at their disposal, to discover the tales that were buried inside the data. From the moment they began their first project, the crew realized how important it was to make the information easy to understand. They knew the people who made the decisions didn't have the time or interest to comb through spreadsheets filled with hundreds of rows and columns of data. They require a visual representation of the data that will enable them to swiftly understand its most crucial elements. The team was able to present the data in a way that was both visually appealing and easy to understand because of the extensive range of visualization styles that Power BI offers, including pie charts, bar charts, and line graphs.

Their newly developed ability to create visually appealing visualizations caused the analysts to observe a substantial change in the way decisions were made. Decision makers may independently examine the data by focusing on certain aspects and using filters to gain deeper insights, all the while presenting their findings through interactive dashboards powered by Power BI. With Power BI's interactive functionality, stakeholders could test hypotheses, ask questions, and make judgments based on the data, which simplified the process of making data-driven decisions. The team soon concluded that data visualizations were a gateway to the investigation and discovery of the data rather than just a means of presenting the data. Thanks to Power BI's interactive features, they were able to explore the geography of the data, uncovering hidden linkages, identifying outliers, and identifying patterns that would have remained hidden otherwise. Throughout their investigation, they found that the ability to chop and dice the data, filter it using a range of criteria, and observe the visualizations react dynamically in real time was an extremely useful tool. Up until they understood that data visualization could be utilized to create engaging tales, the analysts made significant progress. With the aid of Power BI's features, like tooltips, custom layouts, and annotations, they were able to construct a narrative around the data. They were able to highlight the key topics and lead stakeholders through the findings as a result. They concluded that by using visuals, they could captivate and engage their audience, increasing the significance and memorability of the data. The group also used Power BI's tools for information sharing and teamwork. They used the platform to publish reports, dashboards, and data visualizations to the

Power BI service. This gave members of the team and other stakeholders the ability to see and engage with the data. The newly discovered cooperation encouraged the sharing of information across the business, as well as alignment and the making of well-informed decisions.

Furthermore, Power BI enabled the analysts to keep an eye on real-time data streams and respond quickly to changing circumstances. With access to live data connections and refresh capabilities, they may create real-time updating visualizations. These graphics offered current information on significant parameters. As a result, they were able to take advantage of fresh opportunities, deal with mounting obstacles, and make changes quickly. Ultimately, the group of analysts discovered that Power BI data visualization was more than just a technique or instrument; rather, it was an effective way to exchange, examine, and utilize data to get better outcomes. It turned their analytical journey from a sea of statistics into an engaging tale, which allowed them to uncover the real worth of their data and make a significant contribution to the decision-making process of their business. Let's now talk about the data visualization capabilities that Power BI offers to help us use our data to tell that story. Consider them as individual alphabet letters. Once you've mastered the art of creating words with them, you'll eventually create stories with them as well as learn how to make the most of each visualization via practice and patience.

The Visualizations pane

You can create visualizations, change them by adding the required data points, format your visualizations, and add additional analytics capabilities that Power BI offers in some of these visuals in the Visualizations pane. You can add, modify, or format them to accomplish any of these tasks with your visualizations. The three main parts of the Visualizations window are the Fields, Format, and Analytics sections.

Fields

Because all of the visualizations in the Fields section take a different set of inputs, it is important to remember that each one will seem different from the others. A matrix will not have the same visual representation as a bar chart, which will not resemble a map. Power BI will attempt to reallocate the selected fields and measures to the new visual if you have already added fields to it, but there is no guarantee that it will function exactly as you had intended. This is especially true if you decide to change the type of the visual yourself. If you choose a visual that is already on the canvas and then click a different visualization in the Visualizations pane, you will be able to alter the kind of visual that is already on the canvas. That sums it up well. Common elements that are present in many of the images in the Fields window include Axis, Legend, and Values. An axis indicates how you have classified your data. The data is arranged into subsections with their distinctions highlighted by a legend. The values are the actual numbers that you want to combine across different categories. The "Drill through" choices section is permanently present at the bottom of the Fields tab. With the help of this amazing feature, you can take a visual and apply the filters that are currently being applied to it to another visual that is on a different page. This will lead you directly to the report page with its collection of visuals. "Drill through" describes a very useful technique for transferring insights from one area of your report to another while keeping things consistent with the data that is being viewed.

Format

A paint roller-like icon used to stand in for the Format window in previous iterations. Right now, the icon for a graphic that hasn't been selected yet appears all over the page like a paintbrush. Conversely, the tool looks like a paintbrush overlaid on top of a bar graph when a visual on the canvas is selected. The format feature allows you to alter the general look and feel of a visualization to better meet your specific needs. The Format options are contextual to the currently updating visualization, just like Fields' settings are. There are a lot of options available, and many of them should look very familiar to you if you have experience working with PowerPoint. Each part in the Format tab has an arrow that you may use to expand or collapse that area. This is quite helpful when it comes to navigating. For this exercise, forget the notion that some of the tools under Format have specific uses; instead, concentrate on the idea that Format is where you go to make your visualizations genuinely stand out.

Analytics

Not every visualization can be used with the Analytics features, which are available by clicking the image of a magnifying glass and looking at a graph. Remember that no custom visuals can utilize the Analytics section. This is another important thing to remember. This feature allows you to add average, median, trend, percentile, minimum value, maximum, and constant lines for comparison, as well as lines to indicate when something is below a threshold, as well as lines for anomaly detection. Only for graphics where Analytics is functional is this available. There is a lot of capability available under Analytics, but getting the most out of it depends on the context, so don't be afraid to experiment to find out what does and doesn't work for you and the project you're working on.

Visual Interactivity

The ability to interact with visual elements inside a report or dashboard, like tables and charts, is referred to as "visual interactivity" in the context of Power BI. Users can choose and filter individual data points or categories, delve deeper into details, and dynamically change the visual representations of the data to explore and study the data. Some of Power BI's interactive features enhance the user experience overall and enable deeper data exploration.

The following is a list of important visual interactive features that are available in Power BI:

1. **Selection and Highlighting:** Users can select categories or data points inside a graphic by clicking on them; the selections they make will then be highlighted. To present a cohesive

view of the data, Power BI highlights the selected elements and adjusts the other report graphics accordingly. As a consequence, users can focus on specific elements and comprehend how those elements impact the entire report.

2. **Filtering:** To focus on certain subsets of the shown data, Power BI users can apply filters to their visualizations. The user can choose a specific value or range of values to filter the data, or they can utilize sophisticated filtering tools. A report's corresponding graphics are changed to match the filtered data when a filter is applied, creating a uniform perspective throughout the document.

3. **Drill-through:** Power BI users can drill down into related information by clicking on data points or categories, which is made possible by the drill-through actions that can be defined in the software. Users are thus given the ability to explore data structures and go more deeply into certain parts of the data.

4. **Cross-filtering and Cross-highlighting**: Both of these features are supported by Power BI, allowing users to cross-filter and cross-highlight across different visualizations. It filters or highlights the matching data points in other related visuals when a user chooses data in one visualization, and it does this automatically. Users can explore the relationships and correlations between the various data items because of this behavior's interactive nature.

5. **Bookmarks and Buttons**: Power BI gives you the ability to develop interactive navigation via the use of bookmarks and buttons. Bookmarks save the visuals in their present form, including any filters, options, and drill-through levels that have been applied. After that, users can move between the many bookmarked views using buttons, which provides a guided experience for the data exploration process.

6. **Tooltips**: Power BI tooltips provide more information and insights to users when they hover their mouse cursor over data points in visualization. You can set tooltips to display different types of data fields, calculations, or user-defined expressions based on your choices. When tooltips are used to provide context-sensitive information without overcrowding the visualizations, the overall quality of the interactive experience is enhanced.

7. **Q&A Natural Language Queries:** The Q&A feature of Power BI allows users to ask questions about the data they have access to using natural language inquiries. This feature makes natural language inquiries possible. To deliver pertinent visual representations and insights, Power BI analyzes the queries. Users can ask questions verbally or in writing. This feature makes it unnecessary to use pre-made visualizations by offering an interactive and user-friendly way to navigate data.

Enable the visual interaction controls

The ability to customize how the visualizations on the report page filter and highlight one another is available after you can alter a report. This will enable the visual interaction controls.

1. Select a visualization to make it active.
2. Display the **Visual Interactions** options.

Within Power BI Desktop, go to the **Format** menu and then click **Edit Interactions**.

3. Every single one of the other visualizations on the report page gets a new filter and highlight icons thanks to Power BI.

The treemap facilitates cross-filtering between the map and the line chart. Additionally, the treemap cross-highlighting the column chart as well. The chosen visualization's interaction with the other visualizations displayed on the report page can now be adjusted. The report page's parameters can be used to accomplish this.

Change the interaction behavior

Select each visualization on your report page individually to become acquainted with how they work together. Examine the effects of selecting a single data point, bar, or shape on the other visualizations. If you determine that the behavior being displayed does not sit well with you, you have the option to change the interactions. You and everyone else who consumes the report will have the same visual interaction experience because these changes are retained in the report. Select a visualization to activate it to get started. Please notice that all of the other visualizations on this page now feature interaction icons. The next step is to identify the influence that the chosen visualization should have on the other options. You can repeat this process for each of the additional visualizations that are included on the report page.

Options for selected visualizations

- To employ the currently chosen visualization as a cross-filter for another of the visualizations on this page, click the filter icon that is located in the top right corner of that visualization. Line charts, scatter charts, and map data are the only types of charts that can be cross-filtered. They cannot be cross-highlighted in any way.
- Select the highlight icon if you want the currently chosen visualization to highlight one of the other visualizations on the page. This can be done by clicking the icon.
- Click the "**no impact**" symbol on the toolbar if you do not want the currently chosen visualization to have any effect on any of the other visualizations shown on the page.

Column and Bar Charts

Columns and bar charts are two of the most common types of visualizations used in Power BI. These charts are used to show categorical data and compare results across a variety of categories.

Both kinds of charts provide the data in the form of horizontal and vertical bars, with the length or height of the bars standing in for the respective data values:

1. **Column Chart**: The bars in a column chart are aligned vertically along the x-axis and are shown in a column format. The height of the bar correlates to the data value that is connected with that category, and each bar in the graph represents a different category. Column charts are often used to compare results across a variety of categories or to monitor changes over time.
2. **Bar Chart:** The use of horizontal bars that are parallel to the chart's y-axis defines a bar chart. The length of each bar in the chart indicates the quantity of data for that particular category, although each bar itself represents a separate category. The column chart and this are comparable. When comparing data in a specific order, such as ranking, or when the category titles are lengthy, bar charts are frequently utilized. The display of financial data is another common use for bar charts.

To create a column or bar chart in Power BI, you can follow these steps:

1. **Prepare your data:** Make sure that your data has both a categorical column that represents the categories and a numerical column that represents the values that are linked with each category. This is an important step in the data preparation process.
2. **Open Power BI Desktop**: Launch the Power BI Desktop application on your computer.
3. **Connect to the data source you want to use:** After loading the data into Power BI, connect to the data source you want to use, which might be an Excel file, a database, or a cloud service.

4. **Drag and drop the desired fields:** Drag the numerical column (Sales Amount, for example) to the Values field well after dragging the category column (Product Category, for example) to the Axis field well from the Fields pane.

5. **Select the chart type:** Choose the sort of chart you want to use by clicking the "**Column Chart**" or "**Bar Chart**" button in the Visualizations window. This option is based on your taste. The chart will be generated by Power BI automatically and shown on the canvas.

6. **Customize the chart:** Use the formatting options found in the Visualizations tab to change the chart's appearance. This can be accomplished, among other ways, by altering the chart's legends, axes, colors, and labels. Additional elements, such as trend lines or data labels, can also be activated.

7. **Interact with the chart:** By selecting specific bars and columns, applying filters, and swiping down to more detailed views, users can engage with the chart.

Using column and bar charts in Power BI helps you display and compare data across categories more efficiently. As a result, you'll be able to understand your data more thoroughly and gain additional insights. In column and bar charts, constructing the x- and y-axes is frequently rather simple. We can then compare the data along two dimensions to obtain some information after taking them into account. Some charts have an additional y-axis option that lets us add a second y-axis for comparison purposes. **Power BI is equipped with the following visuals by default in the column and bar chart category (listed in the order that they appear in the Visualizations window, from left to right and top to bottom, skipping past visuals that aren't relevant to this section of the text):**

- Stacked bar chart
- Stacked column chart
- Clustered bar chart
- Clustered column chart
- 100% stacked bar chart
- 100% stacked column chart
- Waterfall chart

Stacked Bar and Column Charts

The stacked bar and column charts arrive at the same conclusion with different verticalities. What distinguishes your y- and x-axes from one another? As a general rule of thumb, use columns when measuring against continuous data, like time, and bar charts when comparing discrete values. But this isn't a strict guideline. We will examine the differences between students whose first class in the department is this one and those who are not in this chart. We want to see how many office hours each group attended, as well as their average score. The bar and column examples are both shown in the figure below. A summary of the components that make up the visualization is formed by the numbers you stack on top of each other in these two charts to construct the visualization—in this case, the average assignment grade and the total number of hours each group spent in the office. This gives us a total value that makes it simple for us to compare multiple columns and get results that might not have made sense at first. When comparing the two charts side by side, the inputs from the Visualizations tab are the same. You create an axis. You can add a legend as a category to further segregate the bar or column, the numbers you want to examine, small multiples, and tooltips. The tooltip appears when you move the mouse cursor over a certain region of the image. When the tooltip is empty, Power BI will create a list of values for it based on what is shown in the visual. Think of it as a quick table you may show for a specific set of facts to help readers understand the image. You can also provide information in the tooltip that isn't always displayed in the image.

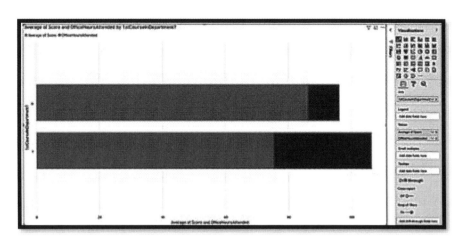

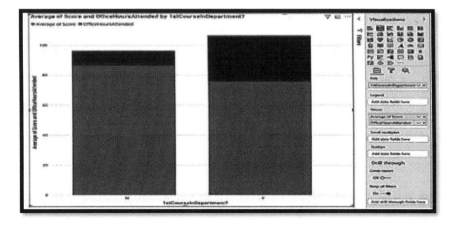

Clustered Bar and Column Charts

In the field of data visualization, Power BI has developed into a formidable instrument for processing and presenting big, intricate data collections. Clustered bar and column charts are the most effective visual aids for comparing data within categories. The data is displayed as either horizontal bars or vertical columns, with each category being represented by a unique color or pattern. It is easy to compare data side by side when the bars or columns are grouped. One of the main advantages of clustered bar and column charts is their simplicity. They give the facts in an easy-to-understand visual format, which facilitates consumer comprehension and evaluation. The labels on the chart's axes indicate the categories that are being compared, and the bars or columns visually represent the data associated with each category. Because of their simplicity, clustered bar and column charts are great for users of all skill levels.

Here are the steps to create and use clustered bar and column charts in Power BI:

Step 1: Import or connect to the data source

To view the information visually, use Power BI and either import or connect to the data source. This can be done with a variety of data sources, including Excel spreadsheets, CSV files, SQL databases, and cloud-based services like Azure SQL Database or SharePoint.

Step 2: Select the clustered bar/column chart visualization

After the data source is attached, choose the visualization of the clustered bar/column chart from the visualization window on the right. It is represented by horizontal bars or vertical columns.

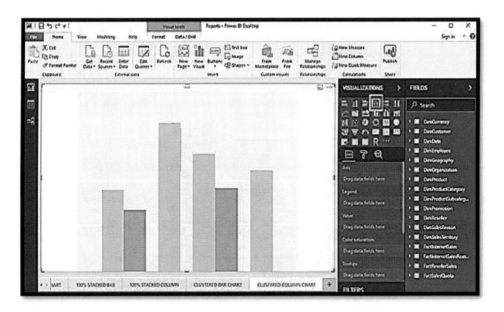

Step 3: Assign data fields to appropriate axes

Drag and drop the category field (such as product categories or periods) onto the axis part of the depiction of the clustered bar/column chart. This field will be used to select the categories along the axis. Decide which numerical field(s) to include in the visualization's value section (e.g., sales, quantities). These parameters will dictate the width of the columns or the height of the bars.

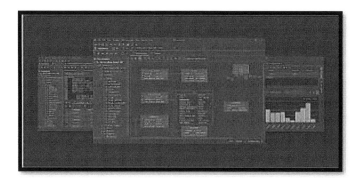

Step 4: Customize the chart appearance

A multitude of customization choices are available in Power BI to enhance the visual appeal of the clustered bar/column chart. You can alter the colors, fonts, titles, legends, and axis labels of the chart by selecting it and using the formatting options provided in the formatting box.

Step 5: Apply sorting and filtering

To logically order the categories, you can sort the axis field. This can be done by first choosing the axis field in the visualization pane, and then choosing the relevant sorting choices. You may also apply filters to the data by selecting the filter pane and indicating the filters you want to use. This helps to focus the data according to specific conditions displayed in the clustered bar/column chart.

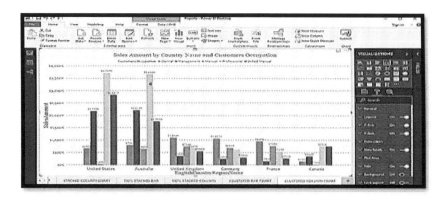

Step 6: Interact with the chart

You can interact with the clustered bar/column chart once it has been made and altered to better analyze the data. You can examine tooltips providing in-depth information about certain data points by hovering your cursor over the bars or columns. You can also dig down to further related visualizations or pages in your Power BI report by clicking on the chart.

100% Stacked Bar and Column Charts

The greatest options for displaying the relative contributions of various groups or categories to a total are column charts and 100% stacked bar charts. Each category or group is shown as a portion of the whole, with the height of the bars or the length of the columns indicating the percentage of each category around the total. These graphs offer a clear visual representation of the various categories' contributions to the composition as a whole. One of its primary advantages is the ability to show relative proportions and trends using 100% stacked bar and column charts. Because the data is displayed as a % of the total, these charts make it easy to compare groups or categories, regardless of the overall number. This is especially helpful when comparing datasets of various dimensions or sizes.

Small Multiples

Small multiples are highly useful when examining patterns, trends, or distributions within a dataset across multiple categories or dimensions. By arranging many charts in a grid or matrix format, small multiples give a complete view of the data and facilitate easy subset comparison. This type of visualization helps find correlations, outliers, parallels and contrasts in the data more effectively than a single chart. One of the key advantages of small multiples is their ability to reduce cognitive load and improve data comprehension. Using small multiples instead of relying on a single complex display breaks up the data into more manageable chunks. As a result, users can concentrate on each subset separately while keeping the larger context in mind, which makes it simpler for them to grasp and analyze the data.

Small multiples are highly useful when examining patterns, trends, or distributions within a dataset across multiple categories or dimensions. By arranging many charts in a grid or matrix format, small multiples give a complete view of the data and facilitate easy subset comparison. This type of visualization helps find correlations, outliers, parallels and contrasts in the data more effectively than a single chart. One of the key advantages of small multiples is their ability to reduce cognitive load and improve data comprehension. Using small multiples instead of relying on a single complex display breaks up the data into more manageable chunks. As a result, users can concentrate on each subset separately while keeping the larger context in mind, which makes it simpler for them to grasp and analyze the data.

Waterfall Chart

A waterfall chart, often called a bridge chart, shows how values rise from an initial level to a final level through a series of intermediate positive and negative elements. It shows how every factor influences both the overall change and the final figure. Waterfall charts are frequently used in financial analysis to display cash flows, income statements, and other financial metrics.

Benefits of Using Waterfall Charts in Power BI

Waterfall charts provide numerous benefits for data analysis and reporting purposes.

1. Waterfall charts offer a holistic perspective on the cumulative effect of both favorable and unfavorable values on a metric. This facilitates users' comprehension of the diverse factors that impact the ultimate result.
2. With waterfall charts, each component is shown as a separate bar, making it easier to identify the factors that have the greatest overall impact. This exercise makes it easier to focus on important variables and understand their implications.
3. A very useful tool for improving data storytelling is the waterfall chart. The transmission of intricate data patterns and trends is made easier by their aesthetically pleasing and intuitive character. They can tell stories based on data to a variety of audiences.
4. Waterfall charts are a useful tool for comparing multiple scenarios or periods in a side-by-side manner. This feature facilitates expeditious comparisons and analyses of the effects of diverse factors across multiple dimensions.

Creating a Waterfall Chart in Power BI

Now let's explore how to create a waterfall chart in Power BI:

1. **Data Preparation:** An essential element in the Power BI process is data preparation. Making sure that the system has all of the necessary data is essential. This could mean importing data from several sources and carrying out any necessary data transformation and cleaning procedures.
2. **Select the Visualization:** To choose the appropriate visualization, launch Power BI Desktop and navigate to the "**Visualizations**" pane located on the right-hand side of the screen. From there, opt for the waterfall chart visualization.
3. **Drag and Drop Fields:** Place the required data fields onto the canvas by using the drag and drop feature. Generally speaking, you need a category field (like periods or goods) and a value field (like revenue or profit) that correspond to each other.
4. **Configure the Chart:** To configure the chart, navigate to the "Visualizations" pane and proceed to assign the category field to the "Axis" section while the value field should be assigned to the "**Values**" section. The Power BI software can automatically generate a rudimentary waterfall chart.
5. **Customize the Chart:** To alter the chart's visual presentation, open the "Visualizations" tab and make use of the formatting options available. Colors, axis labels, data labels, and tooltips are just a few of the properties that can be altered to suit an individual's preferences and requirements.
6. **Add Additional Fields:** To improve the chart's quality, you have the option to add supplementary fields into the "**Legend**" and "**Tooltip**" segments of the "Visualizations" panel. This facilitates a more comprehensive examination and furnishes a backdrop for the information.

7. **Utilize Analytical Features**: Power BI provides an array of analytical features within the "**Analytics**" pane. Consider utilizing features such as data labels, constant lines, and trend lines to enhance the visual representation of the chart and extract more profound insights from the data.

8. **Save and Share:** After you have finished modifying the waterfall chart to your specifications, please save the Power BI report. You may also choose to distribute the report to other pertinent parties. The report can then be shared with colleagues for group analysis and reporting, exported, or made available to the Power BI service.

Line and area charts

Like column and bar charts, line and area charts have their primary centers on the x- and y-axes. The difference is that it is relatively simple to identify patterns or do comparisons using lines or regions, which makes it possible to find data points that overlap in a time series or to see where certain categories meet. In addition, we will explore a set of Power BI charts in this section that combine line and column charts.

The list of visualizations in this particular category should be read from left to right, top to bottom, with the exclusion of any visualization that do not belong to this section.

- Line chart
- Area chart
- Stacked area chart
- Line and stacked column chart
- Line and clustered column chart
- Ribbon chart

Line Chart

A line chart bears a resemblance to a column chart, albeit with a more pronounced ability to discern trends due to the visual clarity of lines as opposed to columns. Line charts are most effective when used with a continuous axis. This is because, in the event of a gap, the line chart will discontinue the line and resume it for the subsequent value in the axis series.

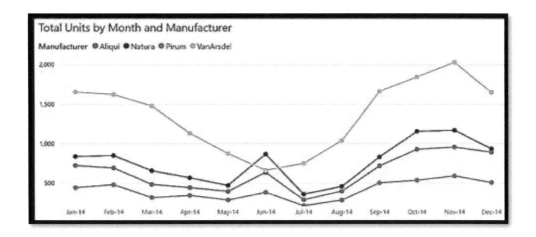

Total Units by Month and Manufacturer

Manufacturer ● Aliqui ● Natura ● Pirum ○ VanArsdel

When you compare the options for column and line charts in the Visualizations window, you'll notice that they are very similar to one another. It is important to remember that the line chart has an extra Secondary values option. Plotting two y-axes against one another is a distinguishing feature of line-type charts, and it is made easier by the previously mentioned section. This particular feature can be useful when comparing the trends of two variables that may differ significantly in terms of their orders of magnitude.

Creating a Line Chart

Choose a report canvas: Create a new report or open an existing one. The report canvas serves as the workspace where you design your visualizations.

Select the line chart visualization: To add a blank line chart to the report canvas, navigate to the "Visualizations" pane located on the right-hand side of the screen and select the line chart icon.

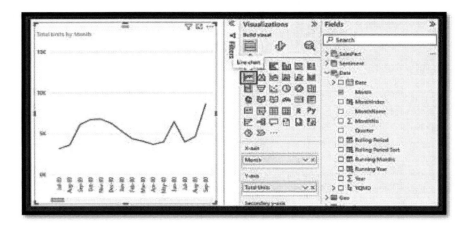

- **Assign data fields**: To assign data fields, kindly drag and drop the relevant fields from your dataset onto the corresponding sections provided in the "Visualizations" pane. It is customary to place the date or time field in the "Axis" section and the numerical values in the "Values" section.
- **Customize the chart appearance**: Power BI offers several modification options to enhance the line chart's usability and visual attractiveness. The chart's look can be customized with these settings. Axes, gridlines, legends, colors, and captions can all be changed to suit your unique requirements and personal tastes.
- **Add lines to the chart**: The chart can have more lines added to it: Many lines can be included in a line chart. Under certain conditions, the values on the lines may differ greatly, which when combined produces an unpleasant display. This time, we'll look at how to add more lines to our current chart and then learn how to format the chart when the values that the lines represent are different.
- **Add more lines:** As an alternative to showing the total units as a single line on the chart, it would be advantageous to divide them up by area. This strategy would offer a more thorough perspective of the data and make it possible to comprehend each region's performance more fully. Simply drag and drop the **"Geo > Region"** choice into the designated "Legend" well to add more lines.

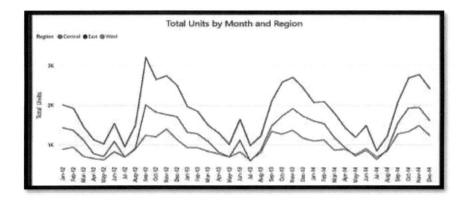

- **Add additional fields**: To enhance context or facilitate comparison, it is advisable to append supplementary fields to either the "**Legend" or "Tooltip**" sections located within the "**Visualizations**" pane. To compare sales data across various regions, it is recommended to position the region field within the "Legend" section.
- **Apply sorting and filtering**: The ability to sort and filter data in a line chart is provided by Power BI's sorting and filtering feature. To arrange the data points in either ascending or descending order, utilize the sorting options. Apply filters to highlight specific periods or focus on specific subsets of data.

Area Chart

The category selections on an area chart are the same as those on a line chart. You can think of an area chart as a line chart with values filled in where the line should be. There are two uses for the area chart that work well in different situations. The first use case deals with circumstances in which data is present but changes over time, and the goal is to provide the reader with an idea of the percentage of these changes. The analysis of population variation across time serves as a prime example of this phenomenon. An area chart can also be utilized to facilitate a clearer visualization of the overlapping of two or more values or to identify instances where there is no overlap, which I find to be the more intriguing scenario.

Stacked Area Chart

A stacked area chart is a graphical representation that displays the changes in data over time. It is a type of chart that is commonly used to show the composition of. The cumulative values of multiple categories are displayed along a continuous axis, like time, in a stacked area chart. It's a good idea to compare each category's contribution to the total and show the overall trend of the figures. A visualization tool in Power BI that allows the user to see numerous data series in a stacked fashion and see both their individual and combined contributions is the stacked area chart. Each data series is represented by a colored region, and the total value of each categorization is shown as the sum of the regions at any given x-axis point. Time, including dates and periods, is often represented by the x-axis, while the numerical values associated with each category are indicated by the y-axis. This chart illustrates the relationship between several categories and their total values over a while. It offers a way to examine trends, spot patterns, and understand the relative importance of each category as a whole. There are numerous ways to customize the look and feel of a stacked area chart with Power BI.

To enhance the visual aid and convey the desired information, one can adjust color schemes, add data labels, apply filters, and personalize legends, tooltips, and axis characteristics, among other formatting options. Think of a situation where you are running a company that provides the silver, gold, and platinum subscription models. In this case, the stacked area chart makes sense because it offers a comprehensive perspective of the aggregate as well as the specific subscription categories by layering the silver, gold, and platinum areas.

Line and Stacked Column Chart/Clustered Column Chart

What happens to column charts that are stacked and clustered when a line is added? The analysis can be expanded by taking a column chart and using a different axis to overlay a line value. The line in the graphic below shows the average score broken down by race, while the total sum of all the scores is displayed in a clustered column. Looking a little closer reveals that the majority of people in my class are White. On closer inspection, it is noticeable that the kids who identify as Black or African American have the highest average score.

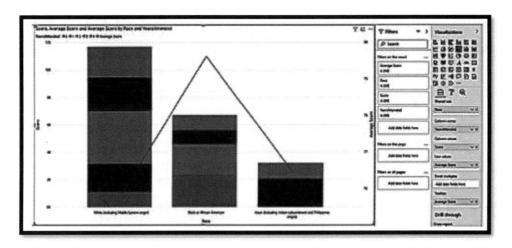

The presence of the second y-axis indicates that the disparity in mean scores across my ethnic groups is relatively minor, spanning from approximately 76 to a maximum of 80.

Ribbon Chart

A tool for graphical representation that shows data in the shape of horizontal bars is the ribbon chart. It is frequently used to show advancement. One visual feature in Power BI that makes it easier to compare and analyze data over time across different categories or groups is the Ribbon Chart. The information is displayed as stacked ribbons, with each ribbon's height representing the relative amount or value of the associated category at a particular moment in time. When presenting trends and patterns in data, ribbon charts are a very useful tool, particularly for dealing with categorical data. Ribbon Charts in Power BI offer a range of key features and benefits that can enhance data visualization and analysis. These charts provide a clear and concise representation of data trends, allowing users to easily identify patterns and insights. With their intuitive design and interactive capabilities, Ribbon Charts enable users to explore data dynamically and engagingly, making it easier to draw meaningful conclusions and make

1. **Comparative Analysis:** A comparative study shows that Ribbon Charts make it simple to compare data between several groups or categories. It is simpler to spot trends and

patterns in the data when the proportions or values of each category are represented by ribbons.

2. **Time-based Insights:** One axis that Ribbon Charts have by default is intended for the display of dates or times. Because of this characteristic, they are very well suited for the examination of data over a specific period. The graph can show how the relative proportions of the categories have changed over time, making it easier to identify patterns, trends, or seasonality.

3. **Interactive Exploration:** Users may dive down, filter, or highlight particular categories or eras with Power BI's Ribbon Charts, providing an interactive exploration experience. The inclusion of interactivity enables a deeper analysis and assessment of the data, enabling users to get insightful knowledge and respond to specific questions.

4. **Flexibility and Customization:** Power BI provides a multitude of customization options for Ribbon Charts, allowing for enhanced flexibility. Individuals can alter the visual components of a chart, including colors, labels, tooltips, and legends, to improve its legibility and effectively communicate information.

5. **Integration with Other Visuals:** Ribbon Charts may be used to create complex dashboards and reports by integrating them with other elements and graphics on the Power BI canvas. These can be linked to filters, slicers, or additional visualizations to provide a cohesive analytical experience.

It is noteworthy that Ribbon Charts, despite their efficacy in data visualization within Power BI, may not be universally applicable in all scenarios. When selecting the appropriate visualization type, it is imperative to take into account the characteristics of the data, the intended message, and the target audience.

Donuts, dots, and maps.

Donut charts, dot plots, and maps are three distinct visualization techniques frequently employed in Power BI to present and evaluate data.

Let us examine each one of them.

1. **Donut Charts:** Donut charts are round representations that resemble donuts and have a hole in the middle. Donut charts, or circular diagrams, are used to show how different classifications are distributed or compared inside an entire unit. A useful tool for displaying the proportionate distribution or composition of data is a doughnut chart. Each group is represented by a section of the donut, and the size of the portion corresponds to its percentage of the total. Donut Charts can be made more visually appealing and clear by modifying their labels, colors, and tooltips, among other customization choices.

2. **Dot Plots:** A simple but effective way to display and contrast data points along one axis is via a dot plot. Each data point is represented by a distinct dot or marker on the chart, which is either vertically or horizontally oriented. When it comes to showing the distribution, ranking, or comparison of values within a dataset, dot plots are a very useful tool. By using

them, discrete or categorical data can be handled efficiently. Dot plots can be customized with labels, colors, and markers to meet individual requirements. This makes it possible to convey more information or highlight specific data points.

3. **Maps:** Maps are a form of visualization that employs geographic data to depict information spatially. The Power BI platform provides users with the convenience of built-in mapping capabilities, enabling them to showcase their data on interactive maps. Maps are a valuable tool for displaying data that is regionally or location-based. Data such as regional sales data, client distribution, and population density can be included in this. A variety of visual components, including heat maps, bubbles, choropleth maps, and filled maps, can be used with Power BI maps to present data. Tooltips, drill-down features, and interactive components can be added to maps to enhance their functionality and make it easier to explore geographical data and provide thorough insights.

The Donut Charts, Dot Plots, and Maps visualizations provide a variety of ways to display and examine data in Power BI. This makes it possible for users to share information efficiently and derive insightful knowledge from their datasets. Power BI users may create engaging and informative reports and dashboards by choosing the best visualization format, which takes into consideration the properties of the data and the intended analytical results.

Funnel Chart

The funnel chart is a versatile visualization tool. Fundamentally, a funnel chart serves the purpose of contrasting a set of data against another set of data, to determine their proximity or divergence.

Below are the essential features and characteristics of Funnel Charts in Power BI.

1. **Sequential Representation:** Funnel charts show the steps or phases that make up a certain process. Each stage is represented by a trapezoid or horizontal bar, the width of which reflects the quantity or value of data at that particular level.
2. **Data Reduction:** The application of Funnel Charts illustrates the progressive reduction of data as it moves from one stage to the next. The bars' width gradually decreases with each phase, indicating a proportional decline in the amount or value of information.
3. **Conversion Analysis:** Funnel charts are a common tool used in conversion analysis research. These diagrams are a widely used tool for evaluating the drop-off rates that happen at different points in a process. Using bar width comparison, bottlenecks or regions where data or potential consumers are lost during process progression can be easily identified.
4. **Focus on Proportions:** Funnel charts place more focus on relative proportions of data between phases than they do on absolute values. When using these charts, proportions must be your priority. The application of visual aids makes it possible to quickly and easily compare the relative sizes of each step, which highlights the significance of conversion or drop-off rates.
5. **Customization Options:** Power BI offers a range of customization options that can be utilized to elevate the visual appeal and functionality of Funnel Charts. Individuals can

78

personalize the colors, labels, tooltips, and additional visual components to enhance the chart's aesthetic appeal and informational value.

6. **Interactivity and Drill-Down:** Drill-down functionality is one of the interactive features offered by Power BI's Funnel Charts. By enabling users to apply filters or dive down into particular stages, the graphic facilitates user involvement and offers a more thorough comprehension of the data. Because of this approach's intrinsic flexibility, the user can actively explore and analyze the underlying data.

Funnel charts are a highly effective means of visually representing and analyzing data in situations where a sequential flow or conversion process is present. They assist in identifying areas of improvement, optimizing conversions, and making decisions based on data. Funnel Charts in Power BI offer a lucid and user-friendly means of visualizing and comprehending data, whether it pertains to sales, marketing, or any other process characterized by a defined flow.

Scatter Chart

A tool for data visualization in Power BI called a scatter chart shows data points as discrete markers on a Cartesian coordinate system. This approach is used to investigate trends, patterns, and correlations between two numerical variables. When comparing data across various dimensions or analyzing large datasets, scatter charts are a very useful tool. With scatter charts, one variable is plotted on the x-axis and the second variable is plotted on the y-axis using a two-dimensional Cartesian coordinate system. This makes it easier to see and analyze the relationship between the two variables. On the chart, each data point is represented by a distinct marker or dot. The values of the associated variables can be inferred from the data point's placement on the Cartesian plane. The detection of correlations between two variables is made easier with the use of scatter plots. The degree to which changes in one variable are related to changes in the other can be determined by looking at the correlation between the variables, which can be positive, negative, or nonexistent.

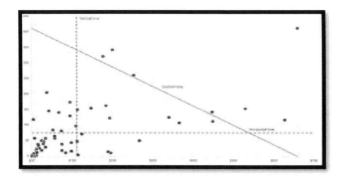

The density or concentration of data points within a particular region of the chart can be shown using scatter charts. This method can help reveal patterns or clusters within the data and help identify areas with considerable or inconsequential data density. By giving each marker a unique color, shape, or size, it is possible to incorporate many data series or categories. This function makes it easier to compare data between different groups or dimensions in a single chart. When the cursor is over each data point in the chart, tooltips displaying further information about that particular data point appear. Users can engage with the chart in several ways, including by choosing individual data points, adding filters, and diving down to examine certain data subsets. It also makes it possible to add trend lines or regression analysis to provide more details about the relationship between the variables. The purpose of trend lines is to provide the overall trajectory or trend of the data with a visual representation.

Pie and Donut Chart

Both pie charts and donut charts are examples of circular data visualizations that are commonplace in Power BI and other analytical software. They are useful for illustrating the composition or distribution of categorical data, and they are successful in doing so.

An overview of Pie Charts and Donut Charts is as follows:

1. **Pie Chart:** Pie charts are circular diagrams that have been divided into sectors, each of which represents a distinct category or a portion of the total. The size of a sector in the chart corresponds exactly to the quantity of information it "represents". Pie charts are a useful tool for visually representing the relative contributions of different categories to a dataset. They can be customized with labels, colors, and tooltips, among other things, which makes them easier to read and adds additional information.

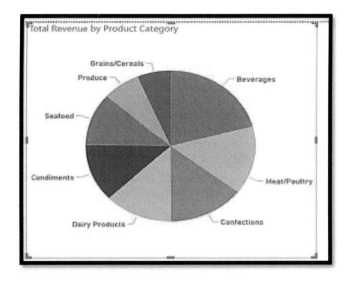

2. **Donut Chart:** The Donut Chart is a Pie Chart version that features a hole in the middle to resemble a doughnut. The distribution of categories is displayed in the inner ring of the chart, while the total or 100%, is displayed in the outer ring. In terms of how proportions are visually represented, Donut Charts and Pie Charts are similar. However, the Donut

Chart's central hole may allow for the display of additional data or information. You can use this section to show a total, a sum, or any other relevant data that may be needed.

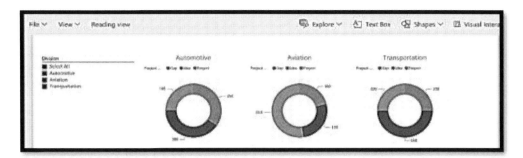

Both Pie and Donut Charts have their uses and considerations:

- **Comparison of Proportions**: Pie and Donut Charts are useful tools for making a comparison of the proportions or percentages of various categories included within a dataset. They give a visual picture of how each category contributes to the overall.
- **Limitations with Data**: It is important to remember that Pie and Donut Charts might not be suitable for datasets with a large number of categories or proportions that are similar. A chart that has too many categories may appear cluttered and challenging to read. Other chart types, such as treemaps or bar charts, might be more appropriate in situations like this.
- **Data Labels and Exploding Slices**: Data labels can be added to pie and doughnut charts to show the exact percentages or figures that correspond to each category. This can improve clarity and readability by presenting the data in a more condensed manner. Furthermore, specific sectors or slices might be "exploded" to draw attention to a single data point or to showcase a particular category. To accomplish this, click the **"explode" button.**
- **Interactivity and Drill-Down**: Power BI offers interaction with these chart types. Users can interact with the chart by choosing or filtering certain categories to explore more comprehensive information or to examine related data in various visuals. This can be done in a variety of ways.

When utilizing Pie or Donut Charts, it is critical to assess the dataset, the number of categories, and the insights you hope to convey. Knowing the context and goal of the visualization being used can help one choose the right kind of chart to communicate the information that is needed.

Treemap

The goal of the Treemap data visualization technique, which is available in Power BI and other analytics apps, is to display hierarchical data as layered rectangles. Rectangles of various sizes and colors are used to indicate the many levels of a category or dimension in the hierarchical structure in which the data is presented. Treemaps are one of the most helpful tools for representing the relative proportions and patterns found inside hierarchical data structures. Treemaps help display hierarchical data structures because they use stacked rectangles to represent each level of the hierarchy. In the display, the root node is represented as the largest rectangle, and its progeny are displayed as smaller rectangles than the root rectangle. Sub-levels of this layering are also present, making it possible to visually examine the hierarchical relationships between the nodes. The size of each rectangle in the Treemap indicates the percentage or weight of the data that it represents. Rectangles with larger sizes are considered more precious than those with smaller sizes. As a result, the categories in the hierarchy that are most important can be quickly identified.

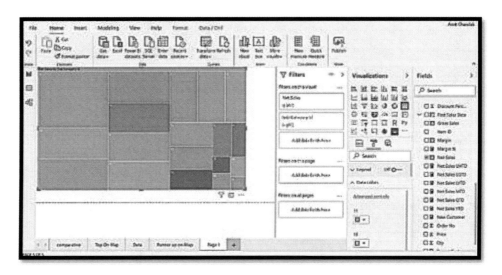

To transmit more information, treemaps can use color as an additional encoding technique. Color can be used to symbolize a distinct dimension, or it can be used to emphasize certain categories according to particular standards or measures. It has interactive elements in its design. Customers can focus on specific subsets of the data by using filters, collapsing or expanding branches, or drilling down into particular levels of the hierarchy. This feature allows for dynamic investigation and analysis of the hierarchical data, and it can be accessed through an interactive interface. Treemaps using Power BI can be personalized so that customers can customize colors, labels, tooltips, and other visual elements to suit their needs and enhance the Treemap's aesthetic appeal. A tooltip can appear when the mouse is over a rectangle in a treemap, offering labels or data values This improves the readability of the visualization as well as one's capacity to comprehend it. Treemaps are one of the most useful methods for visualizing hierarchical data, such as file directory systems, product categories, organizational hierarchies, and portfolio breakdowns. Because the hierarchical structure provides a compact and efficient manner of displaying the proportions and relationships contained within the data, users can see patterns, outliers, and trends within the data. To ensure that the visualization effectively communicates the data and insights that you need to convey, it is crucial to consider the level of hierarchical complexity as well as the readability of the labels or tooltips while working with Treemaps.

Map Visuals

The map graphics in Power BI can be used to display and analyze location-based or geographical data. Because they provide a visual representation of data points projected on a map, users can investigate geographical correlations, patterns, and trends. A range of requirements and types of geographic data can be accommodated by Power BI users with its alternative map displays.

Here are some keymap visuals in Power BI:

- **Basic Map**: The Basic Map visual presents a conventional map view and includes the capability to plot data points or shapes on the map. It can handle many different types of maps, such as road maps, satellite images, or a mix of the two. Users have the option of representing their data spatially using individual points, lines, or polygons that can be plotted.
- **Shape Map**: With the Shape Map graphic, users can plot data on any shape of a map, including states, regions, or nations. Additionally, users can alter the map's shapes. It is capable of handling both predefined borders for a range of geographic areas and customized polygons. Shape map visualizations assist in displaying data at different administrative levels or in areas that the user has specified.
- **ArcGIS Map**: Complex mapping features are made possible by the integration of the ArcGIS Map visual with Esri's ArcGIS platform. What the ArcGIS Map visual offers is these capabilities. It offers additional data layers, which could contain information about the weather, company locations, demographics, and possibly more. ArcGIS maps allow users to combine many layers of geographic data to produce interactive and educational visuals.
- **Filled Map**: The Filled Map visual is used to show data in a choropleth style, in which geographic areas are shaded or filled dependent on the value of a given measure. This kind of data presentation is also known as a heat map. It is very helpful for comparing data from various places as well as determining geographical patterns or trends.
- **Heat Map:** The Heat Map is a graphical depiction of data density that highlights the concentration or intensity of the data using colors or gradients. It aids in locating locations on the map with high or low data densities. Heat maps can be used to examine data that varies spatially in intensity, such as customer dispersion, population density, or any other type of data.
- **Bubble Map**: The Bubble Map is a visualization that presents data as bubbles or markers on a map, with the size of each bubble reflecting a particular measure or value. It makes it easier to see the distribution, size, or comparability of data over a variety of geographic regions.

Thanks to the dynamic and drill-down features provided by the map graphics in Power BI, users can zoom in or out, apply filters, and review detailed information about specific locations or data points on the map. Additionally, they include supplementary features like tooltips and legends to enhance the user's comprehension of the data and their ability to analyze it. Make sure the geographic data is correct, properly formatted, and geocoded before working with the Power BI map graphics. Users can successfully analyze and convey geographic information inside their reports and dashboards by making use of the appropriate map visual depending on the nature of the data and the intended insights. This allows users to effectively communicate geographic information.

The "Flat Visuals"

Openly displayed information that the reader is expected to learn from the experience is what flat visuals are intended to convey. The slicer, one of these images, is the conspicuous exception to this rule. Generally speaking, these images are cross-filtered rather than cross-filtering each other. Despite their seemingly simple appearance, these images frequently offer a mysterious, extra bit of information to reports, turning the facts into a coherent story. They achieve this by focusing more attention on the specific details of what you want your audience to understand than anything else.

The following examples of visuals can be found in this category:

- Gauge
- Card
- Multi-row card
- KPI
- Slicer
- Table
- Matrix

Gauge

The gauge is one of the first types of data visualization available to us. They were utilized in a range of engineering projects and equipment over the majority of the 20th century. Essentially, a gauge tells you how a value is currently doing concerning its lowest value, its greatest value, and its target value. When setting goals and assessing your current progress toward them, the gauge can help you make sense of them quickly. Moreover, it can be useful when you wish to keep the temperature within a specific range to avoid extremes in either direction.

Card/Multi-Row Card

One of the simplest visualizations available in Power BI is the card visual. It's also a name whose meaning is obvious just from its appearance. When given a value, it uses that value to display the object being seen along with a brief description on a square card. The card works well in both of these categories, in my opinion. First, it is easy to understand the text you are reading due to its clear style. This combined with the cross-filtering feature of the card graphic gives you a tool that can quickly and easily highlight a certain value for any set of data. Second, it assists the narrative process by directing the reader's attention to certain values that you believe they should care about. These values can be significant in and of themselves, or they may give the required context that makes the other visuals on your report page more relevant. Either way, it is beneficial to the storytelling process. The multi-row card visual is like the relative of the card visual that your aunt and uncle can't stop talking about during Thanksgiving, but you're not sure if they're really that great after all. The multi-row card aims to shamelessly jam multiple values onto a single "card"-like region. It will appear reasonably neat if all of the numbers are aggregated. On the other hand, the multi-row card will create multiple rows on the card that display the aggregated values for each category value if you have aggregations and then some dimension that categorizes those aggregations. These rows will be shown in the order that the categorical values appear on the card.

KPI

The **key performance indicator** (KPI) visual is one of those things that, on the surface, seems like a wonderful idea, but ultimately ends up driving people crazy. Although it is not quite as confusing as the scatter chart, the KPI visual might be difficult to understand at first. You are measuring something when you look at the value of this field, which acts as an indication. The visual will display the results on an x-axis that isn't currently visible using something called a trend axis. Next is the targeted goal, which we should either surpass or fall short of at this time. A common example of a KPI use case is the comparison of the revenues for the current year and the previous year, broken down by fiscal month. The most annoying aspect of the KPI is that it always shows the value for the most recent value on the axis, regardless of what occurred before it, even though it will depict those data in the chart part of the report. This is a waste of everyone's time.

Table/Matrix

The table is precisely what it appears to be. Here, there are no bonuses or additional features. The table visual in the Visualizations window has a single insert that goes into a values field. Every element is a field or column, and each value is connected to the column it resides in. Incorporating a table visual into a data visualization tool may appear paradoxical, yet the table visual can offer more specific information and context. I frequently discover that a table, as opposed to a multi-row card, works better for me when it comes to accentuating particular data points. Another nice thing done with table visuals is placing them at the end of reports. This makes it simple for analysts who may want to utilize the data from that table for other types of analysis to extract the data from the table quickly and easily. Given that it can have many levels of row properties that can be explored; the matrix is more akin to an Excel pivot table. Although matrices have the potential to be overdone, when used to highlight particular data sets or combinations of data, they can help readers focus on particular items or provide analysts with additional context, enabling the analysts to determine which questions they need to answer as soon as possible. For a considerable amount of time, Power BI exports data from matrix visuals without first arranging the data into a table. This resulted in the loss of matrix formatting. However, as of recently, this is no longer the case; thus, if you need to export data in the format of a matrix, maybe for a presentation or anything else, you can do so.

Slicer

Using a slicer and choosing a column in the Filters pane by clicking the "Filters on this page" button is similar in many ways. The "Edit interactions" feature on the Format tab of the ribbon allows you to change how a visual on a report page interacts with every other visual on the page. Additionally, the "Sync slicers" pane allows you to synchronize slicers across pages of your choosing. The Format tab on the ribbon has both of these functions. As a result, slicers may be made far more flexible and intuitive for readers of your report. This provides you, the author, with an additional opportunity to highlight the particular aspects that, in your opinion, should be emphasized to assist your audience in comprehending how they should be thinking about the content.

Conclusion

To sum up, Power BI data visualization is critical to obtaining pertinent insights and arriving at wise conclusions. Users may create and edit data visualizations in one place, using the Visualizations Pane, which provides a range of visual forms for effective information sharing. With the aid of visual interaction, users may explore and analyze data dynamically and naturally, identifying trends, patterns, and outliers. The decision-making and data analysis processes in Power BI mostly depend on data visualization. Whether through column and bar charts, map visuals, "flat visuals," tables and matrices, slicers, or other graphic forms, data visualization enhances data comprehension, allows trend discovery and facilitates effective communication. By utilizing the power of visual representations, users may improve reasoned decision-making, gain valuable insights from their data, and foster company success.

Activity

1. Why should data be visualized?
2. Configure your visualization pane.
3. Alter the interaction behavior.
4. Employ the use of the charts. I.e. column and bar charts, stacked and bar charts, and clustered and column charts.
5. What are the benefits of making use of the waterfall charts?

CHAPTER 5

AGGREGATIONS, MEASURES, AND DAX

A Primer on the DAX Language

A versatile query language called Data Analysis Expressions, or DAX, can be used to create calculated tables and columns or to get specific results. DAX is the language used by the formula engines in Analysis Services Tabular and Power BI. To retrieve data from the Power BI storage engine, Power BI automatically generates DAX behind the scenes when you develop a new visual.

To be used, DAX must be configured on a column-by-column or table-by-table basis, just like everything else in capability BI. DAX has a remarkable amount of power. This isn't the case with programs like Excel, where every detail is set right down to the cell. Unlike Excel, DAX does not support the editing of individual cells or points in space. Before continuing, the data in a table or column needs to be changed. Remember that our database is fundamentally columnar, thus instead of having a language that can modify and query individual cells of data, we want one that can query columns of data. The ability to query and alter columns is far more powerful because it is faster and eliminates the need to write equations against specific cells, which is a major drawback. Having this ability also makes it easier to work with large amounts of data.

Measures

The idea of measures is one of the most essential aspects of the DAX programming language, and it is very important for both the data analysis and the reporting processes. Measures are, in a nutshell, calculations that are carried out at the moment. They allow us to extract aggregated numbers, run calculations over several rows or tables, and assess sophisticated business logic. Answers to inquiries like "**What is the total sales revenue?**" or "**What is the average customer satisfaction score**?" are often provided using measures. To construct a measure in DAX, we utilize the construct **MEASURE** command or the user interface offered by visualization tools like Power BI. Measures are often connected with a particular table in the data model and are assessed within the context of that table. But through the links between the tables, they can also refer to columns from other tables. Measures are generated using expressions written in DAX, which comprise operators, functions, and pointers to other measures or columns. A wide range of calculations, aggregations, filters, and other operations can be performed using DAX's extensive set of functions. We may create powerful expressions with the help of these functions that can draw insightful conclusions from the data we supply. The ability of measures to dynamically adapt to different levels of granularity in the data they gather is one of their most crucial features. A sales revenue measure, for example, can dynamically change to provide revenue at different levels of aggregation, like by year, month, or product category, or it can present the total revenue for the entire dataset. This system's versatility allows for the evaluation of data at different levels of detail as well as drill-down studies.

Aspects such as the assessment context are also taken into account. The term "**context**" refers to the collection of filters or criteria that are applied to the data before any calculations are carried out. DAX contains methods like **CALCULATE and FILTER** that allow users to change the context and exert control over the calculation of measures. This context awareness makes it feasible to perform more intricate computations and make use of dynamic filtering. Before implementing any measures, it is essential to take into account the different kinds of data and make sure that these data types match the expected results. Numerical, text, Boolean, date/time, and many other types of data can all be worked with by DAX. It is crucial to select the appropriate data type for every measure to ensure consistency and accuracy of the calculations. Conditional logic, branching statements, and iterators can all be used to improve measures. DAX contains methods such as **IF** and SWITCH, as well as iterators such as **SUMX and AVERAGEX**, which allow us to do calculations based on specified circumstances or traverse over a table while applying filters. These characteristics enable us to create dynamic, more complex metrics that meet the requirements of increasingly intricate studies. Measures can incorporate text concatenation, formatting, and other string operations in addition to their mathematical computations. As a result, we can produce visually beautiful measures, have textual context, and are informative. We can also combine data from multiple sources into a single outcome. Finally, the creation of interactive reports and visualizations is based on the metrics. They can be utilized to emphasize key indicators and facilitate data-driven decision-making in charts, tables, and other visual components. Measures give stakeholders the essential data they require to compare, analyze, and gain insightful business knowledge.

Calculated Columns

A helpful component of the DAX programming language is calculated columns, which let users add more columns to a table based on the outcomes of their customized computations. In DAX, a calculated column is defined by a formula applied to each table row. You may find this formula in the header row of the table. Each row that the formula impacts have a corresponding computed column row where the results are saved once the formula has been evaluated column by column. Calculated columns are often produced during the data modeling process, at which point they are irreversibly incorporated into the table structure. References to other columns in the same table as well as DAX operators and functions can be used in a calculation for a computed column. This enables you to perform multi-column calculations or apply complex logic to generate new values. For example, you may create a calculated column that shows the profit margin by subtracting the cost from the selling price. Users can create new data components using calculated columns, which may provide more context or insights. Using computed columns has many important benefits, one of which is this. These columns become an integral part of the table upon addition and can be utilized for many purposes such as filtering, sorting, computations, and more. They can be especially useful when you need to perform computations involving several rows or when you wish to create dimensions using pre-existing data. Making a pivot table is an additional scenario in which they are useful.

The evaluation of calculated columns occurs at the row level, meaning that each row in the table is subject to the formula on its own. This enhancement makes it possible to perform calculations that account for specific row conditions or values. For example, you can create a calculated column that offers customers a rank based on a predetermined set of criteria, or you can categorize clients based on their purchase history. One crucial consideration when utilizing calculated columns is the impact these columns have on the data model's performance and size. Computed columns increase the stringency of the table's storage requirements because the computed values must be kept for every entry. Furthermore, computations involving calculated columns are performed during data refreshes or query executions, which influence the query processing time. Optimizing the use of calculated columns and considering the trade-offs between performance and storage is crucial to making them as efficient as feasible. Calculated columns can also be utilized as measures' inputs, allowing for the execution of more intricate calculations and analyses. Measures are dynamic calculations that are done in real-time. Data from numerous rows or tables may occasionally be combined to create a measure. By using computed columns as measure inputs, you can increase the level of analysis and gain insights that would not be possible with measures alone. This is due to the impossibility of utilizing measures alone. It is crucial to select the appropriate data types for the newly generated column when building calculated columns. Numerous types of data, including text, Boolean, date/time, and numeric data, can be worked with by DAX. Carefully choosing the right data type can lead to both accurate computations and accurate data representation.

Calculated Tables

The ability to create new tables in a data model based on the outcomes of custom calculations or filters is a valuable feature of the DAX programming language. Calculated tables are one such capability. We're going to talk about calculated tables in this discussion, along with all of their benefits and useful applications for data analysis. The **EVALUATE** statement is used to define a table expression, which is then used in the process of producing a calculated table in DAX. The table expression can contain references to previously constructed tables, operators, and DAX functions. The process of evaluating the phrase will result in the creation of a new table that is computed in real-time using the given logic. Within the framework of your data model, virtual tables can be created using calculated tables. Rather than being stored in the underlying data source, these tables are dynamically created based on the computation logic at the time of use. This allows you to create tables that individually reflect a section of the data or modify the pre-existing tables by adding certain filters. One of the main benefits of using calculated tables is that they may make complex data modeling situations simpler to comprehend and deal with. They enable you to create tables that aggregate information from other tables or sources, apply customized filters, or perform computations according to predefined criteria. When executing cross-table calculations, such as creating a table that integrates sales data with customer demographics, calculated tables can be very useful. A table that mixes demographic information about customers with sales data is an illustration of this type of computation.

In addition to being useful for creating summary or aggregate tables, calculated tables can also be used to store previously calculated data. By using these summary tables, the amount of data that needs to be processed can be drastically decreased, which can dramatically speed up the query. If you aggregate the data at a higher level of granularity, you can expedite searches and provide answers more quickly. The other advantage of utilizing computed tables is that they are flexible. Due to its dynamic calculation, computed tables can adapt to modifications in the data model or filters applied to the data. This enables dynamic analysis and reporting, in which the calculated table dynamically updates itself depending on user options or changes in the data that underlies it. Be aware that the intricacy of the data model and performance issues associated with computed tables can be problematic. It's important to remember this concept. Being in charge of storing the outcomes of all computations, calculated tables increase the total memory footprint of the data model. A complex computed table with a large number of data points might also impact query performance. Calculated tables should be used as efficiently as possible, and consideration should be given to the trade-offs these tables offer between memory usage and query performance.

One of the DAX features that can be used in conjunction with other features, such as calculated columns, and measures, is calculated tables. They can serve as a basis on which more intricate computations or analyses are built. When you integrate calculated tables with other DAX language elements, you can create reliable data models that provide in-depth insights and address complex business requirements. In the "role-playing" of dimensions throughout the Power BI creation process, calculated tables are also frequently utilized. The most common scenario is when you have a fact table with multiple dates in it. Depending on the reporting requirement, you need to be able to work with different dates. You can only have one active relationship at a time from the relationships shown on your date table. As a result, using a calculated table, you can create an additional set of dates to create an additional link with that fact table. Afterward, you will have two different data tables that you can use, based on the date that you may need to pull from a particular fact table. Any one of these data tables can be used.

Types of Functions

The DAX functions are arranged into families, or kinds, that denote the intended tasks for each function. A DAX formula is a construction of one or more DAX functions or a construction of one or more DAX functions. The majority of users undoubtedly do not make use of every single DAX feature available, just because there are hundreds of them. Because of this, understanding the hierarchy of DAX functions might be helpful if you ever need to look up information fast on a particular function's operation or if you're looking for a function that works well for the kind of analysis or data manipulation you're trying to do.

The following is a list of the several ways that DAX functions can be categorized:

- Aggregation functions
- Date and time functions
- Filter functions
- Financial functions
- Information functions
- Logical functions
- Math and trigonometric functions
- Other functions
- Parent and child functions
- Relationship functions
- Statistical functions
- Table manipulation functions
- Text functions
- Time intelligence functions

Aggregations, More than Some Sums

When doing data analysis, aggregations entail more than just basic sums; rather, they involve a variety of calculations that give insightful new perspectives on the information under consideration. It requires extracting summary or aggregated values from a dataset and then calculating those values. Although sums are a typical sort of aggregation, there are a great many additional varieties that give quite diverse viewpoints on the data. **We can obtain a more in-depth knowledge of patterns, trends, and correlations by using aggregations, which enable us to study data at varying degrees of granularity.**

1. **Sum**: A fundamental kind of aggregation, summation determines the final value by simply adding up the values of the various components. It is most often used for presenting numerical information, such as sales income, quantity, or cost.

2. **Average**: An aggregation known as the average can be used to get the arithmetic mean of a set of numbers. It provides an understanding of the main pattern in the data and is frequently applied to analyze metrics like average customer spending or average rating.

3. **Count**: The count aggregation determines the total number of items included inside a dataset. It helps comprehend the magnitude or frequency of events, such as the number of orders, customers, or transactions.

4. **Minimum and maximum**: These summaries identify the dataset's lowest and highest values, respectively. Every value in the dataset is compared. They aid in locating boundaries and extremes, such as the lowest and highest temperatures ever measured or the lowest and highest sales figures.

5. **Median**: The number that represents the "**middle**" position in a sorted collection of data is called the median. Since it is less impacted by extreme values, this aggregation is beneficial for studying data with outliers or skewed distributions since it reduces the impact of such factors.

6. **Mode**: The mode of a dataset is the value that appears most often within that dataset. It is used to determine which data points are the most prevalent or well-known, such as the product or method of transportation that is bought the most often.

7. **Percentile**: A technique known as a "percentile" divides a dataset into hundredths to examine the distribution of the values. For instance, the value at the 50th percentile of the distribution equals the median. To compare data points and better understand where they fall within a dataset, percentiles are useful.

8. **Aggregations with Filters**: Calculations can be carried out on different subsets of data by combining aggregations with filters. For instance, determining the overall income for a certain area or the aggregate total of sales for a particular kind of product category.

9. **Weighted Aggregations**: Aggregations that assign different weights to distinct data elements based on their significance are known as weighted aggregations. They are useful tools when analyzing data that have different levels of importance, such as weighted total or average.

10. **Statistical Aggregations:** Statistical aggregations, such as standard deviation, variance, or correlation, provide insights into the variability, distribution, and interactions between data points.

Sum

The time-tested method. Everyone is aware of what a sum is. It's a case of adding. You have always had a solid grasp of the art of adding numbers. You have undoubtedly previously used the sum functions in Excel or other applications that are comparable to it. The good news is that Power BI retains Sum's functionality. We will get the sum, or addition, of the numerical values for a given column of numbers for any particular combination of data that is shown visually. This is so because Sum functions identically in Power BI and Excel. Like with a lot of other data concepts, this one is simplest to understand visually. Given that the goal of our conference is to display data, it would seem more suitable to show rather than to vocally explain. Two tables can be seen in the picture below. Both have a total number of office hours that they have been present for. Both of them arrive at the same total, but their results for each possible combination of data are unique.

The table at the top of the page displays the total number of office hours that various grouped classifications attended. As a result, in this specific case, 22 out of 41 office hours were occupied by participants in the ISOM 210 course, which started on January 4, 2021, who identified as she/her and who had never used Power BI before the course began. In this case, the total is the sum of the values that are included in the **OfficeHoursAttended** column. There is a difference in the table at the bottom. It shows the breakdown by the last name of students as well as the number of office hours attended by the student for a particular assignment ID. It's evident that while the total number of hours stays the same, they are distributed differently. You would notice that no student attended more than one office hour for any given assignment ID if you were to glance at the table with the grades. Even if the sum in this case reduces all of the data to the level of a single cell, the sum is still computing a summation. I wanted to use this example to show you that Power BI will by default conceal data collections that don't yield a result for a given summation. As a result, we know that Ms. Avina only showed up for one office hour, which was for Assignment ID 12. We can ascertain that much faster by analyzing only the data that has an actual value offered, as opposed to viewing outcomes that yield no data at all.

Average

There are various varieties of averages. Power BI generates a simple average to represent the default aggregate that is displayed in the settings pane found under the Visualizations section. The total of a given set of values, filtered by all relevant categories on a visual, is divided by the count of records that are likewise filtered by all relevant categories on a visual to arrive at this simple average. Stated differently, the simple average represents the total of the values on the visual that have been filtered by all pertinent categories. Consequently, we would have an average score of 80 if we had a total score of 240 for a certain set of data, with three recordings making up those 240 points. A value divided by one is itself; it's still theoretically an average if we end up with a combination of categories that only yields one record's worth of data, just like the sum. A value split by one is itself if we ultimately arrive at a combination of categories that only yields one record's worth of data. Two new tables with average scores are shown below. Furthermore, the average number of office hours attended is shown on the right, while the total number of hours attended is shown on the left.

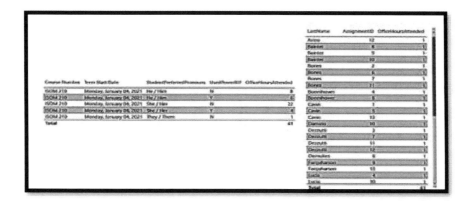

The image you see above has two features that might immediately catch your attention. First off, there is no difference between the two tables' cumulative Average Scores. Second, isn't it a little strange that the number of AverageOfficeHoursAttended is displayed on the right? Even if there are some blank numbers, the average is 1. What does that mean? Why do certain values have blanks in them? For each given assignment, no one attended more than or fewer than one office hour. Blanks, however, are not zeros. True blanks, also referred to as nulls in database language, and are frequently seen in a variety of datasets. The most essential thing to take away from this is that Power BI does not consider nulls to be zeros and simply disregards them when it generates a count of values. If nulls are disregarded while creating a count, our mathematical description for the average in Power BI will still be accurate, and the overall average shown in the table to the right of the picture will continue to make sense.

Right now, figuring out how to calculate Ms. Avina's average is crucial. Does one hour need to be divided by one office visit, or should it be divided by fourteen office visits, with thirteen zeros? If the latter, how many zeros ought to be divided next? The answer to this issue is unique to us as the analyst or report author, and it mostly depends on what we want the average to convey. The second question is why the Average of OfficeHoursAttended column on the right table is returning blank numbers for certain users. The default behavior was not to return values when there would be no data to show. On the other hand, if there is a second aggregate on a visual that does yield a value for a certain combination of data, then all of the other aggregations will still appear, even though they will return a blank result. A simplified version of the image can be seen below, which was produced by copying the right table from the previous image and leaving out the average score from the second copy. You can verify that the inclusion of the second aggregate is the reason for the blank values in the visual when you compare the two tables together. Putting the two tables side by side allows you to observe this. It also supports the previous idea on the elimination of blanks in average calculations.

LastName	AssignmentID	Average of Office Hours Attended		LastName	AssignmentID	Average of Score	Average of Office Hours Attended
Avina	12	1.00		Avina	1	72.00	
Rainier	8	1.00		Avina	2	76.00	
Rainier	9	1.00		Avina	3	72.00	
Rainier	10	1.00		Avina	4	71.00	
Bones	2	1.00		Avina	5	90.00	
Bones	6	1.00		Avina	6	94.00	
Bones	7	1.00		Avina	7	61.00	
Bones	11	1.00		Avina	8	74.00	
Boomhower	4	1.00		Avina	9	54.00	
Boomhower	8	1.00		Avina	10	66.00	
Cavin	1	1.00		Avina	11	66.00	
Cavin	5	1.00		Avina	12	55.00	1.00
Cavin	13	1.00		Avina	13	66.00	
Damato	10	1.00		Avina	14	20.20	
Dezzutti	3	1.00		Rainier	1	75.00	
Dezzutti	7	1.00		Rainier	2	74.00	
Dezzutti	11	1.00		Rainier	3	99.00	
Dezzutti	12	1.00		Rainier	4	100.00	
Dismukes	8	1.00		Rainier	5	93.00	
Farquharson	9	1.00		Rainier	6	100.00	
Farquharson	13	1.00		Rainier	7	64.00	
Luda	4	1.00		Rainier	8	63.00	1.00
Luda	10	1.00		Rainier	9	77.00	1.00
Miyamoto	1	1.00		Rainier	10	88.00	1.00
Miyamoto	2	1.00		Rainier	11	68.00	
Miyamoto	11	1.00		Rainier	12	100.00	
Total		1.00		Total		77.67	1.00

Minimum and Maximum

When it comes to data analysis and visualization, Power BI places a significant emphasis on the ideas of minimum and maximum. They help determine the borders, range of values, and outliers that exist within a dataset. Here, we will discuss the relevance of Power BI's minimum and maximum values, how to compute them using DAX (Data Analysis Expressions), as well as their uses in data analysis and visualization. The borders and extremes of a dataset can be better understood with the help of a dataset's minimum and maximum values.

Let's get into more depth about their importance and how they can be applied:

1. **Data Range and Boundaries:** The range that the data points are positioned in is determined by the minimum and maximum values, respectively. To ascertain the scope and diversity of the dataset, a thorough grasp of the data range is essential. By presenting the lowest and highest values, you can quickly determine the lower and upper boundaries. This might assist you in identifying any potential outliers or unusual data points.

2. **Data Cleaning and Quality Control**: The use of minimum and maximum values is common in data cleansing procedures. Their aid makes it easier to identify anomalies, outliers, and erroneous data items that fall outside of the expected range. By identifying and removing any potential outliers, you can ensure the accuracy and reliability of the data. When you employ minimum and maximum values for data quality control, you'll be able to identify or investigate data points that significantly deviate from the norm. This is due to the practicality of minimum and maximum values.

3. **Visualizing Data Extremes:** Users using Power BI have access to a wide range of visualization methods for effectively displaying data. To clearly illustrate the data's dispersion, a variety of visualization styles, including line charts, column charts, and scatter plots, can be used to display the minimum and maximum values. To further help draw attention to patterns and extremes in the data, conditional formatting and color scales based on minimum and maximum values can be used.

4. **Threshold Determination:** When making decisions, minimum and maximum numbers are frequently utilized as benchmarks or thresholds. For example, when conducting a sales study, you may choose to focus on products with the highest sales or set a minimum sales target. By matching actual statistics to these standards, you may evaluate performance, identify areas for development, and make decisions based on this knowledge.

5. **Data Normalization**: The minimum and maximum values are essential components of the data normalization process, which entails adjusting the data to fit within a predetermined range. By ensuring that all variables are measured on the same scale, normalization prevents certain variables from being disproportionately influential in the analysis owing to the bigger values they represent. You can assist with fair comparisons and reliable analysis by rescaling the data by utilizing the lowest and maximum values as the scaling factors.

6. **Machine Learning and Modeling**: Feature scaling is frequently necessary when working on machine learning tasks to ensure fair comparisons over a range of features or variables. Utilizing minimum and maximum values allows you to scale features within a predetermined range. As a result, bias is lessened and models can precisely determine how relevant the attributes are. For algorithms that rely on distance-based computations to decide results, such as support vector machines and k-means clustering, feature scaling is very crucial.

7. **Conditional Formatting**: Strong conditional formatting capabilities in Power BI allow users to highlight data based on how it relates to minimum and maximum values. Applying conditional formatting rules to tables, charts, or cards allows you to graphically highlight

high or low numbers, identify patterns, and draw attention to important data points. This enables you to draw attention to high or low values visually.

The **MIN and MAX** functions of the DAX language can be used in Power BI to do the calculation of minimal and maximum values, respectively. These functions take a column or expression as their input and then return either the lowest possible value or the highest possible value that can be found in the column or expression.

For example, to calculate the minimum and maximum sales amounts from a sales table in Power BI, you can use the following DAX expressions:

- Minimum Sales = MIN(Sales[Amount])
- Maximum Sales = MAX(Sales[Amount])

These expressions will calculate the minimum and maximum sales amounts, respectively, based on the "**Amount**" column in the "Sales" table.

Standard Deviation, Variance, and Median

Important statistical measures such as the standard deviation, variance, and median give useful insights into the distribution, variability, and central tendency of a dataset. These measures can be found in the standard deviation, variance, and median.

Standard Deviation

The standard deviation is a measurement of the dispersion or spread of data points around the mean. It gives the amount by which the data deviates from the mean in numerical form. A higher standard deviation value denotes greater variability, while a smaller standard deviation value denotes less dispersion.

The following are the steps by which standard deviation is calculated:

- Calculate the mean of the dataset.
- For each data point, calculate the difference between that data point and the mean.
- Square each difference.
- Calculate the mean of the squared differences.
- Take the square root of the mean squared difference to obtain the standard deviation.

Standard deviation is useful in several ways:

- It helps understand the spread and variability of data, which is particularly important when comparing datasets or analyzing the stability of a process over time.

- Standard deviation is often used to assess risk or volatility in finance, such as measuring the volatility of stock prices.
- In quality control, standard deviation helps determine if a process is within acceptable limits or if there is excessive variation.

Variance

Variance is an additional measure of data dispersion, similar to standard deviation. The average squared difference between each data point and the data mean is calculated to achieve this. The amount that any one data point deviates from the "mean" value is referred to as "variance". Except for the final step, which involves calculating the value's square root, the processes involved in calculating variance and standard deviation are fairly similar.

Variation is helpful in a few different ways:

- It plays a role in the analysis of experimental data to measure the effect of different factors on the variability of the response variable.
- Variance is employed in modeling and optimization problems, such as determining the optimal allocation of resources.
- Variance is used in statistical inference to assess the variability of a population based on a sample.

Median

The value that precisely lies in the middle of a set of data that has been sorted either ascending or descending is represented by the median, a measure of central tendency. It is robust in the face of skewed data since it is insensitive to extreme or outlier values.

The median is calculated in the manner described below:

- Place the values in either ascending or descending order.
- If the dataset has an odd number of values, the median is the middle value.
- If the dataset has an even number of values, the median is the average of the two middle values.

The median is a very helpful statistic in the following circumstances:

- The median, as opposed to the mean, provides a more accurate representation of the core value when dealing with skewed data or datasets containing outliers.
- When extreme values can significantly affect the mean but less so the median, it is frequently applied to scenarios involving income distributions, real estate prices, or other skewed economic indicators.

- The median is also used in data analysis to describe the distribution of ordinal or ranking data, as well as to compare the central tendency of several groups. These two applications use data ranking.

You can compute any of these statistical measures by utilizing the DAX functions that are available in Power BI:

- **Standard Deviation**: The STDEV.P or STDEV.S functions in Power BI can be used to find the standard deviation of a column or expression. When analyzing data that is representative of a subset of the population, STDEV.P is used; when analyzing data that is indicative of the entire population, STDEV.S is used.
- **Variance**: In Power BI, the variance of a column or expression can be computed using either the VAR.P or VAR.S function. Data from a sample are entered into VAR.P, while data from the population are entered into VAR.S.
- **Median**: The MEDIAN function in Power BI determines the value that represents the columns or expression's median. When the data are sorted, it gives back the value that is in the center.

Count and Count (Distinct)

Count and Count (Distinct) are two forms of aggregation that are very helpful and can be used for any data type. They can be applied to the counting of text, date, or numeric data instances. They can also be used to tally the quantity of data instances. Duplicate instances of that data will be counted by the selection Count; however, the selection Count (Distinct) will not. The main difference between the two options is this. This count is performed concerning the data column that is now being mentioned. The graphic below shows four instances of counting and counting (distinct). First, on the upper left corner of the screen, you will find a list of the overall results for each assignment. Because we are not aggregating the score for that table, we are first retrieving the raw values and then carrying out a count of the score as well as a count (Distinct) of the score to determine the total number of occurrences of each score associated with that assignment. It's important to remember that Power BI creates an alias for most aggregates to help readers identify the aggregate if it isn't a sum. However, Power BI aliases Count (Distinct) in the same way that it aliases Count; as a result, I manually aliased Count (Distinct) to make sure the graphics are clear. Any object in a visual can be given a new name by double-clicking it in the Visualizations pane's Values section, followed by the new name. An alias is made in this manner.

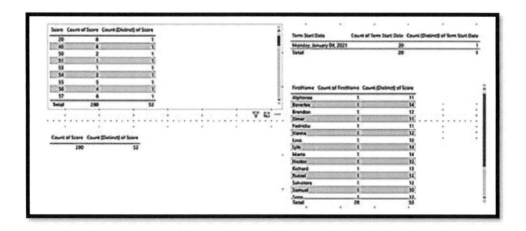

Take note of the three distinct counts shown in the example in the upper left corner: the raw score, the number of times the score appears in the dataset, and the distinct count, which is one for each value. In total, the sum represents 52 different values. Conversely, in the visual representation, when all values are listed, the unique count of each value will always be one. The visual in the lower left corner of the image is the same as it was previously, but the score value has been removed. The total number of scores (280) and the number of distinct score values (52), respectively, are displayed here. The sample in the top right corner gives us the number of times a specific date—the word "start date" in this case—has occurred. We are currently working with a single-term start date because the dataset only includes data for one academic year. There are twenty instances of that value in the table it comes from. Note that under no circumstances will the distinct count ever equal 1 because of the way this table was constructed. This is so because a value is defined in the table, and its distinct count will always be 1. An alternative perspective on the situations we've been discussing is provided by the example in the bottom-right corner. We have a list of the first names of the pupils, together with the count of those names, which is 1, for each name. This is not a count of unique names; it simply so happens that none of the names occur more than once. However, after that, we can look at the Count (Distinct) of scores and determine how many distinct scores each person has gotten. Given that there are 14 assignments, we would anticipate a significant number of separate counts of scores for each individual, but as you can see, it is not always 14 either. During the semester, several students received the same score on many occasions.

First, Last, Earliest, and Latest

Inside the domain of data analysis, specific functions, and concepts—like first, last, earliest, and latest—are frequently employed to identify specific values or dates contained inside a dataset. These functions reveal information about the first and last values as well as the earliest and latest events that take place within a specific context. The meanings of the terms "First," "Last," "Earliest," and "Latest," as well as their applications and how they are used in various data analysis situations, will all be covered during this discussion.

- **First**: To find the first value or record within a dataset or specific grouping, utilize the First function. The function can be used to discover the initial value or record to do this. It helps identify the initial value or occurrence in a sequence of occurrences. The First function is highly useful when running analysis on time-series data or data that has been arranged based on a certain criterion.

For example, in Power BI, you can use the First function as follows:

- First Customer = FIRSTNONBLANK (Customer [CustomerName],
- Customer [Date])

Based on the order of the "**Date**" column, this expression will return the first non-blank value that can be found in the "**CustomerName**" column of the "**Customer**" database. It assists in determining which client was the first one recorded or which customer had the earliest date.

- **Last**: The Last function contains the analog of the First function, which is called the Last function. It represents the record or value that ends a dataset or a certain grouping. The Last function aids in identifying the value or occurrence that comes last in a sequence of events. It is a strategy that is frequently employed when undertaking a data analysis in another way or when attempting to determine which event occurred most recently.

For example, in Power BI, you can use the Last function as follows:

- Last Sale Amount = LASTNONBLANK(Sales[Amount], Sales[Date])

This expression retrieves the most recent non-blank value of the "**Amount**" column in the "Sales" database depending on the order of the "**Date**" column in the "**Sales**" table. It helps determine the amount of the most recent sale that was recorded.

- **Earliest**: The Earliest function focuses on locating the earliest date or value inside a dataset or a particular grouping. It does this by searching for the earliest date or value. In the process of dealing with time-series data, it is often used to create the earliest occurrence of an event.

For example, in Power BI, you can use the Min function to calculate the earliest date as follows:

Earliest Date = MIN (DateTable[Date])

This expression will provide the earliest possible date value that can be found in the "Date" column of the "**DateTable**" table. It assists in determining the date that was recorded first inside the collection.

- **Latest**: The date or value that is the most recent occurrence inside a given dataset or specific grouping is found using the Latest function. Finding the most recent value or instance of a particular event is particularly useful.

For example, in Power BI, you can use the Max function to calculate the latest date as follows:

- Latest Date = MAX(DateTable[Date])

This expression retrieves the most recent possible date value from the "**Date**" column of the "**DateTable**" table. It is useful in determining which date was the most recent one recorded in the dataset.

Applications of First, Last, Earliest, and Latest:

- **Temporal Analysis**: When analyzing time-series data, which can include information on sales, market prices, or weather patterns, these functions are frequently utilized. They assist in identifying the first and last values that occurred throughout a specific period, the earliest or most recent occurrences, and whether events came first or last.
- **Customer Analysis**: In customer analysis, the first and final functions are frequently utilized to identify the initial and final interactions or transactions made by customers. You can use this information to have a better understanding of customer behavior. This data can shed light on several subjects, such as turnover, loyalty, and customer behavior.
- **Data Monitoring**: The Earliest and Latest capabilities help monitor updates or changes to data over time. Analysts can follow the development or progression of certain variables or metrics by determining the earliest and latest values or dates.
- **Report Visualizations**: Reports and visualizations can display the First, Last, Earliest, and Latest values to highlight certain data points or to provide a summary of the data. For example, the first and last sale amounts, the earliest and latest dates noted, or the beginning and ending numbers in a time series can all be seen on a dashboard.

Measures and DAX Fundamentals

To have a deeper understanding of the individual data points, we aggregate data. Sometimes we need to make sure the calculation is done in a specific way or that future users will be able to view an explicit calculation in our data model. Sometimes all it takes to understand the function of an aggregate is the name of one of its columns. In both cases—whether you are dragging a column into the Values section to acquire a total or average, or you are creating a DAX measure to do a calculation—what is frequently misinterpreted is that a measure is being utilized to produce an aggregate. Regardless, an aggregate is being created.

Implicit and Explicit Measures

Implicit Measures

Implicit measures are those that are determined by Power BI automatically based on the data model and visuals. Another name for implicit measures is automated measures. These metrics are acquired by extrapolating them from the domains and connections that the model describes. Based on the results of this analysis and an examination of the data structure, Power BI automatically determines which aggregation functions to apply.

Characteristics of Implicit Measures in Power BI

- **Automatic Generation**: Power BI will generate implicit measures on its own without any explicit user input. They are created following the structure of the data model and the fields that are used in the visualizations.
- **Aggregated Functions**: Common aggregated functions like total, count, average, maximum, and minimum are frequently used in implicit measurements. This is a result of implicit metrics not being mentioned clearly. Power BI considers the type of data in the field to determine which aggregate is appropriate to utilize.
- **Contextual Evaluation**: Implicit measures are evaluated within the context of the visualizations. Power BI takes into account filters, slicers, and other visual interactions to provide accurate results.

Applications of Implicit Measures in Power BI

- **Quick Analysis:** Efficient exploratory data analysis is made possible by implicit measures. Users only need to drag and drop fields into visualizations; Power BI will take care of the necessary computations automatically. This frees users from having to explicitly identify measurements and allows them to focus on visually expressing the data.
- **Standard Aggregations**: Basic aggregations that are frequently used in data analysis, including totaling the number of orders, summing up the sales, or figuring out the average rating for each product, are provided by implicit measures. They achieve this by executing the appropriate aggregating techniques automatically, which in turn greatly simplifies the process of creating basic visualizations.

Explicit Measures

Explicit measurements are calculations created by end users in Power BI using the Data Analysis Expressions (DAX) language. User-defined measurements are another name for these computations. Explicit measures require manual creation and definition, in contrast to implicit measures. Compared to implicit measures, this allows consumers more freedom and control over the reasoning underlying the calculation.

Characteristics of Explicit Measures in Power BI

- **User-Defined**: These explicit measures are generated by the users themselves by utilizing DAX expressions. Users are responsible for defining the calculation logic, specifying the aggregation functions, and customizing the calculations following the analytical needs that are unique to them.
- **Customized Calculations**: When employing explicit measures, users can do intricate computations that are outside the purview of standard aggregations. They can employ complex functions, create conditional logic, carry out time intelligence computations, or implement company-specific rules.

- **Reusability**: It is not necessary to repeat calculations in different visualizations when explicit measures may be reused across different reports or visuals, ensuring consistency in calculations. It is also possible to export and import explicit measures into different programs.

Applications of Explicit Measures in Power BI

- **Advanced Calculations:** To complete complex calculations and analysis, explicit measures are necessary. The user can use statistical functions, build complicated business measures, compute growth rates, do segmentation analysis, and produce custom KPIs.
- **Time Intelligence**: Power BI includes a broad collection of functions for time intelligence, which enables users to define explicit measures for year-to-date calculations, period comparisons, moving averages, or other time-based studies. These functions can be accessed via the Power BI interface.
- **Business-Specific Metrics:** Explicit measures enable the development of metrics specific to the business and tailored to the requirements of the enterprise. Users can design calculations for profitability ratios, conversion rates, client retention rates, and any other critical performance indicators pertinent to their specific organization setting.

DAX Syntax Fundamentals

To get a grasp on the fundamentals of DAX syntax, we will begin with a simple calculation that uses the AVERAGE function applied to a single column.

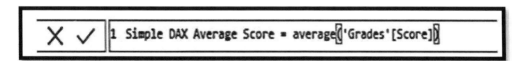

Starting from the left and working our way right, we have the measure's name, which in this case is "Simple DAX Average Score." The equals symbol sets the title apart from the calculation that will follow in the sentence body. Our task is to compute an average. Subsequently, the function will accept certain conditions, a column reference in this case. The initial set of parentheses separates the function from the arguments or conditions that it is looking for. The table name that we want to supply is the next item, followed by the function wrapped in single quotes and the column name that we want to supply enclosed in brackets. When the second set of parentheses is used, it indicates that all of the function's parameters have been provided before. Put all of that together, and let's try to make it sound a little bit more like English, shall we? There is a DAX measure called **Simple DAX Average Score**. This DAX measure is referred to as the Average function and it calculates its results by utilizing the Score column from the Grades table as its calculating parameter. This will return the average score from the Grades table in our scenario, and it is susceptible to being changed by any context that is relevant to the situation. To give you an idea, any table name with a space should always be encircled by single quotes, and the names of any columns should always be enclosed in brackets. It is excellent practice to surround the names of your tables in single quotes when creating your own DAX, whether or not the table names contain spaces. From a technical point of view, this means that every one of the basic aggregations we looked at earlier uses the same basic DAX syntax for their different functions. There is no difference between the **Sum, Average, Count, DistinctCount, Min, and Max** values. Simply calculating the minimum or maximum allows one to determine the first, last, earliest, and latest positions. The following is how that syntax looks.

- *FUNCTION('TABLE'[COLUMN])*

That sums it up well. You will then be provided with a straightforward explicit measure that will have any additional context in the visual as well as any relevant slicers on your worksheet applied to it for filtering.

CALCULATE

One way to think of the CALCULATE function concerning DAX functions is like a Swiss army knife. Like a lot of other things in life, 20% of knowledge is sufficient to tackle 80% of DAX problems. If you can understand CALCULATE, you will have gone a long way toward achieving that early level of proficiency. The operation of the CALCULATE function is simple. It is a wrapper whose filtering capabilities have been improved, and it evaluates an expression in that environment. What does it involve precisely? Filter contexts can be saved for subsequent usage after functions have been evaluated. When working with SQL, take into consideration the potential of employing a WHERE clause.

You could wish to restrict the results to those where X = Y or Z > 100, for example. You can feed this WHERE clause–type parameters into your DAX formula using CALCULATE, which enables you to do so in an explicit manner. This guarantees that they will always be applicable, independent of the situation. There are countless other situations that you can think of when this could be helpful. Are you curious about the comparison between this year's sales and those at the same period last year? With CALCULATE's assistance, you can succeed. You likely need to assess how one product's sales figure stacks up against another set of products. You can accomplish it. Would you like to offer a calculation that is dynamic and meets the filter context requirements based on the results of another calculation, like the date from the day before? You can do that.

Syntax: The syntax of the CALCULATE function in Power BI is as follows:

- CALCULATE(<expression>, <filter1>, <filter2>, ...)
- **<expression>** represents the calculation or measure to be evaluated or modified.
- **<filter1>, <filter2>**, and so on are optional parameters that define the filters or conditions to be applied to the calculation.

Examples of CALCULATE Function Usage

- **Applying a Filter to a Calculation**: Let's say we have a Sales table that has columns like "**SalesAmount**" and "**ProductCategory**." We want to determine how much money was generated in the "Electronics" area as a whole, but we are only going to include the money that was earned in 2022.

```
Total Sales 2022 =
CALCULATE(
    SUM(Sales[SalesAmount]),
    Sales[ProductCategory] = "Electronics",
    YEAR(Sales[SalesDate]) = 2022
)
```

In this demonstration, the CALCULATE function alters the SUM calculation by adding filters that are determined by the column titled "ProductCategory" as well as the column titled "SalesDate." Only sales that fall under the category of "Electronics" and those that take place in 2022 will be included in the calculation.

- **Applying Multiple Filters**: If we want to expand upon the previous example, we can do so by adding a further filter that is determined by the sales area. We want to determine how much money will be made in sales for the category of "Electronics" in the year 2022; however, we are only interested in the "North" area.

```
Total Sales 2022 North =
CALCULATE(
    SUM(Sales[SalesAmount]),
    Sales[ProductCategory] = "Electronics",
    YEAR(Sales[SalesDate]) = 2022,
    Sales[Region] = "North"
)
```

In this particular instance, the **CALCULATE** function uses many filters so that the calculation may be simplified. The only sales that are taken into account are those in the "**Electronics**" category, throughout the year 2022, in the "North" area.

- **Nesting CALCULATES Functions**: Use of the CALCULATE functions in nested calculations may result in increased complexity. For example, let us imagine we wish to find the average revenue generated by sales in the "Electronics" category, but we do not like to use any data for 2023. One of our other objectives is to compare this average to the ordinary general sales amount.

```
Average Sales Electronics =
CALCULATE(
    AVERAGE(Sales[SalesAmount]),
    Sales[ProductCategory] = "Electronics",
    NOT(YEAR(Sales[SalesDate]) = 2023)
)


Overall Average Sales = AVERAGE(Sales[SalesAmount])


Comparison = [Average Sales Electronics] - [Overall Average Sales]
```

This example shows how to use the CALCULATE function to get the average income from sales in the "Electronics" category while excluding revenue from sales in 2023. The total quantity of average sales is computed separately. The final stage of the computation compares the "Electronics" average against the overall survey average to find the difference. Through the use of Power BI's CALCULATE tool, users can alter computations depending on specific conditions or filters flexibly and dynamically. Users can do complex data analysis, produce tailored calculations, and obtain deeper insights into their data by using this function.

We Heard You like DAX, So We Put Some DAX in Your DAX

If you enjoy using Power BI's DAX (Data Analysis Expressions), you'll be happy to learn about some sophisticated methods that combine DAX functions inside of DAX expressions. This makes it possible to do computations and analyses that are even more complex and powerful. In this article, we'll explore the realm of nested DAX expressions and provide some illustrations of how you may improve your data modeling and analysis by using this feature.

Nested DAX Functions

"Nesting" DAX functions is the process of using one DAX function as an argument or parameter within the context of another DAX function. This technique will enable you to perform complex computations, alter data, and create custom metrics that are outside the scope of individual functions. It gives you the ability to combine and link many functions to produce the intended outcome.

Examples of Nested DAX Expressions

Let's explore a few examples to illustrate the power of nested DAX expressions:

- **Calculating a Weighted Average:** Imagine that you have a Sales table that has columns such as SalesAmount and Quantity. You can use the following nested DAX statement to determine the weighted average sales price, where the contribution that each sale makes is proportionate to the number of sales that it represents:

```
Weighted Average Sales Price =
DIVIDE(
    SUMX(Sales, Sales[SalesAmount] * Sales[Quantity]),
    SUMX(Sales, Sales[Quantity])
)
```

Using the SUMX function, the nested DAX expression in this example loops over each row in the Sales database and multiplies the SalesAmount by the Quantity for each sale. The total of all of these values is then divided by the total of all of the quantities to determine the weighted average sales price.

Calculating a Rolling Total: You can use the nested DAX expression that is shown below to generate a running total of sales for a certain period:

```
Rolling Total Sales =
CALCULATE(
    SUM(Sales[SalesAmount]),
    FILTER(
        ALL(Sales),
        Sales[Date] <= MAX(Sales[Date])
            && Sales[Date] > MAX(Sales[Date]) - 30
    )
)
```

The layered DAX expression in this example combines the capabilities of the FILTER and CALCULATES functions. For every row in the Sales database that meets the requirement specified by the FILTER function, it determines the overall SalesAmount. Based on the maximum date that is applicable in the current situation, this function selects rows from the Sales table where the date falls within the last 30 days.

- **Applying Conditional Logic**: You can utilize nested DAX expressions to apply conditional logic and produce dynamic calculations depending on particular criteria.

These capabilities are made possible by DAX. Consider, for instance, the following example, which computes a specialized measure dependent on a condition:

```
Custom Measure =
IF(
    [Total Sales] > 1000,
    [Total Sales] * 0.1,
    [Total Sales] * 0.05
)
```

This nested DAX expression we have here applies a condition using the IF function. If the Total Sales measure is greater than 1000, the Total Sales are multiplied by 0.1 in the computation; if not, they are multiplied by 0.05. This makes it possible to do dynamic computations based on the specific situation. Benefits and Application Areas: In Power BI, nested DAX expressions offer several benefits and a plethora of options for data modeling and analysis.

These advantages and possibilities are as follows:

- **Improved Calculations**: The use of nested DAX expressions makes it possible to do more complex calculations, which may include the combination of some functions and logical operations.
- **Flexibility**: When you stack DAX functions, you have more control over the calculations and can adapt them to match particular needs or business logic. This is made possible by the fact that you have more control.
- **Advanced Analysis**: Nested DAX expressions allow you to execute advanced analysis, such as weighted averages, rolling totals, complicated conditional calculations, and many other types of analyses.
- **Reusability**: Once you've generated nested DAX expressions, you can reuse them across many measures, visuals, or reports, which will save you time and ensure consistency.

Row and Filter Context

Power BI and other data analysis tools are built on the fundamentals of row context and filter context. They play a crucial role in understanding how computations and aggregates are performed in connection to the evaluation environment.

Row Context

The data point in the current row that is being taken into account by a calculation is referred to as the "row context". When you create a calculated column or measure in Power BI, the calculation gets applied to every row in the table or visualization you are working with. Which values from which rows are used in the calculation at any given time depends on the row's context. **For instance, if you have a Sales table that has columns such as SalesAmount and Quantity, and you develop a measure to compute the overall income for each row, as an illustration:**

- Total Revenue = Sales[SalesAmount] * Sales[Quantity]

The row context will proceed to iterate over each row in the Sales database, compute the total income by multiplying the SalesAmount by the Quantity for that particular row, and then show the result as appropriate.

Filter Context

A series of filters or conditions may be applied to the data in the course of evaluating a calculation's accuracy. This is the definition of "filter context." Filters can be applied automatically or manually by the user based on interactions with slicers, graphics, and other filtering techniques. When a calculation is made, Power BI considers the filter context to determine which data rows are included in the calculation and which rows are excluded. The filter context defines the range of the calculation as well as the subset of data that it operates on. **For instance, if you build a measure to compute the overall quantity of sales for a certain product category, the following will occur:**
- Total Sales = CALCULATE(SUM(Sales[SalesAmount]), Sales[ProductCategory] = "Electronics")

The condition **Sales [ProductCategory] = "Electronics"** establishes the context for the filter. Only the rows that satisfy this criterion will be considered for inclusion in the calculation of the total amount sold, while the results of the calculation will exclude the results of any other product categories.

Interaction between Row and Filter Context

The row context and the filter context in Power BI work together while doing calculations. The computation considers the filters that have been applied in the filter context and evaluates each row in the row context. The filter context will change based on the region you select, for example, if you have a table visualization that shows the total sales for each product category and you add a slicer to filter the data by that area. This is thus because the data being filtered defines the filter's context. The total quantity of sales will be determined when the row context has finished iterating over each row and combining the information from the filter context with the row context. To guarantee correct calculations and interpretations of data, it is essential to have a solid understanding of the relationship that exists between the row context and the filter context. By modifying the filter context using functions like **CALCULATE, FILTER, or ALL**, you can control which data is included or excluded from the calculation, offering greater flexibility in data analysis. This allows you to select which data is included or omitted from the calculation.

One Final DAX Example

Let's examine one more DAX example to show you the depth and breadth of what this language is capable of. Our computation of the customer retention rate, which is based on the sales data, will be based on a hypothetical scenario. Suppose we have a Sales table with columns for SalesAmount, SalesDate, and CustomerID. The ratio of all customers to all customers who have made purchases in the current year and the previous year is known as the customer retention rate, and it is something we need to find out. This ratio shows the proportion of consumers who have made purchases in both years.

To calculate the customer retention rate using DAX, we can follow these steps:

1. Create a measure to count the distinct number of customers who made purchases in the current year:
- **Current Year Customers = DISTINCTCOUNT(Sales[CustomerID])**
2. Create a measure to count the distinct number of customers who made purchases in the previous year:
- **Previous Year Customers = CALCULATE(DISTINCTCOUNT(Sales[CustomerID]), SAMEPERIODLASTYEAR(Sales[SalesDate]))**

In this measure, we use the CALCULATE function along with the SAMEPERIODLASTYEAR function to calculate the distinct count of customers for the previous year.

3. Create a measure to calculate the customer retention rate:
- **Retention Rate = DIVIDE([Previous Year Customers], [Current Year Customers])**

A decimal representation of the retention rate can be obtained by using the DIVIDE function to determine the ratio of customers from the previous year to customers from the current year. We can get the client retention rate by integrating all of these different measures. To do the required calculations and comparisons, the measures make use of DAX functions such as **DISTINCTCOUNT, CALCULATE, SAMEPERIODLASTYEAR, and DIVIDE.** Once the metrics have been established, the customer retention rate can be displayed in a Power BI report using a card visual or any other suitable type of visualization. With the addition of filters and slicers to the report, the retention rate will dynamically change, offering valuable insights into customer behavior and loyalty over time. It is noteworthy to mention that this example illustrates the basic procedures needed to calculate the client retention rate. You may need to put extra logic into the calculations, depending on the unique data model and needs that you have. Alternatively, you may need to improve the calculations further. Gaining a deeper comprehension of DAX functions and how to use them will help you make the most out of your data and obtain insightful conclusions that will help you make wise decisions. Because of its expressiveness and versatility, DAX is an excellent tool for business intelligence and data modeling in Power BI. It enables you to carry out intricate computations and analyses.

Conclusion

Comprehending the DAX language is essential to utilizing Microsoft Power BI's full analytical power. An overview of the main ideas, operations, and syntax that make up DAX has been given in this introduction. We have now finished our thorough introduction to the DAX language, which includes information on measures, calculated columns, calculated tables, aggregations, implicit and explicit measures, DAX syntactic basics, the CALCULATE function, row and filter context, and useful examples. With this knowledge, users can use Power BI's DAX capabilities to turn their data into actionable insights and significant business results.

Activity

1. What are the types of functions?
2. Differentiate between deviation, variance, and median.

CHAPTER 6

PUTTING THE PUZZLE PIECES TOGETHER: FROM RAW DATA TO REPORT

Your First Data Import

1. Open the Power BI Desktop.
2. To obtain data, select the "**Home**" tab of the Power BI Desktop application and then choose the "**Get Data**" button.
3. The data source should be Excel; select "Excel" from the list of options that appear in the "Get Data" box. If Excel is not one of the programs displayed, you can search for it by typing its name into the field provided, or select "More..." to view further possibilities.
4. Choose the Excel file by using the "**Navigator**" window to go to where your Excel file is stored, and then select it after you've found it. After that, choose the "Open" option to continue.
5. You will get a preview of the sheets and tables that are accessible in the Excel file in the "**Navigator**" box. From there, you can choose the data that you want to import. Check the boxes next to the individual sheets and tables that you wish to import to choose them for import. You can also examine a preview of the data by clicking on the "Preview" button.
6. After choosing the sheets or tables that you want to work with, you have two options available to you: load the data or edit the data.
   - **Load**: If you want to load the data straight away, you may do so by clicking the "Load" button. The chosen data will be imported into Power BI, at which point you can begin the process of displaying and analyzing the data.
   - **Edit**: Select "**Edit**" if you want to make any changes to the data before importing it. You can then modify or manipulate the data, among other things. By doing this, you'll be able to perform a multitude of data modifications, such as merging tables, deleting columns, renaming columns, and more, within the Power Query Editor.
7. **Visualize and analyze your data:** Using the fields and tables available in the Power BI Desktop, you can start creating dashboards, reports, and visualizations as soon as the data has been imported or after you have finished shaping it in the Power Query Editor.

Select and Transform the Data When You Import

Before entering your data into Power BI, you can adjust and shape it using the "**Choose and Transform Data**" tool, also referred to as Power Query. You may create calculated columns and carry out several data manipulation operations with this tool, including cleaning, filtering, merging, and appending data. You can choose to use this capability when importing data into Power BI Desktop.

The "Choose and Transform Data" option can be used in the following manner:

1. Launch Power BI Desktop and choose the "Get Data" option located in the Home tab of the program.
2. Select the desired data source, be it an Excel spreadsheet, a CSV file, a SQL database, or any other supported source.
3. In the "**Navigator" window**, select the tables and sheets that you want to import from the designated data source.
4. Instead of selecting "**Load**," you should click the "**Transform Data**" button. The window for the Power Query Editor will open when you do this.
5. A glimpse of your data will appear for you to peruse in the Power Query Editor. You can do a variety of data transformation activities in this section. **The following are examples of frequent tasks:**
   - **Removing columns:** Right-click on a column header and select "Remove" to remove unnecessary columns from the dataset.
   - **Filtering rows**: Use the filtering options in the column headers to filter rows based on specific criteria.
   - **Changing data types**: choose a column, right-click, and select "**Change Type**" to convert the data type of a column.
   - **Merging tables**: If you have various tables with related data, you can merge them by defining relationships between common columns. Use the "**Merge Queries**" or "**Append Queries**" options under the Home tab to merge tables.
   - **Creating calculated columns**: Use the "**Add Column**" tab to create new columns based on calculations or expressions using existing columns.
   - **Splitting columns**: If a column contains combined data, you can split it into multiple columns using the "**Split Column**" option.
   - **Renaming columns**: Right-click on a column header and select "**Rename**" to provide a more meaningful name to the column.
   - **Applying transformations**: Power Query provides numerous transformation options under various tabs, such as Home, Transform, Add Column, and View.
6. As you make changes, the data preview that appears in the Power Query Editor will be updated in real time, allowing you to assess the results of your changes as you go.
7. After finishing the data conversion and shaping process, select "**Close & Apply"** from the Power Query Editor's Home tab. Your modifications will be saved as a result. In the process, Power BI will load the data and the transformations will be applied.
8. Now that the data has been converted, you can use Power BI to build dashboards, reports, and visualizations using the data.

Consolidating Tables with Append

In many cases, the data originates from multiple tables or sources; thus, one of the most important steps in the process of preparing the data for analysis is to combine all of these tables into a single table. Users can condense their data further by using the Append tool in Power BI, which offers a quick and simple way to join tables vertically. Appending tables in Power BI is the process of merging the rows of several tables into a single table. This process works incredibly well when dealing with linked data or data that is dispersed across several sources or files. By linking tables, users can create a cohesive dataset that simplifies the evaluation and display of the consolidated data. To do this, a unified dataset is created.

Here, we will look into the processes and things to keep in mind while consolidating tables using the Append function in Power BI.

Step 1: Accessing the Power Query Editor

Once the desired tables have been imported, Power BI will display the data preview window. Users can import all of the available tables in this area, or they can choose which tables to import by checking the boxes next to those tables. Rather than just importing the data, use the "**Transform Data**" button to open the Power Query Editor. The Power Query Editor will then appear. This editor provides a wide range of tools for modifying the data before adding the tables, enabling the tables to be adjusted and improved.

Step 2: Selecting and Appending Tables

The Power Query Editor's "Queries" window, which is on the left side, is where tables are displayed. Locate the first table you wish to include in the combined table, and then select it. Click the **"Append Queries" button** on the "Home" page of the Power Query Editor to attach tables. This button allows you to append tables and appears as two tables stacked on top of one another. A dialog box will appear with a list of the tables that are available for use. Holding down the Control key while clicking on the desired table or tables will allow you to select which ones to attach. Click **"OK"** in the dialogue box to start the adding process.

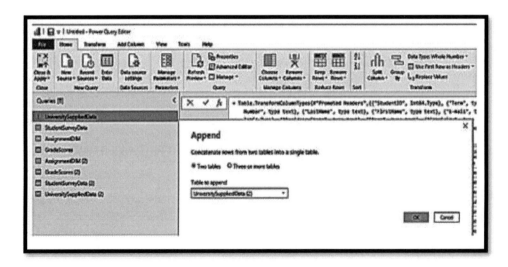

Step 3: Repeating the Append Process

Should you require additional tables to be added, you will have to repeat the process by selecting the next table in the "Queries" window and completing steps 2 and 3. Using Power Query, the entries from each table will be added beneath the pre-existing consolidated table. By adding tables frequently, users can integrate data from many sources, blend time-series data, or combine similar information for a comprehensive study.

Step 4: Data Transformation and Cleanup (Optional)

Before starting the add process, it is imperative to make sure that all of the tables that are being consolidated have a similar format. To achieve data harmony, Power Query Editor offers an extensive set of data transformation and cleaning features. Users can remove unnecessary columns, filter rows according to certain standards, change the kind of data, divide or merge columns, do computations, and perform other necessary data preparation tasks. The procedures involved in this transformation help maintain the integrity of the data contained in the consolidated table and help align the tables.

Step 5: Applying the Consolidation

When all the tables you wish to attach have been appended and any necessary transformations have been carried out, click the "**Close & Apply"** button on the Power **Query Editor's Home tab**. This step will apply the consolidation procedure and save the alterations. Power BI will create a new consolidated table with all of the rows that were added from the previous tables in the following steps. The data analysis and visualization process will be simplified as a result.

Considerations for Consolidating Tables with Append

Consolidating tables using the Append function can give some advantages; nevertheless, to conduct an accurate and useful analysis, it is essential to take into consideration the following factors:

1. Verify that the tables that are being added contain comparable structures, including column names, data types, and order. This will ensure that the data will be consistent. The inconsistency of the structures may result in the misalignment of the data and incorrect analysis.
2. **Data Quality:** Before adding tables, any necessary data cleaning and quality checks must be completed. This is because of the requirement for data quality. It's essential to remove duplicate entries, address missing values, and fix data anomalies to ensure the accuracy of the study.
3. **Performance**: There is a possibility that performance may be impacted if you append huge tables that include a significant number of rows. Applying filters or changes to the append process may help minimize the size of the dataset and improve query speed. This can be done to optimize the append process.

4. **Data Refresh**: If the original tables are changed frequently, you should make sure that the consolidated table is also kept up to date. To preserve the authenticity of the aggregated data, the data refresh settings in Power BI need to be configured.
5. **Data Relationships:** Building the relationships between the consolidated table and any extra tables that are relevant to the circumstance should come next after you have consolidated the data. This makes it possible to analyze data effortlessly and makes Power BI's advanced features, including drill-through and cross-filtering, possible.

The Append function in Power BI offers a reliable way to combine data from several tables or sources into a single dataset. This function may be used to combine tables into a single dataset. The Power Query Editor allows users to modify and mold data, assisting in preserving the integrity and coherence of the combined table. By carefully considering the quality, structure, and performance of their data, users can fully utilize Power BI's analysis and visualization capabilities to get insightful knowledge and realize the full potential of their data.

Utilizing Merge to Get Columns from Other Tables

Based on shared fields or relationships between the datasets, users can combine columns from multiple tables into a single table using Power BI's Merge function. Additional information can be added and your dataset can be improved by including data from other tables when tables are merged.

Here's a step-by-step guide on using the Merge function in Power BI:

Step 1: Open Power BI Desktop and ensure that you have imported the tables you want to merge using the "**Get Data**" option.
Step 2: Locate the table to which you wish to add columns from other tables inside the Power Query Editor.
Step 3: To choose the table, locate the "Queries" pane on the left-hand side of the screen and click on the table's name.
Step 4: Go to the Home tab of the Power Query Editor and choose the "Merge Queries" option. It seems to be two tables connected by a line with an arrow in the middle.
Step 5: You will see that the "Merge Queries" dialog box has two drop-down selections. These menus are titled "Table" and "Merge Kind."
- **Table**: Select the table you want to merge with the currently selected table from the drop-down list. This is the table you wish to add, and it is the table that has the additional columns you want to add.
- **Merge Kind**: Decide what kind of merging operation you want to do. Rows that match and rows that do not match between the tables are handled differently by the merging process depending on which of the four options—"Inner," "Left Outer," "Right Outer," and "Full Outer"—is selected.

Step 6: Select the required columns from each table to define the merging requirements. The names of the columns will cause Power BI to provide suggestions for new columns automatically. Check to see if the columns you've chosen to combine include data that already matches, or that they may act as the merge's keys.

Step 7: Choose the options for the merging procedure according to your personal preferences. You can choose to maintain every column from both tables, or you can choose to keep only a portion of each table's columns. Depending on your needs, you can either keep the combined columns as a nested table or expand them.

Step 8: Click on the "**OK**" button to perform the merge operation.

Step 9: Depending on the merge criteria you specify, Power Query will merge the selected table with the other table. A combined table with columns from the two original tables is the result. Rows will be matched using the merge key, and the right values will be inserted in the merged columns once a match has been made.

Step 10: If you still have other tables that need to be merged, you will need to repeat the procedure by choosing the next table in the "Queries" pane and then proceeding with steps 3 through 9.

Step 11: Power Query will merge the chosen table with the other table based on the merge criteria you provide. The outcome is a merged table that contains columns from the two original tables. The merge key will be used to match rows, and after a match has been made, the appropriate values will be added to the merged columns. The merged columns from other tables give extra context and insights to strengthen your analysis and decision-making. After merging tables, you can utilize the combined dataset to create visualizations, analyze data, and produce reports in Power BI.

Building Relationships

You're probably going to use the data from all of your tables in some sort of analysis if you have several tables. To do proper computations of results and present accurate data in your reports, relationships must be established between these kinds of tables. In the great majority of cases, you won't need to do anything. That's what the autodetect function does for you. However, there are times when you might have to start connections from scratch or modify an already-existing relationship. Regardless of the situation, it is critical to comprehend relationships in Power BI Desktop and how to construct and modify them.

Autodetect during load

In Power BI Desktop, when you query two or more tables at once, the tool searches for relationships between the tables and attempts to build them for you when the data is loaded. Cardinality, the direction of the cross filter, and the "Make this relationship active" setting are preconfigured relationship choices. When you perform a query in Power BI Desktop, it looks up potential associations between the column names in the tables you are querying. If there are, such relationships will be forged on their own. Power BI Desktop does not establish the relationship if it cannot determine with a high degree of certainty that there is a match. Nevertheless, you can still manually establish or update relationships by using the **Manage Relationships** dialog box that is available to you.

Create a relationship with Autodetect

- On the **Modeling** tab, select **Manage Relationships** > **Autodetect**.

Create a relationship manually

1. Navigate to the **Modeling tab** and pick **New > Manage relationships** from the drop-down menu.
2. To establish a link between two tables, select a table from the first table drop-down list in the Create Relationship dialog box. From the drop-down menu, select the column you want to use in the relationship.

3. Using the "second table" drop-down menu, choose the other table that will take part in the relationship. Click the **OK button** once you have chosen the alternative column you wish to use.

Cardinality (direction), Cross filter direction, and Make this relationship active for your new relationship are all automatically configured by default in Power BI Desktop. The term "cardinality" describes the direction of a filter's application. If, however, you feel that changes are necessary, you can make them here. The following error will appear if there are no unique values in any of the tables chosen for the relationship: A unique value must be present in one of the columns. Any relational database technology must have a separate, unique list of key values for at least one table in the relationship.

There are a few different solutions available if you come across that error:

- Use Remove Duplicates to create a column with unique data. Adopting this method has drawbacks because there is a chance of information loss due to the removal of duplicate rows. The duplication of a key (row) frequently has a good reason.

- Include an interim table with the list of distinct key values in the current model. After that, this table will be linked to the two main columns that make up the connection.

You also have the option of using the Model view diagram layouts, where you can construct a relationship by dragging and dropping a column from one table to a column in another table.

Edit a relationship

In Power BI, there are two methods for editing a relationship. Using the Editing relationships tool in the Properties pane of the Model view is the first method. This lets you select any line joining two tables, and then in the Properties pane, go over the many possibilities for relationships. To view the relationship choices, make sure the Properties box is expanded.

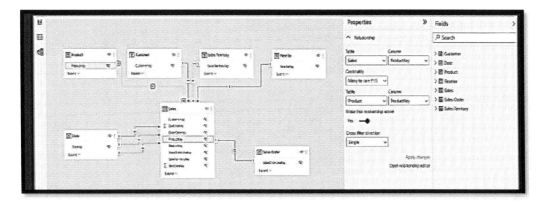

The second approach to update a relationship is by utilizing the Relationship Editor dialog, which can be opened in a variety of different ways from inside Power BI Desktop. **The Relationship Editor dialog can be opened using any one of the methods presented in the following list:**
From the Report view do any of the following:
- Select the **Manage Relationships option** from the Modeling ribbon, then select the relationship you wish to change and press the **Edit button.**
- Select **a table first from the Fields list.** Next, select the **Manage Relationships option** from the Table Tools ribbon. Lastly, choose the relationship that needs editing and press the **Edit button.**

To edit a relationship, select it first using the Table tools ribbon's Manage relationships option, located in the Data view's ribbon, and then pick **Edit.**
From the Model view do any of the following:
- After choosing the relationship from the Manage Relationships submenu of the Ribbon's Home tab, pick **Edit** from the drop-down menu that displays.
- Double-click **any line between two tables to link them.**
- To get the Properties option, right-click on any line joining the two tables and select it from the context menu.

- First, pick a line that connects two tables, and then choose the **Open relationship editor** from the Properties pane.

Additionally, you may update a relationship from any view by right-clicking on the table, choosing Manage relationships from the context menu, choosing the relationship, and then choosing Update. You'll be able to adjust the relationship in this way. A screenshot of the Edit relationship window may be seen in the image below.

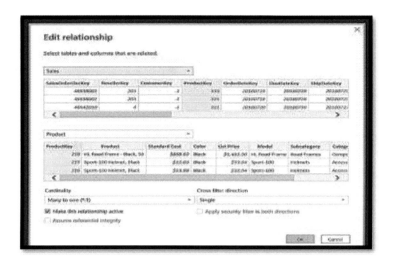

Editing relationships using different methods

The Edit Relationships dialog, which is currently in preview, offers a more assisted experience when making changes to relationships in Power BI. Each table provides a preview of the data. As you choose the columns, the window will automatically determine their relationship and offer appropriate cross-filter and cardinality selections. Using the editing options available in the Properties pane is a time-saving way to change relationships in Power BI. You are not given a preview of the data; instead, you are just presented with the names of the tables and columns that you might select. The relationship choices you make are only assessed once you click the **Apply Changes button.** Using the Properties pane and its streamlined technique can assist reduce the number of queries executed while altering a relationship? This can be an important factor to take into account in scenarios with a lot of data, especially when using DirectQuery connections. There is a chance that the relationships created with the Properties pane will be more complex than the relationships created with the Edit relationships dialog. In the Model view diagram layouts, you can also choose many relationships at once by holding down the Ctrl key and selecting multiple lines at once. This will allow you to choose multiple sets of relationships. The **Properties** pane is where you can make changes to common properties, and clicking **Apply Changes** will execute those changes in a single transaction. You can erase either a single relationship or several relationships at once by using the erase key on your keyboard. Because you can't reverse the delete operation, a dialog box will ask you to verify that you want to get rid of the relationships.

Important

Currently in preview is the ability for users to update relationships within the properties pane. Both the product's functionality and documentation are subject to change while it's in preview. In Power BI Desktop, go to the File menu, select Options and Settings, click Options, and then choose Preview features to enable this function. Lastly, click the checkbox next to the Relationship pane option in the **GLOBAL section.**

Configure more options

More parameters can be configured whenever a relationship is created, edited, or edited again. Power BI Desktop automatically configures additional options based on its best estimate, which can be different for each relationship depending on the data that is included in the columns. This is the default setting for the software.

Cardinality

The Cardinality parameter can be changed to any of the following values based on your preferences:
- **Many-to-one (*:1)**: The most common sort of relationship and the default type is the many-to-one relationship. It means that whereas a column in one database could have multiple instances of a given value, the column in the other linked table—also called the lookup table—can only contain one instance of a given value.
- **One-to-one (1:1)**: In a one-to-one relationship, each column in one table only has one occurrence of a given value, and each column in the other associated table also only has one instance of a given value.
- **One-to-many (1:*)**: A column in one table can only ever have one instance of a given value in connection with a one-to-many structure, whereas the column in the other related table can contain many occurrences of the same value.
- **Many to many (*:*)**: Using composite models eliminates the need for unique values in your tables because many-to-many relationships can be established between them. It also removes the need for previous workarounds, like adding extra tables just for connection creation.

Cross filter direction

The Cross filter direction option can have one of the following settings:

Both: Filtering can be done on both tables more effectively by treating them as a single table during processing. When used on a single table with many lookup tables surrounding it, both alternatives work effectively. An illustration of this would be a sales actuals table with a department lookup table included. This arrangement—which consists of numerous lookup tables plus a core table—is frequently referred to as a star schema configuration.

- However, if you have many tables that contain lookup tables, you shouldn't use both options (particularly if some of those lookup tables are shared). In this case, to carry over with the previous example, you also have a budget sales table that records the allocated budget for every department. Furthermore, the budget and sales tables are connected to the department-specific table. Both options are not something you should utilize when configuring anything similar.

Single: This is the most usual and default direction, which implies that filtering decisions made on related tables affect the table that is being used to aggregate information. When you import a data model from Power Pivot into an older version of Excel than **Excel 2013**, all of the relationships will only have one direction.

Make this relationship active

When the checkbox is checked, the relationship becomes the default relationship for the time being. When several relationships can be created between two tables, Power BI Desktop can use the active relationship to automatically create visualizations that include both tables.

Understanding additional options

Whenever a relationship is created, Power BI Desktop will automatically define additional parameters based on the data in your tables, regardless of whether the relationship was created manually by the user or using autodetect. These new relationship options are located in a section at the bottom of the interfaces for both the Create relationship and Edit relationship dialog boxes.

In most cases, Power BI will automatically configure these parameters, and you won't need to make any changes to them. However, there are some scenarios in which you may find it useful to specify these parameters on your own.

Automatic relationship updates

You can control how Power BI handles relationships and makes automatic adjustments in your models and reports. Go to **File > Options & Settings > Options from the Power BI Desktop**. Then, select **Data Load** from the left pane. This gives you the ability to see how Power BI handles relationship management choices. Relationships' available choices menu is displayed.

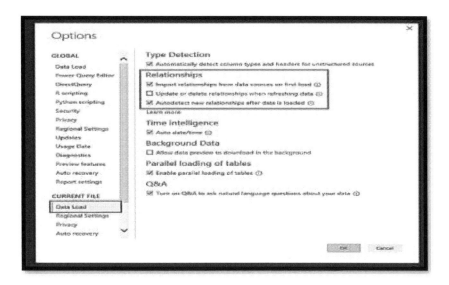

Three options can be selected and enabled:

- **Import relationships from data sources on the first load**: By default, this option is enabled, allowing relationships to be imported from data sources at the time of the first load. Power BI looks for relationships—such as primary key and foreign key relationships in your data warehouse—that have been defined in your data source when this option is enabled. Any relationships of this kind that are found when you first load data into Power BI are reproduced in the internal data model of the software. If you select this option, you can work with your model immediately without having to search for or define such associations yourself.

- **Update or delete relationships when refreshing data**: You have the option to update or remove relationships that already exist when refreshing data; by default, this option is deselected. If you decide to enable this feature, each time you refresh your dataset, Power BI will look for updates to the relationships between the data sources. If any of those associations alter or end, Power BI will update or remove the pertinent nodes from its data model to maintain consistency.

Caution: If you are using row-level security that is dependent on created relationships, choosing this option is not something that we advocate doing. If you get rid of a relationship that your RLS settings are dependent on, your model can end up being less safe as a result.

- **Autodetect new relationships after data is loaded**

Identifying Our Relationship Columns

Establishing proper relationships between tables in Power BI requires that you first locate and identify the columns that represent those relationships. These columns are the keys that link and tie the many tables to one another, hence they are very important.

Identifying the relationship columns can be done in some different ways, including the following:

1. **Data Understanding:** To begin, you should comprehend both the structure and the content of your tables. Determine the fields or columns that are shared by many tables and include information that is connected. Search for columns that have names, data types, or value ranges that are similar to one another since this may suggest a probable relationship.

2. **Data Modeling Best Practices:** The Best Techniques for Data Modeling: It's crucial to adhere to data modeling best practices while creating your data model in Power BI. One such method is to employ surrogate keys or unique identifiers that can also serve as relationship columns. Primary keys, foreign keys, and natural keys are examples of these types of columns; they are all used to uniquely identify items in various tables.

3. **Source Documentation or Data Dictionary:** Consult any available documentation or data dictionaries when working with your data sources. These resources frequently contain details about the connections between tables, including the specific columns in charge of creating those links.

4. **Analyzing Data Dependencies:** Examine the business logic and data dependencies that are present in your dataset. It is critical to comprehend both the columns that enable these linkages and the links that exist between tables conceptually. For demonstration, in a scenario where there is data related to sales, the "CustomerID" column might serve as the relationship column between the "Customers" database and the "Sales" table.

5. **Visual Exploration:** Use visual exploration techniques in Power BI to visually analyze the data and identify potential relationship columns. Create visuals such as scatter plots, bar charts, or matrix visuals to observe patterns and correlations between columns across tables.

6. **Collaboration and Expert Input:** Interact with stakeholders that possess in-depth knowledge of the data, such as domain experts or data analysts. Together, with their experience and understanding of the data domain, determine which relationship columns are acceptable.

Time to Get Building

Using the **Manage Relationships Wizard**, which can be accessed from the ribbon in the Model view, is the first available choice. Once the wizard opens and we click the New button, we select our two tables and click the names of the columns in each table to decide which columns will be the starting point for the relationship that will be built. The relationship is formed when we approve of the message.

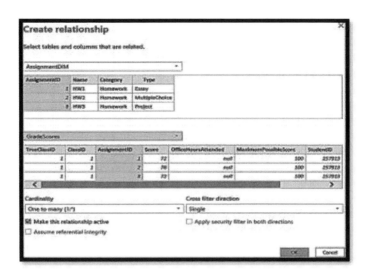

Using the second strategy, relationships can be built faster. In the Model view, you may establish a relationship between two tables by selecting a column in one, pressing the mouse button, and dragging it to the desired column in the other table. After that, you let go of the mouse button, and the relationship was solved. The drawback of this approach is that it increases the possibility of mistakes like dragging to or from the wrong column. It is also more prone to error when you have tables with numerous columns and you must drag into areas of a table that have to be scrolled through to locate the proper column; this can rapidly become monotonous, and when it becomes tedious, errors arise. We need to have a primary data model that looks like the illustration below after those relationships have been constructed. As a result, we can create a star schema, which is made up of multiple dimension tables interacting with our fact table in the form of a star. This enhances optimization while also simplifying the model's reading and understanding. The fact table (or tables) that interest you can be filtered, and you can see right away which tables can do so and how the filter works (i.e., one way or both ways).

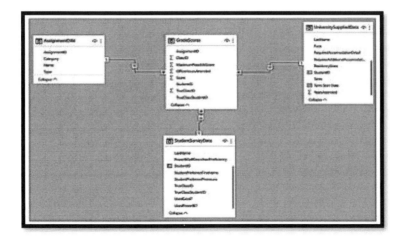

Let's Get Reporting

We've got our data in, we've had it converted, and we've got it modeled. Now that we have this opportunity, we can begin gathering the information that will satisfy our curiosity. There are a plethora of inquiries that we can make.

We Need a Name...

Here are some words of advice: Looking through the reports, I frequently discover that something as simple as a title that makes clear what the reader is looking at may have a big impact. This title can be used as the report's title if it is something we use repeatedly on different pages; if not, we might choose to use different titles for each page. We also have the option to have a whole page in the report serve as some sort of title introduction. Each approach has advantages and disadvantages, but for this example, we will merely provide a clear title for the report at the top of the page. We will do this using the good old-fashioned text box. Inside the Report view, the **"Text box"** option can be found inside the **Insert portion** of the ribbon. We are aware that a text box does not provide anything particularly fascinating, yet it is useful. I have positioned the text box at the top of my reporting area, justified it in the center, and added some amazing italics to it because I can't get enough of them, as seen in the image below. I made it much larger than it was originally because I like the Segoe font better than the Power BI default font and because I want it to look nice and be readable.

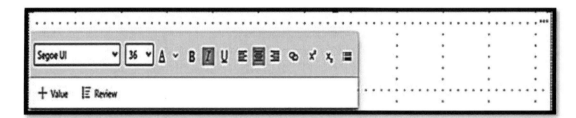

Cards Help Identify Important Data Points

We will begin by highlighting specific values that I believe are valuable for understanding how our cohort of students performed. I am also interested in "lines" of information. I just can't help but like building with blocks. The first card in our deck contains a tally of the number of students for whom ISOM 210 was the very first class they took inside the department. This makes use of the column in the database labeled **"1stCourseInDepartment**?" On the other hand, if you create a card graphic and put that column into it, you would most likely see something that looks like the picture that is below;

```
┌─────────────────────────────────────┐
│                                       │
│                 N                     │
│                                       │
│     First 1stCourseInDepartment?      │
└─────────────────────────────────────┘
```

Let's talk about a few recent events that have happened here for a bit. First of all, since this is not a number column, there is no default summary attached to it. In card graphics, data is always summarized in some fashion. Here, the data is shown as the first table result that matches our filter context, which in this case is nothing because there is no filter context. Consequently, we need to change the summary to read "count" instead of "first." To accomplish this, click the down arrow next to the column name in the Fields list of the Visualizations pane. From the drop-down menu that appears, select the desired summary type—in this case, count—from the list. Although we've made great progress, as the image below illustrates, there is still more work to be done before we get the desired outcome.

```
┌─────────────────────────────────────┐
│                                       │
│                27                     │
│                                       │
│    Count of 1stCourseInDepartment?    │
└─────────────────────────────────────┘
```

The fact that the card now shows the count rather than the word first is a positive development. We must offer context for the filter. We would want Power BI to provide us with a count; however, we are only interested in the count of the "Y" values. We can see that there is now no meaningful filter context when we look at this visual's Filter pane at the moment. Let's provide some more contexts by dragging the column into the Filters section of this visual area of the Filter pane. Then, make use of the Basic filtering option to pick just the values that are "Y." It is important to point out that the Count version of this field already exists since it is the one that is being shown here. To get the column's base values to filter, we will need to add it once again to the Filter pane. When we carry out those steps, we can arrive at the number 24 we need. Let's create an alias for the column name by double-clicking on the column name in the Fields section of the Visualization pane. Then, rename the column to anything you'd want it to be called.

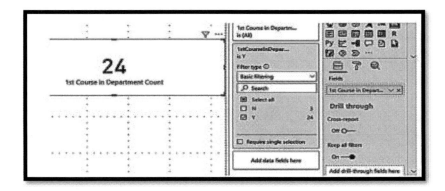

Bars, Columns, and Lines

Imagine that you are the sales manager for a retail firm and that you have been tasked with the responsibility of evaluating how various goods in your inventory have performed.

To bring your data to life, you turn to Power BI and its visualizations.

1. **Bars**: You may compare the sales figures of different products that fit into different categories by using bars. For example, to display the total sales for every product category—such as apparel, accessories, and electronics—you can create a vertical bar chart. A visual depiction of each category's overall sales success will be shown by the rise and fall of its bar. By comparing the bar heights, you can quickly ascertain which categories are performing better than others. This gives you the knowledge you need to manage your inventory and choose your marketing strategies with knowledge.

2. **Columns**: Now, let's use columns to examine your product analysis in greater detail. Let's say you want to see how many units are sold of each distinct product that fits into a particular category. Creating a chart with vertical column formatting will allow you to group the elements into sections based on attributes like brand or price range. Following that, each category's sales data will be displayed in the columns adjacent to one another. This visualization will allow you to assess how well each of the numerous product groupings that make up a category is performing and identify the specific products that are driving sales. It allows you to focus your efforts on promoting specific products or expanding the range of goods you offer.

3. **Lines**: Now let's talk about lines. Suppose you want to track changes in your organization's average monthly income over a year. In Power BI, you may display the months on the horizontal axis of a line chart and the revenue data points on the vertical axis. The lines that depict the evolution and variance of revenue over time will elegantly connect the data points. By closely scrutinizing the line chart, you can find seasonal trends, identify periods of rise or fall, and gain insights into the overall trend of revenue. Financial forecasts, the detection of potential bottlenecks, and the assessment of the effectiveness of marketing campaigns can all be aided by this data.

Conclusion

Several crucial processes are involved in turning raw data into an extensive report in Power BI. Building the report itself, importing and processing data, combining tables, creating relationships, and so on are the steps involved in going from raw data to a thorough report in Power BI. To make this process easier, Power BI offers a comprehensive toolkit with an intuitive interface that makes every stage of the process possible. Users may convert unstructured data into meaningful insights and facilitate data-driven decision-making and efficient information sharing by utilizing Power BI's features.

Activity

1. Import your first data.
2. Consolidate tables with the use of append.
3. Use Merge to get columns from other tables.
4. Create a relationship with Autodetect.
5. Modify a relationship.
6. Alter relationships making use of diverse methods.
7. Make the relationship active.

CHAPTER 7

ADVANCED REPORTING TOPICS IN POWER BI

AI-Powered Visuals

To further improve Power BI's capabilities, Microsoft has already included four AI-powered visuals in Power BI Desktop. It is expected that the business will keep funding the development of more AI-powered visuals. These images may be used by the online service as well as the desktop version. As seen in the image below, they are situated in the Visualizations window. The images consist of **"Key influencers,"** "Decomposition tree," "Q&A," and **"Smart narratives,"** in that order from left to right. Now, let's take a look at each one individually.

Key Influencers

The Key Influencers visual provides Power BI users with the capability to perform causal analysis. Investigating the connections between different elements and the impact these connections have on a particular metric is required. Power BI uses strong machine learning algorithms to identify the key influencers on its own, based on the data that is sent into it. With this visual, users may make data-driven decisions by quickly determining the primary reasons for a statistic.

Benefits and Significance: The Key Influencers visual has a significant amount of importance for companies and organizations operating in a wide variety of fields.

It gives users the ability to:

1. **Identify influential factors**: The Key Influencers graphic allows users to determine which variables or dimensions have the greatest impact on a certain measure of interest. With this insight, businesses can focus their attention on the areas that matter most, leading to more effective strategies and superior results.
2. **Acquire actionable insights:** If organizations have a firm understanding of the major influencers in their respective industries, they may gain actionable information to improve operations, marketing campaigns, product offers, and more. With the help of these insights, organizations can make informed decisions and focus their efforts on the elements that have the biggest influence on their success.
3. **Optimize your marketing strategies**: The Key Influencers graphic can assist marketers in determining the aspects that have the most significant influence on the actions of their

customers. Businesses can adjust their marketing plans to target certain groups more successfully by evaluating client segments, demographics, campaign data, and other characteristics, which leads to improved customer engagement and conversion rates.

4. **Improve the overall customer experience**: Businesses can identify the factors that significantly affect the degree of customer satisfaction by knowing the major influencers. By examining customer feedback, support interactions, product use statistics, and other pertinent attributes, businesses may establish a hierarchy of needs and develop customized experiences that tackle the most pressing issues.

Using the Key Influencers Visual in Power BI

Now let's explore how to use the Key Influencers visual in Power BI effectively:

1. Assemble your dataset and make sure it contains all the necessary dimensions and measurements. For the most accurate analysis possible, your data should be cleaned and arranged.
2. Open your report in Power BI or create a new one by launching it. After that, access your report or create a new one in Power BI.
3. Get the Visualizations window open. Navigation: Navigate to the Visualizations pane on the right side of the Power BI interface.
4. Choose the **Key Influencers visual** by navigating to the Visualizations pane and selecting the "**Key Influencers**" visual icon with your mouse. It is similar to a scatter plot that also includes a target symbol.
5. You can choose the measure to be studied by dragging and dropping the desired metric into the "Analyzing" area. You are interested in learning more about this metric or outcome, such as revenue, sales, or customer satisfaction levels.
6. Drag and drop the potential dimensions or influencers into the "Explain by" box to select the influencers. These are the elements of the scenario, sometimes referred to as variables or factors, including the type of product, the location, or the marketing campaign, that you believe could have an impact on the measurement.
7. **Visual creation and customization**: Power BI will automatically analyze the data and build a visualization that displays the key influencers. This visualization may then be customized by the user. The graphic may present a ranking of influencers based on their effect, coupled with a bar chart or table that corresponds to the ranking. Utilizing the many formatting options available in the Visualizations tab, you can personalize the look and style of the graphic.
8. **Consider your options and get new perspectives**: Conduct an examination of the data provided by the Key Influencers graphic. Utilize the newfound understanding to comprehend how variables relate to one another and how they affect the measure of your choice. Make use of these insights to guide you in making evidence-based decisions that will produce favorable outcomes.

Let's work with an example

We will be demonstrating the "Key influencers" visual from a separate dataset from Microsoft known as **AdventureWorks. AdventureWorks** is a sample database shipped with Microsoft SQL Server. Additionally, there are several examples of AdventureWorks being coupled with Power BI. In this specific instance, I will look at the total number of invoices according to the component number, product description, product category, product subcategory, and area name. It is possible to divide this image into several portions. First, let's examine the image that has been supplied below. After that, we will go on to the visual analysis. We will first focus on the variables that have an impact on the organization's overall invoice count. Determining the elements that lead to a rise or fall in that number could yield valuable insights. A rise in invoices should, in theory, translate into an increase in sales. By moving our way down the picture from top to bottom, we can acquire a better understanding of what's going on. To begin, we can choose between "**Key influencers**" and "**Top segments**." At this time, "**Key influencers**" are chosen both explicitly and by default. The second item you'll notice is a question that is framed around the idea of determining what causes the variable under evaluation to increase or decrease. The default choice in this instance is Increase, but I modified it to Decrease to provide more results. Then, a list of selected conditions and an explanation of how each affects the value I'm looking at may be found on the left side of the screen.

This example shows that the Touring Frames subcategory has 43 fewer invoices than the average of all other subcategories. This is because the subcategory under consideration is Touring Frames. The picture's column graph segment, which is the one furthest to the left, contains this specific subcategory, which is indicated. Given that the dimension under consideration is Subcategory, a graph highlighting the specific group that has been selected is displayed to the right of the screen, along with data on the average number of invoices allocated to each subcategory. You'll see that the graph on the right can be scrolled as well, which enables me to view all of the subcategories in this manner.

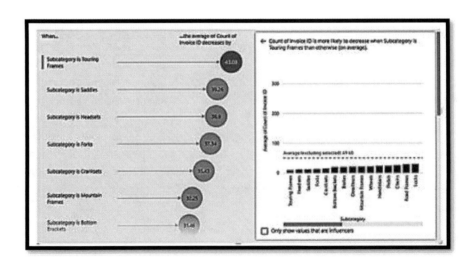

Let's begin by returning to the very top of the visual and selecting the option labeled "**Top segments**." In the picture below, you can get a first glimpse at what it looks like;

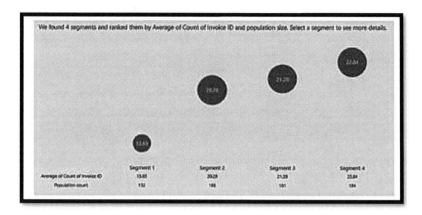

The first line remains unchanged from its prior version. However, the second sentence is written in a somewhat different style. It will be evident to you that the current version of the question has been somewhat modified when it appears in the selection box. Instead of asking "What might be causing a value to increase or decrease," the inquiry here is asking "When is the point of analysis more likely to be high or low?" Although the default setting is set to High, in this case, we will choose Low. For this query, Power BI has shown a tiny scatterplot and provided information on how it is arranged. The figure illustrates that Power BI has identified four sections that it considers to be interesting and worth delving into further. In this instance, it is proceeding from the lowest average invoice count to the highest, while simultaneously displaying the total number of records that are included inside each segment. You will be able to view all of the parts that go into generating that segment on the left when you select one of those bubbles (we'll choose segment 2 in this example). On the right side of the picture below, you can see Segment 2 in comparison to the overall value and the percentage of the data that is contained in the segment that you choose to analyze.

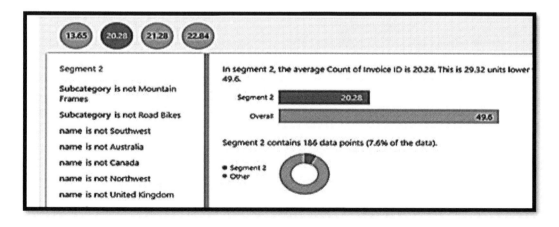

The visual in and of itself is strong; nevertheless, making use of it can be extremely irritating. The visual will update itself after each addition when you add categories to the **"Explain by"** portion of the Visualizations pane. It may have difficulty locating combinations of data that will lead to the identification of noteworthy influencers or segments. It is not necessarily more beneficial to keep adding categories though; the more categories you add, the smaller your population becomes for each combination of categories that you have added. You will want both some degree of human judgment and a thorough understanding of the facts to utilize this visual aid effectively. What does your intuition say you should be the most important? Start there and check if the evidence supports your assumptions. This is a recurring theme that appears throughout the section on artificial intelligence graphics. These objects require human cognition to operate; the AI visuals cannot make them do so on their own.

Decomposition Tree

One helpful feature of Power BI is the Decomposition Tree visual, which allows users to examine and comprehend complex data structures in a dynamic and comprehensible manner. Users can graphically depict the hierarchical relationships that exist among the data by breaking down a measure into its component pieces, which may include dimensions, attributes, or categories. With the aid of this visual representation, the composition and distribution of a measure over multiple dimensions may be fully and easily understood.

Major Benefits of the Decomposition Tree

1. **Hierarchical Analysis**: The Decomposition Tree is a tool for visually representing data hierarchies, which makes it much simpler to examine how different measures are distributed across various levels. It provides consumers with the ability to go deeper into the data, therefore illuminating the underlying elements that contribute to a certain indicator.
2. **Interactive Exploration**: Expanding or contracting nodes allows users to focus on specific levels or dimensions while dynamically exploring the decomposition tree. The interaction allows for a more thorough analysis of the data, which in turn helps reveal insights that would probably remain hidden otherwise.
3. **Contribution Analysis**: The visual presents a concise and understandable description of how each dimension or category contributes to the overall measure. Users can determine the elements that have the most impact on a certain result, which assists them in prioritizing areas in need of modification or optimization.
4. **Comparisons and Trends**: When comparing the various layers or dimensions that make up the hierarchy, the Decomposition Tree is a helpful tool. By comparing the contribution of different categories or dimensions, users can immediately understand trends, patterns, and variances throughout the data.

Using the Decomposition Tree Visual in Power BI

1. To begin, launch **Power BI and then open your report.**
2. Choose the Visualizations tab: Navigate to the right-hand side of the Power BI interface, where you'll find the Visualizations pane.
3. Select the "**Decomposition Tree**" visual icon by looking in the Visualizations window for the "**Decomposition Tree**" visual icon and then clicking on it. In most cases, it takes the form of a tree-like structure.
4. **Define the measure**: To accomplish this, choose the "Analyze" box, then drag and drop the desired measure into the well. This metric shows the outcome or statistic that you should analyze in more detail to gain a better understanding of.
5. Define the hierarchy by dragging and dropping the dimensions or characteristics you wish to include in the decomposition tree into the "**Explain by**" field properly. This will allow you to define the hierarchy. These are the categories or elements that have been taken into consideration in the measurement.
6. **Make adjustments to the visual**: A decomposition tree will be automatically created by Power BI based on the measure and hierarchy that you select. The Visualizations page has layout, formatting, and style settings that you may adjust to make the graphic uniquely yours.
7. **Explore the decomposition**: To zero in on a particular aspect of one of the levels or dimensions, you can interact with the visual by expanding or collapsing nodes within the tree. Analyze the contributions, and dig further into the facts, so that you can get a more in-depth understanding.
8. **Make use of extra features**: Additional features of Power BI's Decomposition Tree visual can be utilized to strengthen the analysis and the way the results are presented. These functions consist of the following: component sorting, element filtering, and aspect highlighting.

Q&A

The Q&A graphic intends to enable end users to pose queries about the data using natural language. With some effort, Power BI will take your query and turn it into a graphic or set of data that answers your question. Although the Q&A style can be quite effective, it sometimes seems to be missing some key components when it is first introduced. I wouldn't quite describe Microsoft's Q&A feature as "natural language" just yet, even though it appears to be improving with almost every new release. A few of the suggested inquiries might not seem pertinent. However, there are numerous things you can do to offer Power BI with just enough context to assist in making the Q&A feature seem more natural. Putting a question-and-answer visual onto our canvas, the first thing we notice is the outcome, which is seen in the picture below;

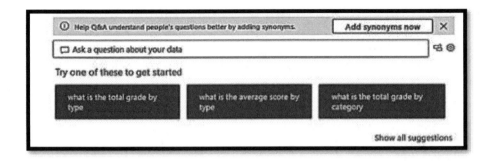

Simply by glancing at the questions that have been posed, we can tell that Q&A performs a decent job of identifying the names of our fields. However, the meanings of those field names may not be immediately clear to other users. For example, "**What is the total grade by the category column**?" is meant to be understood as "**What is the total grade**." In addition, what exactly is meant by the term "**category**"? We are both aware that this is the criterion that determines whether a certain assignment is to be considered homework, an exam, or extra credit. However, can we assume that our audience is aware of this? By examining this specific example, we can see one of the issues with Q&A and the sample questions it generates. It can initially just function with our column names and the relationships between them. It will attempt to apply some basic aliasing wherever possible, but it won't always be sufficient to get us there. However, we can still utilize one of the sample questions to demonstrate the benefits that Q&A can provide. For this example, I'll select the first question from the left, "What is the total grade by type?" In this case, Power BI generates a bar chart that shows the distribution of the total grade metric among the different kinds of assignments. The picture below illustrates that result. Observe that every other image on the canvas interacts with this one, and it can also interact with other images in the same manner that anything else may interact with anything else. Remember the question you asked when you began applying the Q&A to cross-filter across many graphics?

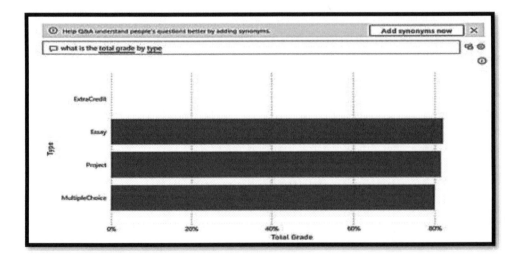

Breaking down the visual itself, there will always be the option to add synonyms unless you click the X next to the button. Let's imagine that you discover a result from a Q&A that you truly like and you want to make it a more permanent fixture in your life. If you want to transform the Q&A visual into a visual of the kind that was created, you can do so by clicking the first button to the right of the text box. The widget right next to it takes you to the settings for the Q&A section. When hovered over, the "i" in the circle displays a brief tooltip that confirms the information that the visual is displaying. A question can be rapidly expanded, changed, or removed because it remains in the text box. When you edit a question, a drop-down choice will appear in the text box that attempts to identify the type of question you are asking by using a search engine. As one might expect, this function becomes better with use; the more you use it, the more precise your synonyms will be. We might give the column headers more approachable titles if we plan to use the Q&A feature a lot. This may facilitate the AI's ability to interpret a column's significance. We may also simplify the wording when users fill in queries by giving specific column descriptors synonyms. This will facilitate understanding of the language. At the top-right corner of the image below, there is a button that says, "Add synonyms now." Selecting that choice will bring up the Q&A configuration box. When we pick the Field synonyms section, we are taken directly to that area, as seen in the picture below. Be aware that it will show every table in the model, including the ones we have hidden with the Report view settings. However, by default, it will not include such tables in the Q&A options.

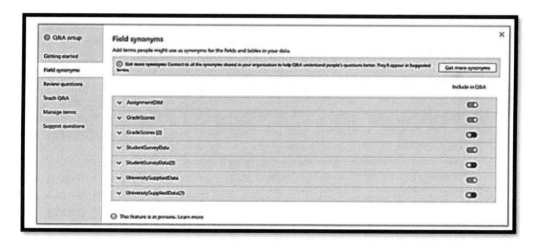

When you choose a table, you will get a list of columns under the heading "**Name**," a list of presently recognized synonyms under the heading "**Terms**," and a list of suggested terms to the right of that heading. At the level of each column, you will continue to see a toggle that gives you the option to include or exclude that column from the Q&A results. If I click the + button that is located next to any of the terms that are labeled as "**Suggested terms**," then that term will be added to the list of terms that are associated with that column instantly. The most effective way to illustrate how this works is to think about the process from right to left. The section referred to as "**Suggested terms**" includes a list of potential alternative names for the Terms section. When a user chooses to use one of the recommended terms, it is added to the "Terms" section.

Power BI will use those terms as true synonyms to identify which column it should use to answer a query when it encounters one in the Q&A area. The name of the object that is referenced in the supplied phrase is shown in the "Name" column. Terms can be used to refer to the names of tables, columns, or measures. It's also worth noting that Power BI comes pre-loaded with a few basic phrases that aren't very informative. It is my suggestion that you test the system with as many questions as you can come up with before implementing Q&A. Examine the returned results, make any necessary adjustments to add synonyms, and then try again. There are many options for fine-tuning the outcomes, and enhancing the quality assurance in your firm is going to be a process that requires iteration. The next two aspects of the Q&A setup are the "**Review questions**" and "**Suggest questions**" functions, respectively. Within the "**Review Questions**" area, you will have the ability to evaluate every Q&A question that has been asked in the most recent 28 days across all of the datasets that you have access to and that have been submitted. This is annoying since it shows all of the datasets that you have access to instead of only the datasets that have questions addressed with Q&A answers. If someone does, however, have a question, you have the option to examine it along with the Power BI response to ensure accuracy and make recommendations about how the answer should be presented for that particular subject.

"**Suggest questions**" gives you the ability to provide questions to your audience, such as the ones that were shown when we first viewed the visual. The distinction lies in the fact that they are questions that you have already evaluated. Consider these recommended questions to be user-friendly cheat instructions that can be used by other users when constructing reports utilizing Q&A visuals. You are aware of the outcomes that will be shown when that particular question is chosen. These can be great starting points for your company to employ Q&A in a sandbox-style setting, to build user trust in the results, and to encourage research. Furthermore, this can aid in offering a specific set of answers to particular questions. Users can select suggested questions inside a single image, which might help them arrange other images on a given report page more effectively. A conference call's question-and-answer period can be a challenging experience, but if you want to make the most of it, it's similar to having a Carnegie Hall performance. It requires a lot of practice, practice, and more practice. You can also deactivate Q&A against datasets in service if you would rather not enable customers to utilize the Power BI service's Q&A feature against a dataset.

Smart Narrative

Something a little bit different is the "smart narrative" graphic, which doesn't act on its own. This visual will appear as a text box and you will receive an error message if you try to insert it into a blank canvas. On a report page with other visuals already present, however, the "Smart narrative" will "read" the other visuals by creating a story from the data points shown in them. After that, this story will help with "reading" the data. It is crucial to remember that any other visual on the canvas can interact and cross-filter a visual with a "Smart narrative," and the "Smart narrative" visual will automatically update its story in response to the various actions. You can also add comments to the "Smart narrative," which will be there independent of any changes to the filter context that would impact the remainder of the narrative. This is possible since the "**Smart narrative**" is still contained inside a functional text box. The so-called "smart narrative" is, in my view, a double-edged blade. It is, on the one hand, a remarkable miracle for the progress of data literacy. This graphic does a great job of simplifying the data so that non-technical users and others who aren't as familiar with the data can understand it. Because it can make the data more accessible, this can be quite valuable to report users. That being said, it is also quite huge and difficult to use. Ultimately, it's just a large text box with the ability to create stories so long you have to drag them up and down to read them completely. The context of your audience and the design choices you make will ultimately determine whether or not the **"Smart narrative"** visual is the best choice because there is a limited amount of design space available.

What-If Analysis

The What-If Analysis is a powerful tool that looks at many situations to assist users in understanding the effects of changes in their data. "What-if" sentences are used to achieve this. Users can test out a wide range of inputs, variables, and presumptions to evaluate the several outcomes that could occur. With Power BI's What-If Analysis function, users can model and visualize the results of modifications made to metrics, key performance indicators, and other data points.

Benefits of What-If Analysis in Power BI

- **Decision-making:** When it comes to making decisions, the **"What-If" Analysis** gives decision-makers useful insights that allow them to evaluate the possible effects of various options or situations. Users can make better options and reduce risks by having a better awareness of the whole range of potential outcomes.
- **Forecasting and Planning**: What-If Users can predict potential futures using analysis by experimenting with different inputs and assumptions. In each of these procedures, this can be useful. Forecasting, budgeting, and strategic planning may all be done more effectively when one is aware of the likely outcomes that could transpire in certain scenarios.
- **Sensitivity Analysis**: This technique aids in identifying the degree of sensitivity of significant variables within a dataset. By adjusting specific inputs and observing the results of those changes, users can determine which variables have the biggest impact on their data.

Techniques for What-If Analysis in Power BI

- **Data Table:** This is a feature of Power BI that allows users to specify and modify certain data that are contained within a table. By adjusting these parameters, users can see the immediate impact of their changes on the computations, metrics, and visualizations.
- **Measure Branching**: This is yet another method available in Power BI that allows users to generate new variants of previously used measures. Users can compare and evaluate many situations inside the same report by simply replicating a measure and adjusting its logic.
- **Scenario analysis:** Power BI provides support for this through the use of measures and parameters. While parameters operate as inputs that users can adjust to replicate different scenarios, measures employ these aspects to calculate outcomes and offer insights into the impact of alterations.

- **Advanced Analytics:** R and Python are two more sophisticated analytics tools with which Power BI can communicate. With the powerful statistical modeling and simulation capabilities these tools offer, users can perform complex What-If Analysis based on sophisticated algorithmic frameworks.

Best Practices for What-If Analysis in Power BI

- **Clearly outline Your Objectives:** One of the first things you should do is outline the goals and questions you want to answer using the What-If Analysis. This will serve as a guide for selecting relevant variables, assumptions, and parameters for the study.
- **Start Simple:** Start with simple situations and gradually raise the difficulty. Beginning with less complicated situations enables users to gain confidence and a better understanding of the mechanics of What-If Analysis before moving on to more complex examples.
- **Work Together and Iterate:** Engage Subject Matter Experts and Stakeholders in the What-If Analysis Process. A greater understanding of the data, as well as the verification and effective implementation of insights obtained from that analysis, are all facilitated by collaboration and iteration.
- **Document and Communicate:** Keep a record of the variables, presumptions, and results of every What-If Analysis scenario. Keep a record of every What-If Analysis scenario's outcome. Effective communication of insights and findings facilitates stakeholders' ability to appreciate the relevance of the results and make decisions based on that understanding.

To perform a What-If Analysis in Power BI, the first step is to create a What-If parameter.

1. After your data has been imported, use the Power BI Desktop ribbon to navigate to the Modeling tab. Numerous tools and functions related to data modeling are accessible from this page.
2. Navigate to the Modeling tab and select the "New Parameter" button from the drop-down menu to create a new parameter. When you perform this operation, a dialog box will open with the What-If parameter that you want to specify.
3. Within the "New Parameter" dialog box, supply the following information:
   - **Name:** Give your parameter a descriptive name.
   - **Data type:** Decimal Number, Whole Number, or Date/Time: Choose the proper data type for your parameter.
   - **Minimum and maximum values:** By establishing the minimum and maximum values, you may ascertain the parameter's value range. This sets the boundaries for the extent of the What-If analysis you wish to perform.
   - **Increment:** When manipulating the parameter value, you can provide the increment by which the value of the parameter should change.

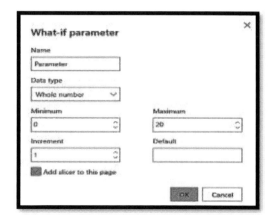

Parameter Setup

The What-if parameter includes several inputs, each of which has to be carefully controlled. Name is evident but also has a distinct impact. No matter which name is chosen, the data model is going to have a pair of objects constructed to accommodate the parameter regardless of which name is used. To build a DAX table, the What-if parameter, after it has been finished, will make use of the **GENERATESERIES** statement, passing in the name of the parameter as its argument. After that, it will generate two separate objects inside that table. One of the objects will be the "New parameter" button that we pressed to bring up the dialog box. This is going to be the initial item. This slicer can be applied to the canvas to change the value of the parameter displayed on the report canvas. A measure that utilizes the SELECTEDVALUE function will be the second thing to be created. The purpose of this measure is to allow you to call another measure and return a parameterized value that may be used in other DAX procedures. In a minute, this will be shown to you. Once we have named our parameter, we need to define the kind of data that it can accept. These types of data include whole numbers, decimals, and fixed decimals. There is a place for a fixed decimal separator in a fixed decimal number. This can come in handy in some cases where rounding might potentially lead to errors or when you are altering very small amounts and your actions could potentially compound errors. Given that we don't detest ourselves to the point that grading would require decimal points, we may move forward with choosing "Whole number." The first and last values in the GENERATES statement, which generates the table and values the parameter will use, are determined by the minimum and maximum values. The first and last values are determined by utilizing the minimum and maximum values. Maintaining the value of zero at some point in the series is, in my opinion, better. Even though it doesn't have to be the lowest or highest number, having 0 as part of the series can be useful when I want to show the baseline value without making any changes. In this particular scenario, I will choose a minimum of −100 and a maximum of 100 for the range.

I then calculated the increment of the change. This describes the selectable period for changing the value. For instance, if I choose 5, the options would be −100, −95, −90, or... 95, 100. The lowest conceivable score would be −100, and the greatest possible score would be 100. For me, it's either

97, 43, or −37; I can't decide. You could choose any whole integer value between −100 and 100 if your increment was 1. Naturally, you should use a data type that is either decimal or fixed decimal if you are going to have an increment that depends on decimals. For the sake of clarity, I will use a one-point increment for this illustration. Lastly, I gave a default value. This is the value that will be displayed when I initially drag the slicer into the canvas from the Fields list. If someone utilizes the Power BI service's "Reset to default" feature, the parameter will also be reset to this value. Additionally, it is the value that will be shown when I drag the slicer onto the canvas for the first time from the Fields list. When using the default value of zero, the slicer will show a blank value at first. Since this is the predicted behavior, there is no reason to be alarmed. One last decision is ahead of us, and that is to choose whether or not we want Power BI to automatically include the slicer that it will build on this report page.

DAX Integration of the Parameter

The OK button has been selected, and I now have a parameter. However, that parameter's value is meaningless! This is a result of the parameter's current inability to change anything. The argument needs to have some value before it can be added to the canvas. For this reason, the measure that was created with our parameter is quite important. We can increase the total by adding the value of a particular parameter by adjusting one of our measures using the slicer on the report page. Go through your measures and then point out where in the figure below we can be able to put the new measure that was developed based on the What-if parameter. We are working with the "**Total Grade Measure**".

```
1 Total Grade =
2 DIVIDE (
3     CALCULATE (    SUM ( 'GradeScores'[Score] ) ) ,
4     CALCULATE (    SUM ( GradeScores[MaximumPossibleScore] ) ),
5     "Extra Credit"
6 )
```

```
1 Total Grade =
2 DIVIDE (
3     CALCULATE (    SUM ( 'GradeScores'[Score] ) ) + [Total Grade Modifier Value],
4     CALCULATE (    SUM ( GradeScores[MaximumPossibleScore] ) ),
5     "Extra Credit"
6 )
```

I'm going to focus on the following query while keeping this adjustment in mind: what if our final grade was X points higher or lower? What effect might that have on the pertinent letter grade? I'm also going to alter the display of my Total Letter Grade metric for this example, showing two decimal places instead of zero. A term slicer, a What-if parameter slicer, and a table showing the overall grade and total grade letter have been added to a very basic website. What happens to our table when we change the grade modifier to a value between -100 and 100? Take a look at the picture below to find out.

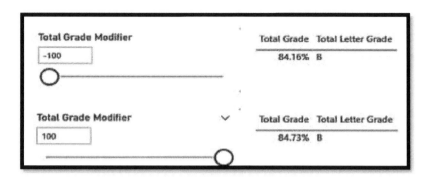

The image illustrates that the 100 points, in any direction, do not determine the success or failure of the class. However, given that we're talking about grades, you may assume that the difference would be more obvious if we decreased the population's overall size. Despite having a higher average GPA, there were only seven students in the summer of 2023, based on my study. Would 100 points increase a letter grade in the summer of 2023? To observe what kind of findings we receive, let's try expanding the study's scope.

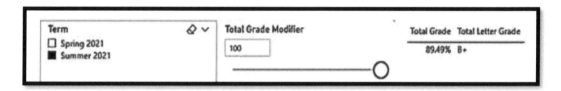

If we gave the students in the summer 2021 class an additional 100 points for their overall score, they would have completed the course with a total grade of 89.49%, which is just 0.01% away from rounding up to an A−.

Parameter Modification

1. **Locate the Parameter Control:** You will need to look for the visual element that represents the parameter in your report or dashboard. This control can take the form of a slicer, a numeric input box, or any other control that enables users to interact with the parameter.
2. **Modify the Value of the Parameter:** By interacting with the parameter control, you can change the value of the parameter.

You can carry out one of the following actions, depending on the kind of parameter control you have:
- **Slicer:** Should the parameter be displayed as a slicer, you can modify the parameter's value or the range it falls inside by utilizing the slicer's available choices. This will result in the

automated updating of the parameter's value and the recalculation of any related visualizations

- ▪ **Numeric Input Box:** If the parameter is represented by a numeric input box, you can change the value of the parameter by clicking on the box and then manually entering a new value. To use the new value, either click outside of the input box or press the Enter key on your keyboard.
- ▪ **Additional Controls:** The parameter control could seem different depending on how it's incorporated into the report or the dashboard. To change the parameter value, it is necessary to first follow the instructions that are included with the control.

3. **Watch the Impact:** Once the parameter's value has been changed, observe the impact of the changes on the parameter-related calculations and visualizations. Power BI will recalculate the affected measures and update the visuals accordingly to accurately depict the modified parameter value. As a result, users can gain an understanding of the What-If scenarios and the dynamic impact that different parameter values have on the data.

4. **Iterative Modification**: Users can iterate and adjust the parameter value several times to explore a variety of use cases and see the changes that correlate to those use cases in the report or dashboard. This repeated procedure enables a greater comprehension of the data as well as the possible results that can be achieved using a variety of parameter settings.

R and Python Integration

Two of the most widely used computer languages in the domains of statistical modeling and data analytics are R and Python. R and Python scripts are easily integrated into Power BI, allowing users to take advantage of the rich libraries and features that these programming languages have to offer. To integrate the two tools, you must first install the necessary language interpreters and configure Power BI to recognize and execute R or Python scripts.

Benefits of R and Python Integration

The addition of R and Python to Power BI will benefit data workers in a variety of ways. Both R and Python offer extensive libraries for data manipulation, machine learning, and statistical analysis that can be utilized to perform intricate computations and obtain insightful knowledge. The range of available data processing and analysis features is increased by this integration with Power BI. Additionally, users can utilize customized analytical models and visualizations created with R and Python thanks to the link. With Power BI reports, data professionals can incorporate custom visuals and models to enhance their visualizations and deliver complex insights in a more comprehensible and visually appealing manner. Furthermore, the amalgamation of R and Python provides expedited procedures for data preparation and manipulation. R and Python are flexible and efficient when it comes to managing missing values, changing variables, or performing intricate data transformations. Before displaying or analyzing their data in Power BI, users can preprocess their data using these languages' potent data manipulation and purification tools.

Practical Applications

Many practical real-world applications are made possible by Power BI's integration of R and Python. For example, data scientists can use R or Python machine learning methods to create prediction models, which they can then incorporate into Power BI. This facilitates forecasting and forecasting in real-time, which helps enterprises make data-driven decisions more easily. Sentiment analysis is an additional application that uses text data analysis to determine an individual's thoughts or feelings about a subject. Businesses can create sentiment analysis models with R or Python and then integrate them into Power BI. Because of this, businesses can keep an eye on how social media trends, consumer opinions, and brand sentiment are changing in real-time. Furthermore, groupings or segments contained inside datasets can be found using segmentation and clustering methods, which can be applied using the computer languages R and Python. Product classification, market segmentation, and consumer behavior may all be understood by utilizing Power BI's visualization features. More domains where the integration of R and Python in Power BI can be quite helpful are time series analysis, anomaly detection, and forecasting. Using the robust time series analysis tools available in R or Python, users can identify patterns, identify irregularities, and make precise predictions based on historical data.

Limitations of Using R and Python

Although the incorporation of R and Python into Power BI delivers a substantial number of benefits, it is essential to be aware of the limits that are connected with the use of these programming languages.

Take into consideration the following restrictions:

1. **Learning Curve**: You must be conversant with R and Python if you wish to work with those languages in Power BI. Before fully utilizing R and Python's capabilities in Power BI, users who are not familiar with these languages may need to take some time to learn about their syntax and related libraries. They might have to put in some time and effort for this.
2. **Managing Dependencies**: Utilizing R and Python inside Power BI may require the management of dependencies and the installation of all required packages and libraries. When working with unique or sophisticated libraries that have compatibility concerns or need specific setups, this can be a hard aspect of the process.
3. **Performance Considerations:** It is possible to run R and Python scripts with Power BI, although doing so can affect performance. This is especially true when handling large datasets or carrying out computationally demanding tasks. Depending on the intricacy of the research, the execution time of R or Python scripts may be slower than the execution time of native Power BI computations.
4. **Security and Governance:** When incorporating external R and Python scripts, extra security issues are brought into play. This relates to governance as well. Companies must check that the Power BI scripts they employ are trustworthy, secure, and compliant with their

organizations' data governance regulations. When bringing in code from outside sources, precautions should be taken to avoid or minimize any possible problems.

5. **Deployment and Maintenance**: Compared to reports that only rely on Power BI's built-in features, deploying and maintaining Power BI dashboards or reports that make use of R or Python scripts can be more difficult. This is because R and Python scripts are more advanced than the built-in functionality of Power BI. If it becomes important to make sure that the required R or Python environments are properly set up and maintained across all of the different Power BI settings, the deployment process can become more involved.

6. **Compatibility and Versioning**: One may be concerned about compatibility problems between different R, Python, and Power BI versions. It is crucial to confirm that the versions of R and Python being used in Power BI are compatible with the ones that Power BI supports to avoid any compatibility issues.

7. **Support and Community**: Despite the sizable user bases of both R and Python, there can be a dearth of tools and assistance specifically designed for using R and Python with Power BI. It's conceivable that more work will be needed to solve specific issues or find solutions related to Power BI integration.

Enabling R and Python for Power BI

Making sure Power BI is aware of the locations of the necessary home directories is the first step toward using R and/or Python with Power BI. This is required so that when certain languages are utilized, Power BI can call the relevant libraries and packages. Select **File > Options & Settings> Options** from the menu bar to accomplish this. This will navigate you to the Power BI Desktop's entire menu of settings and features. This menu has a few more sophisticated choices, but the ones that apply to us are the R scripting and Python scripting settings. When these languages are installed, Power BI Desktop performs a decent job of recognizing where their respective home directories are located. If, however, the software does not discover them automatically, you will have to manually browse them inside the Options box. Please note that clicking on the links in either of these two selections will direct you to the Microsoft page where you may install Python or R. You are prepared to go on to the following stage once it is completed.

R and Python in Power Query

First, we are going to examine how scripts written in R and Python can be used to manipulate data, and then we can talk about R and Python on their own as independent data sources. Scripts written in R and Python can be located in the **Transform** portion of the ribbon, which is the area that is the farthest to the right. The subsection is called **Scripts**. When you click either of these buttons, a dialog window will open where you can paste the relevant R or Python script. Remember that the steps involved in applying an R or Python script to the query must be followed in the right order, just like everything else. The advantage of this is that it may be started at any time until the R or Python script is called, and in both cases, the data from the step before the transformation can be accessed by calling it a "dataset" to access the relevant script. This can be done at any point until the point where the R or Python script is invoked. R and Python do not necessarily have to be considered terminal transformations either. You can direct Power Query to carry out transformations either before or following the execution of an R or Python script. This might be helpful in scenarios when you might find it difficult to do a certain data transformation using the Power Query user interface (UI) or when carrying out a transformation would require some advanced M. In addition to this, you can utilize scripts written in R or Python as your independent data sources. If you choose "**Get data**" and then search for "**script**," you will find possibilities to write scripts in both R and Python. In situations such as this one, when you may already have a well-defined script that you have written from the **integrated development environment (IDE)** of the applicable programming language, you can just copy and paste that script into the dialog box that displays when it occurs. This will launch the R or Python script, which is probably going to contain a URL to some source data, run the script, and display the output as a brand-new query. Subsequently, the outcomes can be altered in the same way as any other Power Query table in any further transformation phases. Once more, this may involve a script modification that sequentially uses one or both languages.

R and Python Visuals

If you have installed the corresponding languages on your computer, Power BI Desktop supports both R and Python visuals. A warning message inquiring if you wish to allow script visuals will show up when you select Visual from the Visualizations pane for the first time. With the use of script visuals, you can create custom visuals in either language that can expand your analysis beyond the representations that are usually available in Power BI, including those that may be accessible through the Power BI custom visual options. Script visuals also allow you the power to do this in a way that can take your analysis to the next level. Furthermore, these images can be fully interacted with both the slicers and the other images on the report page. Moreover, R and Python-generated visuals can be modified using alternative cross-filtering from other visuals. You will be requested to drag fields with the mouse into the Values area of the Visualization pane when you open an R or Python visual for the first time. Power BI uses the fields you drag into a visual to figure out what it calls the "dataset" for the visualized object. We can see how it appears both before and after the fields have been added in the following figure.

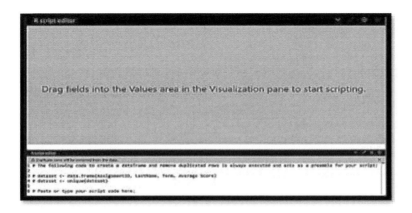

Additionally, you'll notice that duplicate rows in the data will be removed, as indicated by the notification you'll receive for both the R and Python graphics. You will notice something about this. Make sure the script contains all the essential scripts before running it, and then make sure the scripts refer to the "dataset" you generated in the Power BI interface. After completing this, you can click the Play button, which is situated in the script editor bar's extreme right corner. By clicking the arrow next to the menu, you can make the window smaller. If you need to change the script, you can do it in a more user-friendly editor by clicking the arrow that points up and to the right, which will open the IDE for the language you are now using.

Conclusion

The experience of data analysis and reporting is enhanced by AI-powered visualizations in Power BI through the use of machine learning, artificial intelligence, and interaction with R and Python. These features enable users to perform complex analyses, gain deeper insights, and create original visualizations, all of which contribute to more accurate and knowledgeable decision-making. With the power of AI and integration for R and Python, Power BI lets customers make the most of their data to generate meaningful and interesting reports.

Activity

1. What are the major benefits of the decomposition tree?
2. What are the benefits for what-if analysis?
3. Enable R and Python in Power query.
4. What are the limitations of using R and python?

CHAPTER 8

INTRODUCTION TO THE POWER BI SERVICE

The Basics of the Service: What You Need to Know

Microsoft's Power BI Service is a web-based platform that was designed in the cloud and provides companies with the ability to do comprehensive data analysis, data visualization, and report generation. **The following is a detailed review of the fundamental information that you need to know about this service:**

1. **Cloud-Based Accessibility**: Users of the Power BI Service may access their data, reports, and dashboards from anywhere at any time because it is housed in the cloud. With no need for on-premises equipment, users can access the service's functions via a web browser or mobile app, offering greater flexibility and ease of use.

2. **Workspaces for Organization**: Workspaces, which act as containers for linked dashboards, reports, datasets, and dataflows, are where Power BI arranges material. By acting as a single focus for the teams' departmental or project-specific data and analytical needs, workspaces enable teams to collaborate effectively. Furthermore, they offer authority over content distribution and access privileges.

3. **Dashboard Visualizations**: Dashboards are representations of data that are visually engaging and give condensed glimpses of important metrics and insights. Users can pin different visual representations to dashboards, such as charts, tables, or tiles, and organize them in a way that provides relevant summaries of their data at a glance.

4. **Interactive Reports**: With the help of Power BI Service, users may generate interactive reports that can be shared with others using the robust authoring tool Power BI Desktop. These reports can then be obtained by the service as publications. Using the extensive visualization filters, and interactive elements contained in the reports, users are empowered to delve deeper into data exploration and analysis.

5. **Connectivity to Data Sources**: The Power BI Service can connect to a broad variety of data sources in a streamlined manner, including databases, Excel files, cloud services, and many more. By importing data from various sources or connecting to them, users can generate datasets that will serve as the basis for their reports and visualizations.

6. **Data Refreshing**: To ensure that their data is correct and pertinent, users can set up scheduled data refresh capabilities using the Power BI Service. Because users may manually trigger a refresh when needed or establish exact intervals for automated dataset updates, reports, and dashboards will always display the most recent data.

7. **Ease of Collaboration and Sharing**: Working with other users is made simple via the Power BI Service. By adjusting access rights and sharing settings, users may control who has access to their dashboards, reports, and datasets. A few examples of the features that enable easy collaboration and group decision-making are co-authoring, commenting, and email sharing.

8. **Pre-built Content Packs and Apps:** The Power BI Service provides content packs and apps that have already been produced and are tailored for certain applications or services. These packs

come with pre-built dashboards, reports, and datasets that are ready to be used and can be modified to fit the needs of a particular industry or company. They provide a good starting point for tailoring reports and analysis to specific needs and requirements.

9. **Natural Language Query**: One element of Power BI Service is "Q&A," which allows users to interact with the data they have access to by asking natural language inquiries. Intuitive exploration and analysis are facilitated by the ability for users to type or speak queries to retrieve visualizations and responses based on the available data.

10. **Mobile Accessibility**: To supplement the service, Power BI offers mobile applications for iOS and Android devices. These apps guarantee that customers can access and interact with their reports and dashboards while they are on the go. Regardless of the location, the availability of data and the capacity to make flexible decisions are both guaranteed by this mobility.

To begin, you can sign in to the service by entering the credentials for your Microsoft account (or employer account, if you have one). The Power BI service is available to everyone with a "free" license, and anyone can use it. Using this free license, you will have access to "**My Workspace**." You can submit reports in this personal growth section and examine how they appear and work inside the service. Following your successful self-authentication, a home page will appear. You'll discover that this field is quite active. A navigation bar sits on the left side of the screen, a list of Favorites and Frequents appears in the center, and a link to the components and programs you can currently access is located just below it. You can generate new reports, search for items to which you have access, and change the settings controls in the upper-right bar by selecting from a variety of alternatives. This first view is the same view that you would get if you were to select the Home link that is located at the very top of the menu on the left side of the screen.

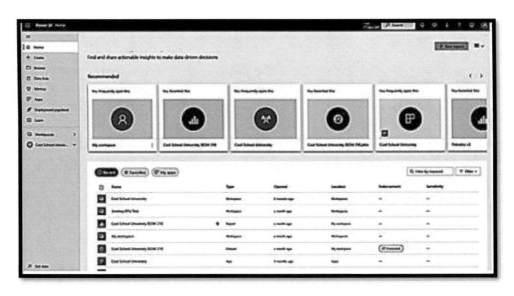

The good news is that everything you need to access in the beginning can be gained from that menu on the left-hand side, which is called the Navigation menu. Therefore, let's travel through those regions and get an understanding of the most significant things that can be found there.

The Navigation Menu

The image below provides a close-up of the Navigation menu. In the black bar at the very top of the screen, you will see what looks like a nine-dot box, the Power BI title, and another link to the Home page. The nine-dot box comes in rather useful. If you pick it, a list of shortcuts that will take you to different Microsoft services will appear in front of you. OneDrive, Word, Excel, PowerPoint, OneNote, SharePoint, Teams, Sway, Outlook, and any other Microsoft applications that you may be able to access with your Office 365 subscription are at your disposal. This functionality can be useful if you're working in Power BI and suddenly discover you need to switch to another part of your Office suite. It can also be useful to have this information readily available when constructing something, such as a dataflow, and you need to refer to the potential location of an item that you wish to draw in from SharePoint or OneDrive for Business.

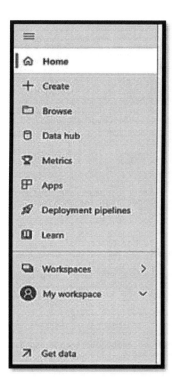

Selecting the Home button below, to the right of the symbol that appears to be home (in the lighter portion of the menu), will accomplish the same thing as clicking on the Home link. Remember that even if there are only a few pixels separating possibilities, Microsoft wants to provide you with as many as possible. In the Navigation menu, you'll see a hamburger menu button directly beneath the nine-dot box. Depending on how much room you need to see the Navigation menu, you can increase or minimize it by clicking this symbol. You can still see the icons that make up the Navigation menu when it is shrunk, and you can use those icons to navigate. You will be provided with explanations of what those symbols imply after you enlarge them.

Home and Browse

The Home section of the Power BI service provides users with convenient access to recommended objects, recently accessed objects, favorite objects, and accessible apps. The topmost section of this page features a pleasant greeting and a button labeled "**New report**" that allows users to generate a new report. Clicking this button will redirect users to the same section as the "**Create**" link located on the Navigation menu. The image below provides a visual representation of this feature. Adjacent to it, there exists a fusion of ellipses and hamburger menu icons, which provides me with the option to select either the uncomplicated or comprehensive arrangement. Although the expanded layout appears largely unchanged, it does feature a selection of valuable learning resources located at the bottom of the page. The entirety of the content presented in this section has been designed using a simplified page layout. At the uppermost part of the page, there is a section labeled "**Recommended**" which displays a list of suggested items. Various items such as workspaces, reports, datasets, and apps can be included in this category. This list may also comprise data elements that are endorsed by your organization, including certified datasets and apps that you may have access to. Displayed below the list of suggested items, you will find a compilation of recently viewed elements, favorite elements, and applications. Switching between views is a breeze - just click the corresponding button. The search functionality allows for easy navigation of the lists by keyword, while the Filter button provides the option to narrow down the search by selecting specific types of objects, filtering by recent activity, or sorting by endorsement status.

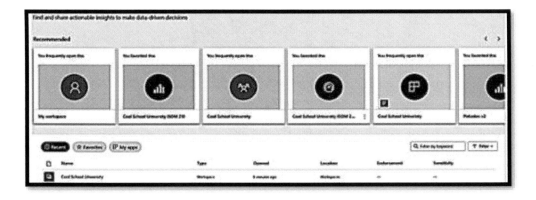

The design of this layout bears a striking resemblance to that of a SharePoint list. The user can view the titles of their **favorite** content. The user can easily identify the type of element, be it a report or a dashboard, along with its owner, endorsement status, and sensitivity labels. Within the Favorites list, it is noticeable that Power BI continues to display the items as starred, despite the possibility of it seeming repetitive. The aforementioned feature can be found within the unmarked column located in the **Recent** section. In case there are any recently added items that you have marked as favorites, you will notice that these particular elements are indicated with a star symbol. Concerning the Home section, the Browse category within the Navigation menu appears to be redundant. The interface displays a comprehensive inventory of accessible items, categorized into subpages such as Recent, Favorites, and Shared with You. The image below showcases Microsoft's unwavering commitment to providing users with a multitude of options to accomplish a single task.

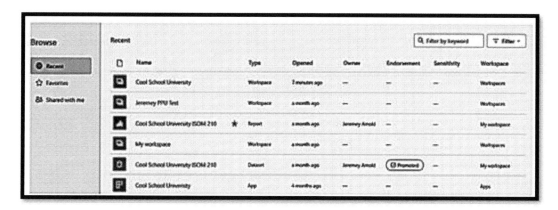

Create

With Power BI, users can construct reports directly within the service. In all honesty, while the option to create reports directly on the web does exist, it is not frequently utilized as compared to the alternative of downloading Power BI Desktop for free and generating reports through that platform. It is highly recommended to utilize Power BI Desktop for authoring purposes. Keeping that in consideration, the Create tab will present you with two alternatives. There are two ways to input data into a table sheet: manual entry or copy-pasting. Alternatively, you can select a pre-existing dataset within the workspace and generate a new report based on that dataset.

Data Hub

The Data Hub is a centralized platform designed to store and manages large amounts of data. It provides a secure and efficient way to. The "**Data Hub**" section provides users with a comprehensive view of their available datasets. This includes a curated list of recommended datasets, a complete list of accessible datasets, and a personalized list of authored datasets. If you possess a **Premium Per User** or **Premium Per Capacity** license, you can also observe the Datamarts feature in the preview. It is worth noting that Microsoft provides hyperlinks within this view that can redirect you to their documentation. This can be helpful if you have any queries regarding specific elements on the page related to dataset discovery and understanding the concept of a dataset. Upon selecting a dataset, a vertical three-dot selection will appear, providing access to an expanded list of options specific to that dataset. This menu provides you with various options to manipulate a dataset. The approach we will be taking is slightly out of order; with the settings section being addressed last as it is a distinct topic on its own. The initial option available to us is to perform an analysis in Excel. Upon your initial attempt, Power BI will prompt you to install an update to Excel to properly read the file format. Upon completion of the task, Power BI will automatically produce an Excel worksheet that is pre-configured with a live connection to the source dataset. Connecting to a Power BI dataset to generate a report from Power BI Desktop is a process that bears resemblance to the one at hand. The data can be accessed in a pivot-table format, allowing for the placement of fields into rows and columns, and the inclusion of measures into the Values section, similar to any other pivot table.

This piece is designed to assist users who may possess the knowledge to utilize the data model you have established, but may not yet feel confident using Power BI Desktop. Perhaps the user requires expeditious pivot-table analysis utilizing Microsoft Excel. From an Excel standpoint, utilizing this function offers the benefit of storing only the data that is visible in the cell on the local device, while the primary data is stored in the cloud. Upon selecting "**Create report**," users will be directed to the web report authoring interface. Here, all tables and measures within the dataset will be readily available for viewing. With the aid of this feature, it is possible to construct a report with an unlimited number of pages, which will be accessible on the Power BI service. It is important to note that the web authoring experience does not provide the option to modify a dataset. In the web authoring experience, it is not possible to add a table or any missing measure. To incorporate your pertinent data elements, you will need to access the primary dataset, append the required information, and subsequently re-release the dataset to the platform. The "**Create paginated report**" function generates a **Report Definition Language (RDL)** file that includes all the essential connection details required to produce a pixel-perfect report, similar to those in SQL Server Reporting Services. This report can then be hosted on the Power BI service. Paginated reports in the Power BI service are created using a distinct software package called Power BI Report Builder, rather than Power BI Desktop. This feature is exclusively available in workspaces with **Premium per User or Premium per Capacity** plans. By accessing the **"Manage Permissions"** feature, you will be able to view a comprehensive list of objects that you have the authority to add or remove users. It is possible to view the individuals who possess direct access to a report, dataset, or workbook. This interface allows for the manual addition of users and provides visibility on pending access requests.

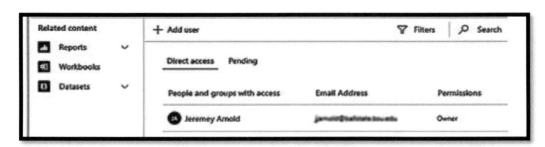

The "**Chat in Teams**" feature generates a link that can be easily shared with individuals, groups, or channels within Microsoft Teams. Upon accessing the dataset, users are seamlessly directed to the relevant section of the Power BI service through Teams integration. In addition to that, it is possible to distribute reports and report pages within Teams. Incorporating analytics into your organization can be seamlessly achieved through Microsoft Teams, leveraging its user-friendly interface that your team is already accustomed to. By utilizing Teams as a communication channel, you can facilitate discussions around the findings of a particular report or dataset. This feature also empowers you, as the author, to promptly offer valuable insights, clarify any doubts, or incorporate suggestions from users to enhance the report. By clicking on the "**View lineage**" option, a fresh browser window will open up, displaying a comprehensive list of all the data elements present within a particular workspace, along with their corresponding dependencies. In the case of a dataset that employs a SQL Server instance, it is customary to present the SQL Server first, followed by the dataset, then the reports based on that dataset, and finally any dashboards that were generated from report elements.

From this perspective, you have the option to generate various other components by utilizing the "**New**" button. By utilizing web-based design tools, you can seamlessly generate fresh elements within a workspace or upload PBIX files directly into it. This versatile tool can be utilized for generating reports and paginated reports, creating scorecards, managing dataflows, and organizing datasets. I highly recommend utilizing Power BI Desktop over the web authorship tool whenever possible. This is the stage where you can create dataflows and scorecards. From a web authorship perspective, this location may seem unusual for housing such functionality, particularly for items that can be better suited to Power BI Desktop. However, it is worth noting that this is the most comprehensive location where these options can be found. Upon clicking on a dataset, a comprehensive list of tables and columns contained within the dataset will be displayed. By utilizing the "**View lineage**" feature, you can gain insight into the flow of data elements from one item to another. This allows you to identify potential impacts that may arise from modifying a dataset, extending beyond your immediate workspace.

Settings

Upon selecting the Settings option for a dataset, users will be directed to a properties page that is conveniently preselected to the Datasets section of the Navigation menu located at the top of the page. On the left-hand side, there is a comprehensive list of all the datasets available in the workspace. To effectively manage your dataset(s), it is crucial to pay attention to the various properties options located on the right-hand side of the screen. These options are specifically designed to cater to the needs of the currently selected dataset. The image below gives us a look at this page.

By clicking on the "**View dataset**" hyperlink, you will be directed to the workspace page of the dataset. By selecting the "**Refresh history**" option, a pop-up window will appear within the page, displaying the refresh history of the dataset. This will indicate whether the refresh was successful or not, and if there was a failure, it will provide a reason for the failure. Some failure messages are helpful. Some are not. It's still a Microsoft product, and Microsoft's error messages can be hit-or-miss in terms of their helpfulness; they're notoriously unfriendly when it comes to troubleshooting in Windows. Next, we can create or update the dataset's description. In cases where data sources are not hosted in the cloud, particularly in Azure, it is typically necessary to install a data gateway to enable the refresh of the corresponding dataset. Suppose that there is a Power BI dataset that is being refreshed from a few Excel files located on the network drive of the user's company. Access to network drives is currently not available on the Power BI service. The data gateway serves as a virtual private network that connects the Power BI service with authorized locations, enabling seamless data retrieval for refreshes. Reviewing each data source and determining whether a gateway is necessary would be a time-consuming task. It is worth noting that Microsoft is the most reliable and current source for this information.

In most cases, the responsibility of managing gateways falls on the IT or security team. Therefore, if your organization is currently utilizing an enterprise gateway, it is advisable to contact the relevant stakeholders to determine whether you need to include a specific data source. A downloadable personal version of the data gateway is offered by Microsoft. Assuming that your local machine is up and running, this version can be accessed. Additionally, if the gateway is operational during the refresh, it will also function properly. It is important to keep in mind that utilizing R and Python data sources and transformations necessitates the use of a personal data gateway, rather than an enterprise one. The reason for this is that the Power BI service requires the execution of the corresponding R and Python scripts from the user's machine. This is because the user's machine is assumed to possess all the essential packages and libraries. Next, "**Data source**

credentials" would be where you configure the credentials required to access the data. Assuming that you are extracting data from on-premises SQL Server, which is configured in your data gateway, you will need to furnish the appropriate credentials in this section. This will enable Power BI to identify the credentials required to pass through the gateway and access the original data source. When a Power BI file is uploaded, it typically retains the credentials that were utilized in Desktop. However, this may not always align with your preferences. It may be necessary to transfer the refresh credentials to a pre-established service account. In certain cases, it may be necessary to modify login credentials, such as when an individual departs from the company or due to a variety of other factors. In case of encountering refresh issues, it is recommended to verify your data source credentials as Power BI can indicate if any action is required. Rest assured that Power BI will efficiently notify you if any further action is necessary. The concept of parameters is quite simple and easy to understand. In case your dataset contains parameters, this is the section where you can adjust their respective values. A common practice is to parameterize server and database names, which can be useful in various scenarios. In the event of an unexpected occurrence such as the need to redirect a Power BI dataset to a backup server or a database name alteration, it is possible to promptly modify the connections by accessing the settings. This process involves a seamless transition of connections, and data refresh and allows for a swift continuation of tasks. This platform allows you to efficiently manage and update all Power Query parameters associated with a specific dataset. Upon updating the parameter values, a refresh will be triggered to incorporate the latest changes to the data state.

For me, the true magic of the Power BI service lies in the process of **"scheduled refresh"**. In this section, you can customize the frequency and timing of your Power BI dataset's refresh against its source data. In non-premium environments, users have the option to schedule up to 8 refreshes, whereas, in premium capacity environments, they can schedule up to 48 refreshes per day. Users have the option to customize their time zone settings, whether it's for daily use or specific days of the week. Once the preferred settings have been selected, they can be saved for future use. Merely configuring a refresh feature does not guarantee its functionality. Before scheduling a refresh, it is imperative to ensure that your dataset has been successfully refreshed in Power BI Desktop and that all dataset settings in service are accurate. Enabling or disabling the **Q&A** feature on a dataset can be achieved through the Q&A toggle switch. In addition, this feature enables users to easily share their synonyms with all members of the organization. The "**Featured Q&A Questions**" feature enables you to showcase select questions to your audience as they peruse reports generated from this particular dataset. With the **Endorsement** feature, you can pinpoint a specific dataset and bring it to the forefront of your organization's attention. Microsoft offers three tiers of endorsement: None, Promoted, and Certified. The default setting is "**none**." If a dataset lacks endorsement, it will only appear in search results without any further visibility. Promoting a dataset can significantly enhance its visibility in search results. This increased visibility can lead to a higher ranking in the search context, thereby increasing its chances of being discovered by potential users. In addition, there is an option to enhance the visibility of the dataset by making it discoverable. This feature enables users who do not have the dataset's access to discover it and request access on their own. Certification of a dataset is a possible final step in the dataset creation process. A dataset that has undergone a thorough review process is referred to as a **certified dataset**, which serves as a reliable and trustworthy label, often regarded as a **"source of truth**." The certified status for a dataset is not set by default by an individual. The aforementioned task is accomplished through various procedures within your company. Every organization has its own set of standards for determining when a dataset is eligible to be classified as Certified. The "**Request Access**" feature allows users to manage how they can request permission to access content associated with the chosen dataset. There are two ways to request access to a dataset. The first option is to send an email request to the dataset owner. Alternatively, you can receive an automatic response that includes a set of instructions to follow to gain access to the dataset. With **Dataset Image**, users have the option to select an attractive image that effectively showcases their dataset in various discoverable locations. Once uploaded, this image will serve as the universal representation of the dataset across your organization's various platforms for dataset discovery.

Metrics

The Power BI service has recently introduced **metrics** as a new feature. With the Power BI service, users can generate measurable KPIs or goal metrics that can be tracked using data. Scorecards are designed to display the performance of a specific metric during a designated time frame. It is important to note that metrics are closely tied to individual users or business scenarios. Therefore, it is best not to delve too deeply into the specifics. If you are considering the implementation of metrics, give it a try to assess its potential usefulness. In a recent development, Microsoft has made it possible for individuals to work with metrics within their workspace. It is recommended that you begin by setting some personal goals before exploring this feature for other areas of the organization.

Apps

An *app*, in the context of the Power BI service, is a collection of packaged content that can be distributed to a broader audience. Apps are developed inside of workspaces, and once they are complete, they can be published to a set of people, an enterprise as a whole, or to a Microsoft 365 community depending on the requirements. Apps can also have different rights than those in a workspace, which makes user management somewhat simpler since the permissions for an app are maintained in a single area. Users can create their applications using a workspace. You can utilize any one of the many applications that are accessible to you, which are referred to as **template apps**. These applications are compilations that were developed by other people and then shared with you and the other members of your company so that you can utilize them. In the picture below, we can see the very first Apps view, which will first give the impression of being empty. After that, we can either add an organizational app or a template app or then inspect the content that comes from those applications. We can view the list of available applications that we can bring into our workplace by using the yellow "**Get apps**" button in any area. This button is accessible in both places. In our demonstration, I have developed an application known as the RLS Test that will serve as an organizational app. The other applications are examples. Using the COVID-19 US Tracking Report template app offered by Microsoft, we will guide you through the process of installing the template app. It is important to note that in the area labeled "**All apps**," organizational apps are always shown first, followed by template apps; yet, the apps in either category are not structured in a manner that makes sense. You'll see that there is a spot where you can opt to pick just applications that have been recommended by the company. When you need to find a collection of data that has been approved by your organization's leadership in a hurry, this can be a useful tool for you.

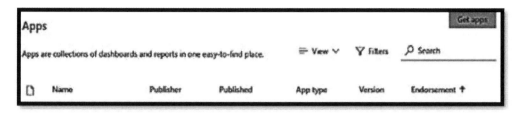

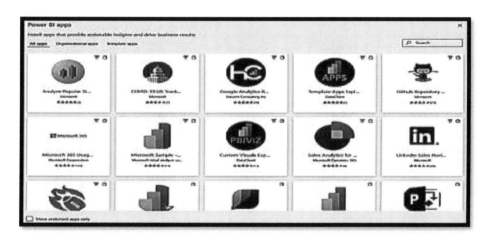

To install the program, just click the proper box, and you will be brought to the right page in AppSource, which is Microsoft's application and custom visual gateway. Installing the application is as simple as that. You should examine the description of the software to see if there are any licensing requirements before downloading it, but in most instances, there will be a large button that says **"Get It Now."** In the case of Microsoft's template programs, a pop-up window will appear before the installation process in which it will request some information from you for the sake of marketing. This doesn't need to be coupled with the same information as your Power BI account itself; thus, if you are uneasy about doing so, you are free to use an email address that you do not often check. When the software or applications have been successfully installed, you will see them here. To get access to them, just click on the link that is provided below its name. Each app will have a list of information associated with it, which may include the publisher, the date it was released, the kind of app, the version number (if applicable), and the endorsement status of the app. You can see the reports that were provided with an app after it has been installed. It's fun for me to browse through some of the template applications to get ideas for the layout of my work, so don't be embarrassed to steal creative concepts!

Deployment Pipelines

You are only able to define Development, Test, and Production environments for a particular Power BI workspace if you have the **Premium per Capacity** plan since that plan includes the Deployment Pipelines functionality. This is a tool that can be used by developers to assist them with difficulties such as user testing and version control. To provide support for a pipeline, workspaces can either be created or assigned; but, as was stated before, any such workspaces must be in the Premium per Capacity tier. In most cases, administrators at the workspace or tenant level, or whatever group within an organization is in charge of managing the **Premium per Capacity** tenancy, are the ones responsible for managing deployment pipelines. If you are on a **Premium per Capacity** tenant and have a need or want to construct a pipeline, you should work with your appropriate administrator to have it put together or seek to have work added to an existing pipeline. If you are not a **Premium per Capacity** tenant, you should not do any of these things.

Learn

Microsoft provides you with connections to training resources, documentation for Power BI, and some example reports to get you started on your learning journey via the Learn site. Learn is a modest learning portal. You can also join the bigger communities around Power BI and Power Platform by using the Learn tab. There are a lot of very awesome users out there who take the time to provide content, answer questions on forums, push new ideas for the product, and host events for practitioners to share what they've learned with others so that others can benefit from them as well.

Publishing Your Work

You will need to take your PBIX file from Power BI Desktop to publish your work. You will then have the option to either utilize the Publish button in Power BI Desktop, which is located on the Home ribbon, or upload a PBIX file to the Power BI service, which can be done through the **Navigation** menu. When we click the "**Get data**" button, the page that appears next is as seen in the picture below.

You will see a menu in Power BI Desktop that provides a list of the workspaces to which you have access. From this menu, you will choose the workspace in which you want to publish the report. In the context of the service, its role is more of an upward pull than an outward push. You will need to submit the PBIX file that is located in the workspace to which you would want to add the dataset and/or report. On the left, we can see the Discover content functionalities, which will make it possible for you to see your organizational apps as well as other template apps that can be directly integrated into the workspace. You can upload your PBIX file by selecting the Files option that is located on the right side of the screen. The Databases & More option gives you the ability to work on the process of creating a dataset from a connection to Azure SQL, Azure SQL Data Warehouse (which is now Azure Synapse), SQL Server Analysis Services, or Spark on Azure. You can do this by connecting to Azure SQL, Azure SQL Data Warehouse, SQL Server Analysis Services, or Spark on Azure. Because selecting File is the 99% of the time when you'll want to utilize this option, the picture below will show us what the service looks like when File is selected.

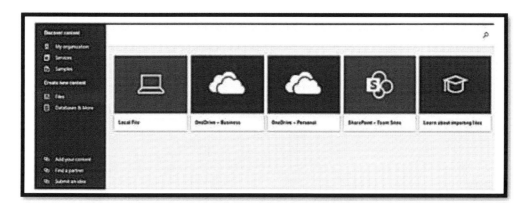

You will notice a few different options once you reach this point. For the sake of this discussion, "**Local File**" refers to the PBIX file that you created using Power BI Desktop. You can establish a dataset in the Power BI service that is linked to either your OneDrive for Business account or your OneDrive account by using the OneDrive connections. These sources are handy from a refreshing standpoint since they do not call for the use of a data gateway to be refreshed. Despite this, I continue to recommend that you construct your report using sources from OneDrive in Power BI Desktop as opposed to doing it here. In a similar vein, the same may be said about the SharePoint option. It is important to keep in mind that even in circumstances in which you could be utilizing OneDrive or SharePoint for the sake of version control; you can still upload PBIX files over those channels. This is one use case that can make it simple to utilize these nonlocal file alternatives. When you pick **Local File**, the classic window for Windows Explorer will come up for you to browse your files. Find the right file, and then upload it to the server. Following that step, the dataset will be visible in the workspace navigation section corresponding to the chosen workspace. **One other point**: Anytime a dataset is uploaded to a workspace for the first time, it will also automatically generate a dashboard with the same name as the dataset. This dashboard will be empty. You can now see that transferring our work from Power BI into a workspace is a very straightforward process; however, what exactly is a workspace and why are they important?

What Is a Workspace?

A workspace in Power BI is nothing more than a storage location for various data assets. A workspace is where datasets, reports, and dashboards are stored. A workspace is also where visualizations are stored. You can send users to a workspace for them to get content, and you can also utilize a workspace as the foundation for an application that you will send users to obtain content. When we publish datasets and the reports associated with them to the service, we are, in effect, publishing them to these workspaces.

My Workspace

Anyone who uses the Power BI service will automatically have a **"free"** customized workspace created for them. You have a responsibility to be aware of a few significant restrictions that apply to this workplace. To begin, to share content that is located in your workspace, both you and the individuals with whom you share need to have at least a Power BI Pro license. This is the case even if you can share the content. Second, it is widely regarded to be a smart practice to not share anything permanently outside of your workplace. This is because access to that workspace can become problematic if you ever leave the business. Additionally, the content in your workspace cannot be used to create an application. Sorry, but you can't utilize this to get around the license requirements set by Microsoft. You also are unable to make a dataflow in Power BI, which is another thing you cannot accomplish. Using one's workstation as one's private testing environment is the most productive way to utilize that space. After constructing your report and determining that it has an appealing appearance in Power BI Desktop, you publish it to the service and then see it there to verify that all of the components are operating as you would want them to. Does the report maintain its professional appearance when viewed on a variety of screen sizes? When you don't have access to the additional capabilities provided by Power BI Desktop, does the navigation of the report flow the way you want it to? These are queries that can be answered right here, in the comfort of your workstation. You can also test your scheduled refresh in this workspace, which can be beneficial before transferring that dataset into a more permanent home in a shared workspace. Alternatively, you can test your planned refresh in this workplace.

Shared Capacity Workspaces

Users who have Power BI Pro or Power BI Premium per-user licenses can share Power BI data components with other users who also have access to a shared capacity workspace if the workspace is set up with that capability. The procedure of establishing a workplace is quite uncomplicated. You will see a list of the workspaces to which you have access when you click the Workspaces button, which is located in the Navigation menu. This will cause a window to appear to the right of the Navigation menu. In this particular scenario, I've created two other workplaces in addition to "**My Workspace**." The first workspace is a **Premium per User workplace**, while the second workspace is a standard shared capacity workspace. A Premium per-user workspace is required for the operation of some functionality. In contrast to a regular Pro license shared workspace, Premium per Capacity workspaces will have a diamond symbol next to their names so you can determine whether it is a Premium per User or Premium per Capacity workspace. Have a glance at it in the photograph that is provided down below. You can start a new workspace by selecting the option that is located at the very bottom of that list.

The newly generated workspace will provide you with alternatives that are suitable for your licensing requirements. In this example, we are going to make use of the premium per-user trial that's free for the first sixty days. The creation of a workspace will trigger the appearance of a pane on the right-hand side of the page. There will be a spot for the name of the workspace and a description of the workspace, as well as a picture that will explain the workplace. Additionally, some configuration options can be found in the advanced portion of this pane. We can choose the individuals who will be included on the contact list for this newly created workspace, affix a OneDrive location to the workspace so that files can be hosted there, and determine the kind of licensing mode that is associated with the workspace (in this example, Pro, Premium Per User, Premium Per Capacity, or Embedded). If your company does not have the appropriate license in place, the **Embedded and Premium per Capacity** options will be grayed out. If you do not have a license for **Premium per User,** then the Premium per User option will likewise be unavailable to you. You have the option of designating the workspace as one that is being used for the creation of a template app, and you also have the option of allowing contributors to change any app that originates from this workspace. When you want more than one person to be able to deploy the updated app yet you have numerous individuals working on the development of a particular Power BI solution, this can be useful. It is essential to keep in mind that both the **Pro and Premium per**

User workspaces can be accessed inside a licensing hierarchy. For example, if I have a Pro workspace, users who have licenses for either Premium per User or Pro will be able to access the workspace and the data items that are included inside it. On the other hand, if the workspace in question requires a Premium per User license to be accessed, only those individuals will be permitted to do so. This rule does not apply to businesses that have Premium per Capacity licensing since that permits an unlimited number of readers inside an organization to access any workspace built on its premium capacity node. Consequently, this regulation is null and void in such organizations.

Dataflows in Shared Workspaces

In Power BI, a "**dataflow**" refers to a shared data element that is kept in a workspace and that can be called upon to serve as a data source for the creation of reports. Consider this to be an ETL process that not only retrieves data from some source and does certain transformations, but also generates a data piece that can be utilized for further analysis outside of the context of a particular model. These days, there are two distinct varieties of dataflows. Refer to the first kind of dataflows as "**classic**," and the second type as "**streaming**." Any workspace that includes one kind of dataflow cannot also have the other type of dataflow inside the same workspace. A set of tables that were produced by the Power Query service inside the Power BI platform constitutes a traditional dataflow. In the section under "**Get Data**," you will discover the possibility of making a dataflow. When we were looking at that page in my workspace, the option that is now there under the heading "**Create new content**" was not there when we first looked at it. Several data sources are not accessible via a Power BI data flow that is available through the Power BI Desktop. It is a rather comprehensive list of the most frequent data sources, although Microsoft does sometimes add new data sources to the Power Query Online platform. When working with a Power BI Desktop file, it can be convenient to have a series of transformations or components of a data model that aren't dependent on a single dataset for execution. Additionally, it is beneficial to have reusable data items so that other individuals within the business may potentially use them as a foundation for their analysis. On licenses for the Pro tier, classic dataflows can be used.

A minimum of a Premium per User license is required to use streaming dataflows. Only users who have a Premium per User license or who are working in an environment that is Premium per Capacity can consume reports that have been shared from streaming dataflows. Power BI is given the ability to call either an Azure Event Hub event or an Azure IoT event by streaming dataflow. You can do "real-time" reporting on data that is generated by any of these scenarios by consuming data from either of those sources and performing transformations on that data in real time. Although this is a wonderful feature, the fact that it can only be used with Azure Event Hubs and Azure IoT Hub restricts its utility, and setting up this kind of event requires a bit more work than usual. I'm hoping that before they make this available to the general public, they increase the number of available options and makes it simpler to make use of them.

Putting Your Data in Front of Others

Therefore, even if we can place our data in a workspace, we still need to make sure that other people can see it. We can do it using one of a few different approaches. Users can join the workplaces that we develop thanks to this option. An app can be made by us. Reports can be linked to either Teams or SharePoint as necessary. If we are using Power BI Embedded, we can also embed report parts into either a website or an application. It is highly recommended that you collaborate with an application developer to integrate reports into an application. An application developer will be able to assist you in overcoming any technical obstacles that may arise. Otherwise, let's begin sharing.

Adding Users to a Workspace

Simply adding someone to our office is the quickest and simplest approach to providing someone access to our data. That is a simple thing to do. When we pick a workspace from the list of available workspaces, we are presented with a view. You should notice an **Access button** in the upper-right corner of the screen. When you click it, a pane will open up on the right side of the screen that enables us to add or delete people and specify the function that each person plays in the workspace. You will also notice a space where you can add individuals or organizations by entering their email addresses. This is helpful since Power BI can very effortlessly interface with your current directory instance in an organizational context, allowing you to search for individuals in your company and validate their email addresses. Simply add them by clicking the **Add** button.

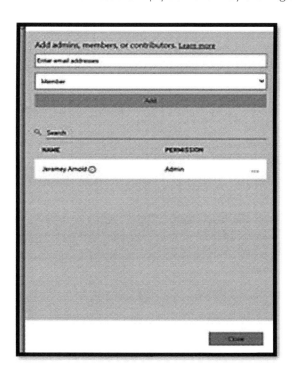

If you have a group of users that you wish to add to a workspace in bulk, you can use security groups to accomplish this task instead. A user can be added at one of these four levels: **Admin, Member, Contributor, or Viewer**. There are several degrees of permissions associated with each position, with Admin having the most privileges and Viewer having the fewest.

Sharing via a Link or Teams

Sharing Power BI reports and dashboards with other people may also be done only by using either Teams or Sharing through a Link. Sharing makes it possible for users to view and engage with the data; this can be accomplished via the use of a simple link or inside a collaborative environment such as Microsoft Teams. Here, we will go further into both approaches and discuss the actions required in sharing content through a link and sharing content using Teams.

Sharing via a Link

1. **Publish your Power BI report to the Power BI service**. To get started, make sure your Power BI Pro subscription is activated and then publish the report to the Power BI service. This makes sure that the report is saved in the cloud and that it can be accessed by other people.
2. **Configure the report's sharing settings:** Change the settings for how the report is shared by going to the Power BI service, selecting the report you wish to share, and then clicking the "**Share**" option. You have control over the sharing settings, so you can decide whether visitors simply have access to read the report or if they can also amend it and work together on it.
3. **Generate a shareable link:** Following the configuration of the sharing options, create a link that can be shared. Depending on the circumstances, you can either establish a safe connection or an anonymous one. Users can view the report via the link even if they do not have the necessary permissions or login credentials.
4. **Copy and distribute the link**: After the link has been produced, you should copy it and send it to the people you desire to receive it by email, chat, or any other mode of contact. Users who are sent the link can easily view the report in their web browser by clicking on the link itself; they do not need a Power BI account to do so.
5. **View and interact with the shared report:** Recipients will have the ability to view and interact with the Power BI report when they access the link that has been shared with them. They can explore the visual representations, apply filters, delve into the data, and get insights from the content that has been given.

Sharing via Teams

1. **Publish your Power BI report to the Power BI service:** Using your Power BI Pro license, begin by publishing the report to the Power BI service. This step is identical to the one that is taken when sharing through a link.
2. **Launch the Microsoft Teams**: Start the Microsoft Teams program, or log in to the service via the online interface.

3. **Create or navigate to the desired channel**: Pick the section of Teams where you want the Power BI report to be shared and click on its name. It can be a pre-existing channel, or it can be a brand-new one that was created just for the report.

4. **Add the Power BI tab:** Within the chosen channel, locate the **"+"** button to include a new tab in the interface. In the app gallery, look for the term "Power BI," and then choose the "Power BI" application. This incorporates a tab for Power BI into the channel.

5. **Connect to the Power BI report**: Following the addition of the Power BI tab, choose the report you want to share from inside the Power BI app. Establish a connection between the tab and the report by supplying the required credentials.

6. **Configure tab settings:** Customize the tab settings to select the first display, such as a particular report page or dashboard. This can be done by configuring the settings for the tabs. You can also choose whether or not members have read-only access.

7. **Save and share with the team**: Once the settings are configured, save the tab. The Power BI report will now be available within the Teams channel for all members to access.

8. **Collaborate and engage with the report**: Members of the team can launch the Power BI tab inside Teams to collaborate and interact with the report immediately there. Through the use of Teams' built-in collaboration tools, users can see visualizations, apply filters, and debate findings.

9. **Receive alerts and keep up to date:** Teams offer notifications for report updates, making it possible for members of a team to be informed when new data is available or when modifications are made to the report.

The distribution of Power BI reports and dashboards is made easier by the availability of customizable alternatives including sharing through a link or via Teams. Sharing a report inside Teams improves cooperation since it incorporates the report into the workflow of a team. Sharing a report through a link is a straightforward and straightforward way of sharing. Select the approach that caters most closely to your requirements, and then begin exchanging insightful observations with others.

Sharing via SharePoint

Sharing Power BI reports and dashboards through SharePoint is a handy way to disseminate data and collaborate on it inside your SharePoint environment. This can be accomplished by using one of the two aforementioned methods. **The following is an in-depth tutorial that will walk you through each stage of sharing content from Power BI using SharePoint:**

1. **Publish your Power BI report to the Power BI service:** To get started, make use of the Power BI Pro license that you have purchased to publish your report to the Power BI service. After completing this step, your report will be uploaded to the cloud and made available to other users.

2. **Navigate to your SharePoint site**: Launch Power BI and go to the SharePoint site where you wish to distribute the report. Make sure that you can change the SharePoint page and that you have the appropriate rights.

3. **Activate the edit mode**: To make modifications to the page layout and content, you must first activate the edit mode on the SharePoint page.
4. **Add the Power BI web part:** To insert a web part into the page, while you are in edit mode, click on the **"+" or "Edit"** button. In the gallery of available web parts, search "Power BI," and then choose the "Power BI" web component.
5. **Customize the Power BI web part**: Once the Power BI web part has been installed, you can customize it by clicking on the "**Add report**" option located inside the web part. You have the option of displaying a previously created report, or you can make a new one. If you choose to use an existing report, you will be prompted to enter the URL of the Power BI report located inside the Power BI service.
6. **Personalize the display options**: Personalize the display options for the Power BI web component by configuring the display options, such as the size of the embedded report, the amount of interaction, and the default report page to display.
7. **Save and publish the SharePoint page:** Once you have finished creating the Power BI web component, save the changes that were made to the SharePoint page. To make the changes to the page visible to other users, you must first click the **"Save" or "Publish"** button.
8. **Verify the embedded Power BI report:** Check that the embedded Power BI report is presented properly on the SharePoint page Exit the edit mode and check to see whether the embedded Power BI report is displayed appropriately on the SharePoint page. The integrated report will now be seen by users who have access to the SharePoint site, and they will be able to interact with it as well.
9. **Collaborate and engage with the report**: Users of SharePoint can explore the integrated Power BI report immediately inside the SharePoint page. To get insights, they can interact with the visual representations, apply filters, and do data analysis.
10. **Manage access and permissions**: SharePoint offers a variety of settings via which users may manage access and permissions for integrated Power BI reports. You can control who can read the report, amend the report, or collaborate on the report depending on the rights settings for the SharePoint site.

Creating an App

Choose the workspace that already has the components of the app you want to build. On the other side of the workspace objects, you will find a toggle that gives you the option to choose whether or not the item should be included in the application. Only the reports and dashboards that make use of a particular dataset will be included in an app; datasets themselves are not shared. The software still gets its information from the dataset, but it conceals the dataset itself from users of the app. Click "**Create app**" in the upper-right corner after you have the things you want to include in your app, and you will be sent to a screen similar to the one shown in the picture below.

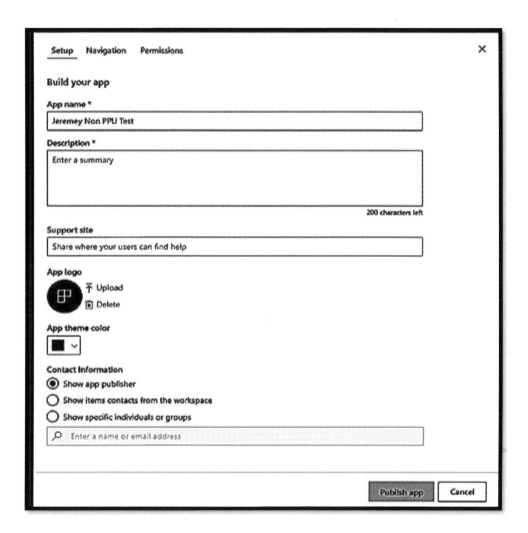

There are controls to choose the app's name, enter a description, create a link to a site where end users can get help or read documentation, and determine app navigation settings (I like the default navigation of the navigation builder, so I tend to leave this alone), and set permissions around who can access the app. These controls can be found in the app's settings menu. Does it apply to the whole organization? Is there a certain kind of user involved here? With build permissions, who can access the datasets that are underneath the application? Is it possible for them to make copies of the reports? Are users able to share, and, as a last question, should this software be automatically installed? You should probably discuss some of these options with someone in your business that is responsible for data governance, since that person may already have rules in place that will assist and guide your options.

Conclusion

Power BI Service offers a comprehensive and robust platform for data visualization, sharing, and collaboration. With its intuitive interface and powerful features, users can harness the full potential of their data to gain valuable insights and make informed decisions. The Power BI Service serves as a centralized hub for managing and accessing data, reports, and dashboards. It allows users to connect to various data sources, including cloud-based services, on-premises databases, and online services, ensuring that data can be easily integrated into Power BI for analysis.

Activity

1. What is a workspace?
2. Add users to a workspace you created.
3. Share a workspace via link or teams.

CHAPTER 9
LICENSING AND DEPLOYMENT TIPS

Licensing

In and of itself, the idea of a license is simple. It is a paid contract that grants you the usage rights of a service for the duration that you continue to pay for it. If the product in issue offers multiple tiers of functionality, you might be able to choose to pay for one level of capabilities instead of another within the service. For the majority of customers, the license for Power BI can be divided into three primary categories: **Pro, Premium per User, and Premium per Capacity.** There are three different types of individual user licenses for Power BI: Free, Pro, and Premium per User (PPU). The type of license you require will depend on the location of your material, how you want to interact with it, and whether or not it makes use of Premium features. The second type of license that can be purchased is the Premium capacity-based license. Workspaces marked as having Premium capacity are accessible to PPU and Pro users with a capacity-based license for Power BI Premium. Subsequently, PPU and Pro users can grant their colleagues, including free users, access to these Premium workspaces.

Power BI service licenses

There are two types of licenses: one that relates to an individual (per-user licensing), and another license (often also referred to as a subscription) that applies to the sort of storage capacity that an organization acquires. It is essential to note the difference between these two types of licenses when discussing licenses. A different subset of the tools and features provided by the Power BI service is accessible with each of the three individual user licenses, which are separate from one another. Premium capacity refers to the set of features and capabilities that are available to Pro, PPU, and free license holders in addition to sharing, collaboration, and other features. It is created by combining the advantages and capabilities of each type of per-user license with the use of a Premium capacity.

Free per-user license

The Power BI service is available to users with free licenses, who can connect to data and create reports and dashboards for their use. They are unable to publish data to other people's workspaces or use Power BI's sharing and collaboration features with other users. However, if the data is stored in workspaces hosted with a Premium capacity subscription, users with a Pro or PPU membership can collaborate and share content with free users.

Pro license

In addition to being able to see and engage with material that other users have uploaded to the Power BI service, users can also create their content by utilizing the Power BI Pro individual license. With this kind of license, users can collaborate with users of other versions of Power BI Pro. Users of Power BI Pro are the only ones who can create content, distribute content to other users of Power BI Pro, or access content created by other users of Power BI Pro—unless the content is housed in a Power BI Premium capacity. If the content is hosted by a Power BI Premium capacity, then users with a Pro subscription can collaborate and share content with users with a free or PPU subscription as well.

Premium per user (PPU) license

All capabilities available in Power BI Pro, as well as the majority of Premium capacity-based features, are available to the owner of a PPU per-user license. Many features, tools, and types of material that are otherwise exclusive to Premium subscribers can be accessed by users with a Power BI PPU license. Exclusively the license holder and any additional colleagues who possess a PPU license can gain access to this. To engage with one another and exchange information within the workplace, for example, each user of a PPU workspace needs a PPU license. If a user has a PPU license, the content that they generate can only be shared with other users who also have a PPU license, unless that content has been placed in a workspace that is hosted in Premium capacity. The following table provides a summary of the fundamental features that are included with each level of license.

Premium capacity

If a user has a capacity-based Premium license—also known as a Premium subscription—they can create and store content in Premium capacity workspaces using their Pro or PPU account. They can then share that workplace with other employees who possess any kind of license. Users with a Pro or PPU license are the only ones who can create and save content using Premium capacities, and even then, only if their company has purchased Premium capabilities.

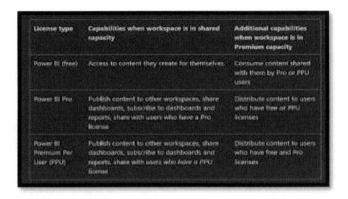

License type	Capabilities when workspace is in shared capacity	Additional capabilities when workspace is in Premium capacity
Power BI (free)	Access to content they create for themselves	Consume content shared with them by Pro or PPU users
Power BI Pro	Publish content to other workspaces, share dashboards, subscribe to dashboards and reports, share with users who have a Pro license	Distribute content to users who have free or PPU licenses
Power BI Premium Per User (PPU)	Publish content to other workspaces, share dashboards, subscribe to dashboards and reports, share with users who have a PPU license	Distribute content to users who have free and Pro licenses

Workspace and App Management

You will need to add users to workspaces as well as applications that you build, regardless of the licensing structure you choose to use for your business since you will be required to do so. I will be using a **Premium per User** license to demonstrate all of the features that are available here.

Workspace Generation and Access Control

There are several methods for gaining entry to a workspace. When you access workspaces through the Home menu screen, they appear as a category of objects that you may add to your Recent list, as shown in the screenshot that follows. Furthermore, on the menu on the left, a line divides the Learn navigation from the **Workspace Management navigation.**

When we click the arrow next to the Workspaces menu item, a second gray vertical box will open, displaying a list of the workspaces to which I have access. Contextually, a button labeled **"Create a workspace"** will also appear in this box, but only if I can create a workspace. If you were on the **Premium per Capacity** plan and the tenant administrator blocked this capability, this would be the

173

situation that would prevent you from being able to establish a workspace the vast majority of the time. Another thing to notice is the upward-pointing arrow in the vertical menu on the line directly below the Workspaces line. When you click on it, details about all of the dashboards, reports, workbooks, and datasets that are contained within that workspace will be displayed, along with the workspace that you are now using. The image depicting my workstation serves as an illustration of how this appears. Looking at this screen, you can see that I have a few datasets and am currently working in "My workspace". You can't see all of the things that are in the workspace from where you are, thus there is a scroll bar shown alongside the information that is provided about what is in the workspace. Selecting a workspace from the list of Workspaces shown on the right-hand side of the menu is yet another method for seeing all of the items included inside a workspace. This will send you to a landing page for the workspace that displays all of the different data components that have been saved in that workspace. We can now go on to the process of workspace creation. Let's begin by making a new workspace by clicking on the button that says "**Create a workspace**" in yellow. When you select that button, a new window will appear on the right side of the screen. This window will provide information on the various possibilities for creating a workspace. To access the advanced settings, you will first need to click the arrow next to the **advanced menu** item. This is because the advanced settings are hidden by default.

It will be evident to you that there is a picture upload option for the workspace. If users would like, you can provide them with a description of the workspace. Next, we reach the advanced configurations. You will first select the people who will be informed of any requests for access to a workspace. Additionally, you may configure the workspace's licensing method, file storage location on Workspace OneDrive, whether or not the workspace will generate a template app, and whether or not contributors will be able to edit the app that was generated from the workspace if one already exists. Most of the time, the workspace administrators are the ones you want to be notified when someone seeks access. On the other hand, the tenant administrator may have more control over the workspaces in Premium per Capacity settings. The company may decide in these types of situations to forward all such queries to the tenant administration or an IT department. We can designate a place on OneDrive for Business for document storage that the workspace will make use of. You can't just use the storage space you have on OneDrive, though. Don't you think that if Microsoft did that, it would be too convenient for individual users? As such, your main attention should be on the SharePoint document library that is part of the Microsoft 365 group. You must create this group somewhere else before proceeding with Power BI. Similar groups can be created via OneDrive for Business, however depending on your situation, Microsoft 365 may not allow you to create as many groups as you would like. If access is limited, contact the administrator of your SharePoint site or your company's information technology department for information on how to integrate OneDrive into your new workspace. The "**License mode**" menu is the next option on our list. Because of the significance of this option to our objectives, it will be the most crucial option we make, as it will decide the capabilities of our workplace. A new feature that was not there previously will appear on the page if you select Premium per User or a higher plan. This is an illustration of uneven design language, to put it mildly. You'll be asked to select the default storage format in which your datasets will be stored. You can choose between the huge dataset storage format and the little dataset storage format. All Pro workspaces use the tiny dataset storage format by default, which cannot be changed. If you wish to have data models greater than one GB, make sure that "Large dataset storage" is enabled in your system.

The next choice is to include a template app in this workspace. This is a choice that you can make now. A template app is under development that will allow you to share material with others outside of your company. Your final choice is also very important if you wish to use elements that you developed in this workspace in an application. After that, we'll discuss permissions and limitations, but for now, this investigation is centered on deciding whether or not a contributor role user ought to be permitted to modify an application that uses this workspace. The workspace administrator or the tenant administrator must respond to the query regarding data governance. In some situations, such as when you're developing something and want to be able to make modifications more quickly, you can approve that feature. But, you should disable it if it will be utilized in regular production to cut down on the number of people who could inadvertently change the files and disturb the workflow. The workspace will become available and the Save button will turn yellow after all the data has been entered. You need to know that Pro Workspaces lack a diamond next to them. Users will always see a diamond next to the name of a **Premium per User or Premium per Capacity** workspace. This is done to assist users in determining the kind of workspace that is being used.

Managing Users in a Workspace

View, Filters, Settings, Access, and Search are some of the features that can be accessed from the home page of any workspace. These options are located in the top right corner of the page. Access is the thing that we are searching for. When we select that button, a pane that looks very much like the **Workspace Generation** window slides in from the right side of the screen. In this pane, we can add people to the workspace.

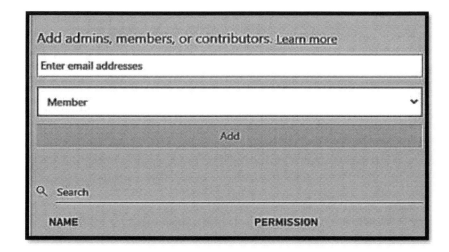

As shown in the image below, Power BI can and will look for people as you type their email addresses or, if you have any, Microsoft 365 groups, if your organization uses Windows or Azure Active Directory. Regardless of whether your business uses Windows or Azure Active Directory, Power BI integrates seamlessly with the instance of an organization's active directory. With a few clicks, you may add entire groups to a workspace. Additionally, you can add several people at once by entering multiple emails in the corresponding fields. Keep an eye out for the line that appears beneath the email address. At this point, we decide what kind of access a user will have to the workspace that we've made available to them. Users in a workspace can be given one of these four roles: **Admin, Member, Contributor, or Viewer**. An individual with a lower position cannot affect the user access of an individual with a higher function due to the hierarchical structure of these roles. An Admin can, for example, kick a Member out of the workplace or remove them from a workspace, but a Member cannot do any of those things to an Admin. Only admins can remove other admins. Administrators and Members can modify workspace elements that are used outside of the workspace or take actions that impact users within the workspace. Contributors can work on items that are contained inside the workspace, but they often cannot engage with the way that external viewers interact with workspace data pieces. Viewers are unable to make any changes to any of the items in a workspace and can only see the things that are present in the workspace.

Establish a minimum of one service account for workspace management. A service account is owned by the company as a whole rather than a particular user, and the login credentials are only accessible to a limited number of people. This service account should be assigned as an Administrator to each workspace even if it isn't usually logged in. You would have to use the Power BI Admin API to elevate someone else to the position of Admin for the workspace if the workspace's single Admin were to depart the firm for whatever reason. Alternatively, you can find the best course of action for you and your organization in this regard with the help of the data governance policies that your firm may have in place. It is crucial to make sure you have a strategy or plan in place so you can regain control of the workplace if employees cause a disturbance.

Remove a user or change their role in a workspace

Right next to the stated permission, there is an ellipsis (three dots) that you will notice. It functions as a button, and clicking it will cause a little pop-up window to appear with a list of the responsibilities that can be transferred to another person. At the very bottom of the list, there is a button that says Remove. They will be removed if you select Remove from the menu. The individual in question will change to the chosen role when you click on it. Given that Power BI doesn't even ask you to affirm your decision to act on the question in the confirmation notification, this part of the process may be a little too straightforward. However, if you do make a mistake, it is simple to correct, as shown by how straightforward it is to add users, as you can see here.

Adding Users to Roles for RLS Implementation

You have arranged your workspace such that only those with permission can use it. As of right now, each dataset in the workspace that has different responsibilities set for it requires you to add them to RLS. Since the real difficulty lies in identifying the jobs in the first place, this is not a particularly tough process to complete. When you are on the workspace landing page, move your mouse pointer over the dataset to which you want to add users or groups using RLS until the dataset name appears next to a vertical three-dot ellipsis option. Click the ellipses, then select the Security tab. When you do this, you will see the list of roles and the individuals who are currently in those roles in the dataset if you have roles selected for your Power BI dataset. You can view any roles that you have established for your dataset by clicking this link. Your Microsoft 365 account allows you to add people or groups. One thing to bear in mind is that if a user belongs to multiple groups, Power BI will treat them as though they had full access to any combination of data that may exist between the various roles they perform. This conduct is comparable to a SQL outer join. The picture below shows the simple user interface for adding users to RLS. Similar to the process of adding users to the workspace, Power BI will make an effort to locate people when you enter the right email address or group name.

You may want users to be able to interact with the data items you've developed at some time, even if you don't intend to bring those elements to the workspace directly. This can be accomplished by incorporating them into an application that is driven by a workspace. A sizable "Create app" button may be found in the top-right corner of the workspace homepage page. We have several options on this first page of the setup procedure. We offer our app a name, a description, and the option to include a link to a help or documentation page so that users may get help from us when they need it. We may also select the color scheme for the app's UI, offer a logo, and, lastly, provide the contact details of the person who should be contacted for app access. By now, all of this should look very familiar since it aligns with our prior experiences with the building of workspaces. You will notice that there are a few more things that need to be taken care of before you click the **"Publish app" button**. The Navigation and Permissions tabs will come after the Setup tab. First, let's review them in the order they were given: Navigation.

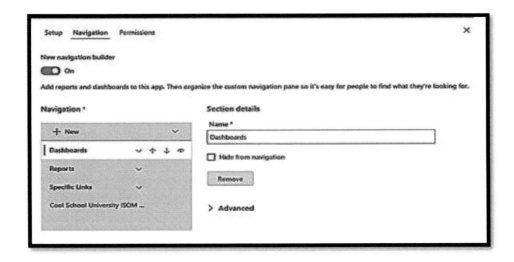

An on/off toggle allowing us to select whether to use the new navigation builder is the first item we see. Give your users a consistent experience if you are starting from scratch with applications by leaving this setting alone. In the future, the previous choice will most likely be eliminated if you are just getting started with apps. An application contains only the data products; it contains none of the underlying core data. For example, we include reports and dashboards in an application but do not give any datasets or dataflows. Looking at the Navigation pane on the left, you will notice that every dashboard and report that is currently in the workspace has been imported into the application. In this case, the generic dashboard that was created automatically when I submitted my PBIX file belongs to me in addition to the actual report. These components are shown in the gray menu located in the left-hand column. It is more appropriate to say that an object has been hidden within an application than that it has been completely removed. By selecting the small eye icon next to the up and down arrows, you can remove items from the list that you do not wish to be included. If there is a slash in the eye, then the object will be concealed. When you click the **+New** button, navigation becomes helpful since you can add a section or a link. A section functions very similarly to a show folder. It is not possible to establish a folder structure with many levels — there cannot be folders inside folders here. You can specify a link to a web page, which may or may not be included inside Power BI, as well as the action that the web browser should do to view the link.

Upon creating a section, you will see locations to name the section and an option to hide the section from the navigation in the area to the right. It is also an option not to display the part in the menu. Creating a link involves naming the app element, providing its URL, selecting how the link should open when clicked, and selecting a group to place the element in so that it can be navigated. By now, your navigation system should be nicely configured and arranged. The next step is to determine who should have access to the app and what underlying rights are granted by access to the datasets that run the app in the background. It's also up to you to decide who gets to use the app. Give yourself some time to comprehend it; it's a lot of information. As you can see, deciding who should be granted access is the first stage. Does it cover the entire company? Are specific individuals or groups inside the organization the target? When we discuss groups, we are referring to Microsoft 365 groups. It is also said by Power BI that everyone who has access to the workspace will also have access to the application. This makes great sense, for the same reason that RLS does not affect a workspace administrator. An administrator can easily get the PBIX for a workspace. Anyone with access to the workplace can examine the content; all they have to do is go there. Next, we determine if users who can access the application will be able to open connections to the dataset that forms the basis of the program and if they can make copies of the reports that are contained in the application and utilize them in their work areas. The order of these two choices is hierarchical. Reports cannot be copied if the underlying datasets to which the app refers cannot be accessed by the user. However, just because you have access to the datasets does not guarantee that you can replicate the reports. One is required, but it is not adequate on its own. Next, we must choose whether or not to allow users to use the share permission to share both the application and the datasets that support it. The lack of a distinct hierarchy also strikes me as odd. Usually, I try to make sure that users may ask the team that controls the program for access to the app somewhere instead of turning on this feature. This is not the case in circumstances where things are freely exchanged. Finally, a link to more Microsoft documentation can be found here, and users who have access to this page can choose whether or not to have this application installed automatically. Because it can be so helpful to end users, automated installation is something that I have no problem leaving switched on. We can then release the app after this. After the application has been packed, which may take anywhere from five to ten minutes on average, it will show up in the Apps area of the Power BI Navigation menu. If you need to update the app, go back into the workspace that hosts the app, and you'll see that the button labeled "**Create app**" has been replaced with the one labeled "**Update app**." That sums it up well. You now own an application!

The Golden Dataset(s)

At some point, when you manage Power BI implementation, you will discover that you have gathered a sizable number of data points. As you expand the amount of these data elements, you will encounter computing difficulties. In an environment where every report is based on its dataset, which is constantly updated, you have a lot of moving parts to monitor. If you have a lot of datasets updating against corporate databases, it could give your poor DBA a heart attack. Therefore, please do not have that many datasets. God forbid. What proportion of the information in both databases is, for no apparent reason, identical? Many of the analysts who were utilizing Power BI and driving this field forward were lacking in strong solutions when the Power BI service started to shine. This is because these inquiries were made before the service was established. But why should this be any different from the thousand other Excel worksheets that are scattered throughout the office? The issue is that, at some point in time, data items become crucial to the operation of the organization. We need to handle them as if they were assets that are vital to the purpose. Therefore, to examine how we needed to handle this issue, we needed to take a peek at the history of Power BI and recall what it is like below the hood. It is the Analysis Services department. How would we oversee the implementation of Analysis Services across the entire company? Either a small number of manageable datasets or a single, comprehensive master dataset would be established. The amount of computer effort that the other parts of our data pipeline would need to perform would decrease if we accomplished this. We can accomplish the same thing with Power BI by creating the master dataset, also referred to as a golden dataset, or by any other name you prefer. We will be in a better position if we can reduce the frequency of large-scale data queries that we run across our databases. The fewer locations at which we are responsible for managing RLS, the simpler the task will be. The fewer datasets we have to handle, the more confident we can feel in putting our finest data pieces in front of our data consumers. This gives us greater peace of mind, as we are aware that there is a greater possibility of being able to respond to the inquiries that users have. We accomplish this goal by making the data more accessible. Does this mean that everything can only be managed using one dataset? Not in every situation. A data mart-like structure could be used to organize data, resulting in a small number of datasets that have been carefully selected to answer specific types of questions while maintaining their position as reusable data pieces. Using RLS as an example, this may be demonstrated. The methods of defining roles using DAX and determining which roles are present in a Power BI dataset are distinct from one another. It is important to keep in mind to access the Power BI service, locate the dataset on the Workspace landing page, hover over it to reveal an ellipses menu, click it, select Security, and ensure that the individuals or groups are added to the roles you have created. You will need to manage those responsibilities in three different locations if you have three datasets that are comparable to one another. What happens if you don't do it even once and one of the datasets doesn't get updated as a result? This suggests that the data is accessible to unauthorized parties.

In certain environments, like a Premium Per Capacity environment, where you may have hundreds or even thousands of report watchers who may belong to dozens of groups and for whom you are trying to control access, there's a considerable risk that this may turn into a more serious issue. Does this mean you should stop considering utilizing Power BI for ad hoc or spontaneous analysis once your organization reaches a certain size? Naturally, no! With any luck, you should be able to utilize your dataset—or a small number of datasets—to quickly find the answers you seek. On the other hand, while looking for data, you may need to think creatively at times. In big settings that use **Premium per Capacity**, Microsoft advises customers to separate the capacity they use for business-mission-critical tasks from the capacity they use for ad hoc exploratory tasks. I think this is a great idea, and even in non-premium situations, it is quite easy to put into practice utilizing workspace management. To ensure they have the data they require, when your users begin creating reports, encourage them to connect to datasets in the Power BI service as data sources in Power BI Desktop. As a result, the dataset's size will shrink. In my experience, far too many organizations with massive datasets have concluded that using Power BI is just too hard. Because they lacked appropriate governance norms, users eventually reached a point where they could no longer remember where all the resources accessible to them were.

On-Premises vs. Cloud Deployment for Power BI

On-Premises Deployment

The term "**on-premises deployment**" refers to the process through which a company hosts the Power BI architecture inside its own data center or on its servers. **The following are some important things to keep in mind while planning an on-premises deployment:**

1. **Data Security:** Businesses regularly regard protecting sensitive information as one of their top priorities. Businesses and other organizations have complete control over their data when they choose on-premises deployment, which guarantees that private data is always maintained inside their network and under their direct supervision. Businesses that handle highly sensitive data or those subject to tight compliance regulations may find this control to be crucial.

2. **Data Governance**: A deployment that is done on-premises gives companies more control over the management of their data. IT teams can develop and enforce compliance procedures, data privacy policies, and access controls based on the unique requirements of each firm. This level of control ensures that the data are managed and shared in a manner compliant with the organization's policies.

3. **Connectivity**: On-premises implementation can be helpful when working with data sources that are situated inside private networks or behind firewalls. Because the Power BI architecture may be kept on-premises, organizations can establish direct connections to these sources without having to expose them to the internet. This tactic provides real-time data access and analysis, both of which could be crucial in particular kinds of business situations.

4. **Customization**: With an on-premises deployment, businesses can tailor the Power BI environment to meet their unique requirements via the addition of new components and the modification of existing ones. This flexibility is especially advantageous for businesses that have specific data needs, intricate data models, or that need to integrate with pre-existing computer systems. It makes it possible to build customized functions such as custom data connections, security enhancements, and other specialized features.

Cloud Deployment

Cloud deployment, on the other hand, refers to the process of hosting the Power BI infrastructure on the Azure cloud platform provided by Microsoft.

Let's look at some of the benefits of using this approach:

1. **Scalability**: Given that cloud deployment offers an unparalleled degree of scalability, businesses may leverage the vast computing resources that the cloud has to offer. Businesses can easily handle enormous volumes of data, accommodate growing user populations, and scale their analytical capabilities in response to demand with cloud-based Power BI. This

scalability eliminates the need for expensive infrastructure design, providing an efficient and cost-effective solution.

2. **Accessibility**: As long as the device has an internet connection, users may view Power BI dashboards and reports on any device, anywhere, thanks to a cloud deployment. Geographically dispersed teams find it easier to make choices in real-time when there is accessibility to resources that promote collaboration and enable remote work. Furthermore, cloud-based Power BI, which makes data insights available on mobile devices like smartphones and tablets, supports mobile apps.

3. **Maintenance and Updates:** Businesses no longer have to worry about the upkeep of their infrastructure or software updates thanks to cloud deployment. Microsoft is in charge of maintaining and updating the underlying infrastructure, which they undertake to ensure high security, performance, and availability. As a result, companies can concentrate more of their efforts on using Power BI for data analysis and less on platform technical upkeep.

4. **Integration and Ecosystem**: Cloud-based Power BI connects easily with other Microsoft Azure services and a broad variety of apps from third parties, enabling businesses to build full data ecosystems. Integration with Azure services like Azure Data Factory, Azure SQL Database, and Azure Machine Learning extends the capabilities of Power BI and makes it possible to implement complex analytics and machine learning scenarios.

When deciding between an on-premises deployment and a cloud deployment, there are a few things to keep in mind. Several aspects should be taken into consideration before settling on either an on-premises or cloud deployment for Power BI.

1. **Security and Compliance**: Examine the compliance guidelines and security requirements that are relevant to your company. In industries where data security is paramount, such as healthcare and banking, on-premises implementation is frequently the preferred option. However, because of advanced security measures and compliance certifications offered by cloud providers like Microsoft Azure, many businesses are now able to evaluate cloud deployment as a viable option.

2. **Cost**: Analyze the one-time and ongoing costs related to cloud vs on-premises implementations. In addition to continuing infrastructure maintenance, on-premises deployment frequently requires higher upfront costs for both hardware and software licensing. On the other hand, subscription-based pricing for software deployment in the cloud allows companies to pay for the resources they use.

3. **Scalability and Growth**: When thinking about the future expansion of your company's data volume, user base, and analytics needs, keeps in mind the scalability of your solution. Deployment in the cloud has the benefit of scalability and flexibility, making it possible for your business to expand smoothly as it expands. If you anticipate large development or if you need the capacity to scale up or down quickly, the cloud may be the most suitable option for you.

4. **IT Expertise:** Examine the IT resources and capabilities that your business has access to. When employing an on-premises deployment option, a higher level of technical proficiency is needed to manage the on-premises infrastructure and ensure its high availability. While cloud deployment reduces the number of tasks related to infrastructure management, it still

requires expertise in both managing cloud resources and integrating them with other services.

Scaling Power BI Deployments for Enterprise Use

Scaling Power BI installations becomes essential for guaranteeing the platform's efficacy and efficiency as enterprises continue to develop and their data analysis requirements get more complicated. **When growing Power BI installations for business usage, the following are some essential considerations and best practices to keep in mind:**

1. Data Modeling and Optimization:
   - **Implement effective data modeling techniques**: It is essential to the system's speed and scalability that an optimal data model be designed. Make use of best practices, such as building relevant associations, intelligently designing calculated columns, and, if required, putting data partitioning into action.
   - **Make Use of DirectQuery and Live Link**: Consider using DirectQuery or Live Connection to create a real-time link to the data sources rather than importing all of your data into Power BI. Large datasets benefit greatly from this method's ability to obtain data dynamically while also assisting in the removal of redundant data.
2. Data Source Considerations:
   - **Optimize data sources**: Ensure that data sources are correctly indexed, and optimize queries to decrease the amount of time spent retrieving data by running them.
   - **Leverage data source-specific optimizations**: You should utilize optimizations specific to the data source to increase speed. Such optimizations include, for instance, query folding in Power Query, aggregations in Analysis Services, and partitioning in SQL Server.
3. Data Refreshment and Gateway Management
   - **Configure efficient data refresh schedules**: Determine the proper frequency of data refresh depending on the constraints placed on the data about its level of freshness. It is important to limit the strain on data sources to avoid doing needless refreshes.
   - **Utilize Power BI Gateways effectively:** It is feasible to connect on-premises and cloud-based data sources using Power BI Gateways. It is important to configure gateways in a way that balances security, resource consumption, and performance.
4. Power BI Premium:
   - **Evaluate Power BI Premium**: Enterprise installations may benefit from the increased scalability, performance, and advanced capabilities that are available with Power BI Premium. You should think about subscribing to Power BI Premium so that you can make use of its features and advantages, like expanded data capacity, paginated reports, and artificial intelligence capabilities.
5. Usage Metrics and Monitoring:
   - **Keep an eye on both usage and performance**: Take advantage of Power BI's monitoring tools and consumption statistics to gain insights into user behavior, report performance, and resource utilization. Determine which areas could have improvement and optimization by using these indicators.

- **Make sure you have alerts and notifications set up**: Establish proactive monitoring alerts so that you can get information about possible problems or performance deterioration, which will enable you to respond and resolve the problem quickly.
6. Collaboration and Governance:
   - **Establish a Role-Based Security System**: Define the proper roles and permissions to exert control over who may access the data, reports, and dashboards. Make sure that sensitive data is safeguarded and that only authorized persons may access it.
   - **Encourage collaboration and sharing**: Share dashboards and reports to create a collaborative atmosphere that appreciates teamwork. This will support the development of a cooperative culture. To facilitate teamwork and information sharing, take advantage of shared workspaces and other resources.
7. Training and Support:
- **Provide training and support**: Invest in training programs that will educate users on the best practices for using Power BI, as well as approaches for data modeling and performance optimization. Make continual help available to resolve concerns and queries raised by users.
8. Consider Future Growth:
- **Plan for Scalability and Future Expansion**: Consider future user growth, data volume, and analytical requirements. Scalability should be considered while designing a Power BI solution, taking into account factors like infrastructure, processing power, and data storage needs.

Best Practices for Power BI Deployment

For an efficient deployment of Power BI, rigorous planning and adherence to best practices are required to guarantee that performance, security, and user adoption are at their highest possible levels. **The following is a list of critical recommended practices for the deployment of Power BI:**
1. Planning and Requirements Gathering:
- **Establish the goals of the project very specifically**: The goals and objectives of the Power BI deployment must be communicated succinctly and effectively. Establish the target audience, the expected outcomes, and the reporting and analysis requirements.
- **Engage stakeholders**: Ensure alignment and improve the effectiveness of requirement gathering by including important stakeholders, such as business users, IT teams, and executives, in the planning process from the beginning to the end.
2. Data Modeling and Design:
- **Implement a robust data modeling strategy**: Take the time and make the effort to create a data model that fits the demands of the business and has a strong organizational structure. Normalize the data, explain the relationships among the data, and consider techniques for performance optimization such as indexing and data division.
- **Use calculated columns and measures judiciously**: You should try to limit the usage of computed columns since it can harm performance. Instead, rely on measures to carry out calculations while the program is running.

- **Apply data cleansing and transformation** Make the quality of the data your top priority by conducting the necessary steps required for data cleansing and transformation.

3. Security and Governance:

- **Implement role-based security:** Establish the roles that users assume and the access rights that they possess to enable the appropriate data to be accessed following those roles. Utilize row-level security, or RLS, to limit user access to specific data rows based on the user's particular context.

- **Establish data governance policies**: Define data governance principles, such as naming conventions, data categorization, and version control. Put in place procedures to ensure that these rules are followed and that data integrity is preserved.

4. Performance Optimization:

- **Optimization of the Data Refresh Schedules**: Establish the ideal frequency and time for data refreshes based on the requirements for the data's current state of freshness. Reducing the load on data sources is crucial to prevent unnecessary refreshes.

- **Utilize Power BI caching**: Make use of the caching mechanism in Power BI to increase the speed of queries and limit the amount of data source access.

- **Make use of aggregations and calculated tables**: One technique to make searches run more smoothly is to use pre-calculated tables and aggregations, especially when working with large datasets. Azure Analysis Services and Power BI Premium are two examples of tools that can be used to achieve this.

5. Data Source Connectivity and Gateway Management:

- **Select the most suitable data connection option**: Evaluate the data connecting options that are available for your data sources, such as DirectQuery, Import, and Live Connection. Your evaluation should take into account the data volume, real-time needs, and performance factors.

- **Optimize Power BI Gateway configuration:** Establish secure and durable connections between on-premises data sources and the cloud by effectively configuring Power BI Gateways. Optimizing the Power BI Gateway's settings will help achieve this. Routinely monitor and maintain gateways to guarantee proper data refresh and communication.

6. User Training and Adoption:

- **Provide Comprehensive Training**: Give users access to resources and training courses that will teach them about Power BI's features, best practices for creating reports, and self-service analytics. You should encourage users to experiment and explore with Power BI to aid with adoption.

- **Encourage user engagement and collaboration**: You should promote the use of shared workspaces, encourage comments and conversations, and share dashboards and reports with other users to foster a culture that values collaboration and information sharing.

7. Version Control and Deployment Lifecycle:

- **Implement version control**: Make use of version control systems like Git to keep track of changes made to the reports and dashboards in Power BI. This not only assures traceability but also makes cooperation easier and permits rollbacks if they are required.

- **Create a deployment lifecycle**: Establish a methodical deployment procedure to oversee the distribution and advancement of Power BI artifacts throughout various settings, such as development, testing, and production. You'll be able to monitor the adjustments and make sure they happen on time thanks to this. Using change management principles is the best strategy to ensure stability and prevent disruptions.

8. Continuous Monitoring and Improvement:

- **Monitor usage and performance**: Keep a regular plan for tracking usage trends, reporting on performance, and making sure that data sources are connected. Make use of Power BI's usage data, audit logs, and monitoring tools to pinpoint issue areas and implement preventative actions to address them.
- **Gather user feedback:** Request that users submit feedback on the dashboards and reports generated by Power BI. It is important to actively seek feedback to discover usability concerns, potential for development, and demands for new features.

Troubleshooting Licensing Issues in Power BI

Common Licensing Issues

- **Access Restrictions:** One common licensing issue is when users are unable to access specific features or reports due to license constraints. For example, users of Power BI's free edition may face limitations on data refresh rates and have limited access to the platform's collaborative features.
- **Problems with License Assignment**: There are situations when users may not be allocated the right license type. As a consequence, they may have restricted access to Power BI or be unable to use it at all. It is of the utmost importance to check that the appropriate licenses have been given to users following the needs of those users.
- **License Expiration:** A further issue may arise if a license is allowed to expire or is not renewed on time. This could lead to the termination of users' access to Power BI tools and reports. It is essential to regularly monitor licenses that are about to expire and to promptly renew them to minimize delays.
- **Sharing and Collaborating Restrictions**: Reports and dashboards might be challenging to share with external users if the required licensing is not in place. There's a chance that sharing capabilities in Power BI Free will be limited, necessitating an upgrade to Power BI Pro or Premium.

Troubleshooting Licensing Issues

- **Checking License Assignments:** The first step in resolving licensing issues is to confirm that users have been granted the right licenses to utilize. This task can be completed using either the Power BI admin portal or the Microsoft 365 admin portal. Licenses can be redistributed as needed if there are any discrepancies.
- **Activation of the License and License Renewal**: Check to see if licenses are current and renewed on schedule. Power BI licenses are frequently included in the price of a business's Microsoft 365 subscription. If users fail to activate or renew their licenses on time, they

may lose access to Power BI features. To avoid any disruptions, it is crucial to regularly verify when licenses are about to expire and to set up automated reminders.

- **Upgrading Licenses**: If customers are encountering constraints as a result of their current licensing tier, upgrading their licenses to Power BI Pro or Premium should be considered. This will allow for more features and capabilities to become available, such as increased possibilities for collaborative work and faster data refresh rates.
- **Troubleshooting Access Restrictions:** Check the licensing restrictions associated with the user's current license type if any specific features or reports aren't accessible. Determine whether the license restrictions or configuration settings are the source of the issue. By altering the license type or configuration settings, the access restrictions can be removed.
- **Seeking Support from Microsoft:** If the troubleshooting techniques do not resolve the license issues, it is advised that you contact the Microsoft support team. They can offer more guidance and counsel to resolve complex licensing concerns. Prepare to provide precise information about the issue, such as any error messages you may have seen and the steps you followed to reproduce the problem.

Tips for Optimizing Power BI License Costs

- **Understand Power BI licensing options**: There are some different licensing options available for Power BI, such as Power BI Free, Power BI Pro, and Power BI Premium. Make sure you are familiar with the capabilities and restrictions of each kind of license before attempting to choose which option will best meet the requirements of your firm.
- **Evaluate user requirements**: Examine the needs and usual behaviors of Power BI users. For many users who only need to view reports and dashboards, Power BI Free can be plenty; as a result, not every user may require a Pro license. It is advised to reserve Pro licenses for clients who require more advanced functionalities including data research, collaboration, and content creation.
- **Leverage Power BI Free**: If your primary goal is to consume reports and dashboards rather than create content or facilitate collaboration, go ahead and use the Power BI Free license. Power BI Free allows users to view reports and access shared content. By lowering the number of Pro licenses needed, it helps businesses save money.
- **Share reports and dashboards efficiently**: Instead of distributing Pro licenses to each user, take advantage of Power BI's built-in sharing features to collaborate on reports and dashboards. Users who do not have a Pro license can still see and engage with reports thanks to shared content, which reduces the number of Pro licenses that are necessary.
- **Think About Purchasing Power BI Premium**: Power BI Premium can be a good value if you have a large number of Pro users or need additional features like paginated reports, AI capabilities, or advanced data refresh choices. With Power BI Premium, users can see and collaborate indefinitely, which eliminates the requirement for separate Pro licenses.
- **Optimize data refresh frequency**: Based on the needs of the users, evaluate and make any necessary changes to the data refresh frequency. Increased resource requirements and higher license costs can result from frequently updated content. Establish an appropriate refresh schedule and frequency for each dataset by analyzing its usage.

- **Implement row-level security**: Make advantage of row-level security, often known as RLS, to limit data access following the user roles or permissions. This eliminates the need for separate reports and licenses by giving you the ability to generate a single report that can be customized to provide varying degrees of data access to various user groups.
- **Monitor license usage**: Use the audit logs provided by Power BI or other specialized monitoring tools to do regular checks on license use and user activities. Find any Pro licenses that aren't being used or aren't being used to their full potential, and then consider reallocating them to other users or, if necessary, downgrading those users to Free licenses.
- **Explore embedded analytics**: If you have users outside your organization who want access to reports and dashboards, you should consider using Power BI Embedded or Power BI Embedded Capacity to handle their needs. These solutions will enable you to integrate Power BI material into your portals or apps without having to buy Pro subscriptions for every external user.
- **Negotiate to price with Microsoft**: Engage in price negotiations with Microsoft or your licensing supplier if you have a big deployment or are planning a substantial expansion. You can also explore possible discounts or licensing solutions that are suited to the requirements of your business during these negotiations.

Conclusion

In conclusion, a thorough understanding of Power BI's licensing and deployment requirements is essential for both installing and utilizing the platform. Organizations can optimize their data analytics and reporting procedures by choosing the appropriate licensing model and using Power BI in a suitable environment. When selecting a Power BI licensing option, it's important to take into account many criteria, including the number of users, their roles and needs, and the functionality that is wanted. There are three different licensing tiers available for Power BI: free, Pro, and Premium. Each has different features and restrictions. Companies should evaluate their requirements and financial constraints to choose the best licensing option.

CHAPTER 10

THIRD-PARTY TOOLS

Get to Know Business Ops

For most programs, you can try to identify each component or extension, download and install each one individually, and then manage your material. In light of this, PowerBI Tips has created the Business Ops external tool manager, which is completely free to download. The heavy work of compiling a huge number of third-party tools into one place and making it easy for you to quickly install and configure the ones you want to use is taken care of by this website. Every time updated versions of the external tools links become available for usage, it is also updated continuously. The installer can be located within the ZIP file that is supplied as part of the download. You will see a user interface similar to the one in the image below once the installation is complete. By going to the Home landing page, you can view the release notes for the version of Business Ops that you have installed. The code is fully open source, so you may view the Git repository if you'd like. With Business Ops, you can install a ton of Power BI add-ons, get instant access to learning resources, create Power BI themes, use a gallery for custom visualizations that you can't get through AppSource, and find links to some of the best DAX resources on the planet.

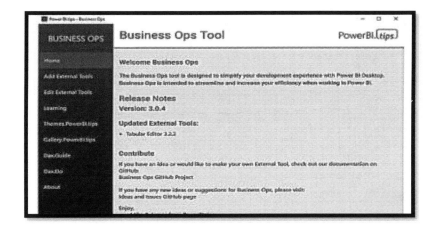

Add External Tools, Remove External Tools, and Modify Display Order

From this location, we can go to **Add External Tools** to see the list of external tools that **Business Ops** has curated. After viewing the list, we can then have those package files uploaded so that Power BI identifies them as external tools. You can do this with the use of a very simple checkbox interface. The scroll bar on the right side of the application may not be the easiest item to see, but rest assured that it exists despite the abundance of information on this page. Using the scroll wheel on my mouse is how I like to navigate when using this. This part will mainly cover the ALM Toolkit, Tabular Editor, DAX Studio, and Bravo. Click the blue **"Add External Tools" button** in the lower right corner of the screen once you have gathered all the tools you wish to add. Leave the remaining tasks to Business Operations after that.

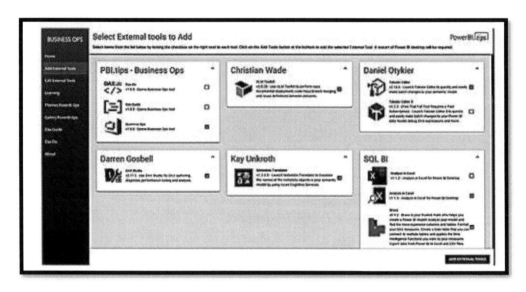

The Business Ops program and its add-ons, like the ones we are discussing here, are installed in the same folder. For certain reasons, this is a bad feature. Furthermore, Business Ops won't make separate entries for each program install it does in your Start menu. The behavior of installing the apps straight from their respective individual installers is different from this behavior. To circumvent this, I install the external tools, open a fresh blank Power BI file, and then use those external tools to force open the software I need to use. Right-click anywhere on the Windows taskbar, and after that, picks the option to **pin to Taskbar**. If you want to create separate shortcuts for your desktop, you will need to open Windows Explorer, browse to the program that you want to create a shortcut for inside the Business Ops directory, and then create the shortcut for the software in the same way that you would in any other version of Windows. In Power BI Desktop, you can adjust the order in which the tools appear in the External Tools area of the ribbon by going to the Edit External Tools section and choosing the relevant option from the drop-down box. If you'd like, you can even remove specific things from the list completely. A JSON file unique to each third-party program is automatically created during installation. By choosing the pencil icon, you can modify the filename. In Power BI Desktop, the accessible tools are arranged alphabetically and from left to right. Every JSON file begins by default with a three-digit code that establishes the order. If an item was installed using this program, you can also uninstall it from your External Tools list. To do this, click the garbage can that is located next to the Edit button. If you delete anything by mistake, you can always go back to **Add External Tools** and everything you currently have there will be grayed out when you do so. You can simply choose the tool you wish to restore and then add it once again.

Learning, Theme Generation, Visual Generation

The generator for custom themes is amazing! You can put together a theme with colors and other visual settings that you can adjust at the global or per-user visual level. After that, you can import it as a custom theme using Power BI Desktop. Additionally, this tool will provide you the hex codes for any color you select, so you may save them for any future reference you may need. On the left side of the page, you will see a color sliding scale. With this scale, you can follow the color sequence of red, orange, yellow, green, blue, indigo, and violet by going from red to violet and back again. At any position along that bar, the square corresponding to the color range you have picked will display a selection of lighter and darker hues for you to choose from, as well as the hex code for the color that you have presently selected. You can enter those codes directly in the input field at the bottom of the page if you already know your hex codes. For example, if the marketing department of your company provided you with your organization's hex-code color scheme, you could enter those codes.

If you check in the app's Gallery section, you may see a list of color schemes that have already been created in the Palette area. You can view an example page of the Power BI Report that illustrates how a color theme looks when coupled with visuals by clicking on any of the color themes listed in this section. This is a very helpful function. Within the Charts area, you will find a collection of custom graphics created with Microsoft's Charticulator, a visual design tool that lets users construct their graphics. You can download and import these custom visuals into the report that you are working on in Power BI Desktop. Importing the PBVIZ file will allow you to do this, after which it may be added as a custom visual. When you choose the **Create My Own** option inside the program, a fully operational version of Charticulator will appear for you to use. It is important to keep in mind that strictly speaking, this is a fork (or a clone of the code source) of Microsoft Charticulator. This is because Microsoft has made a few minor UI adjustments. On the other hand, the behavior of whatever you make in this version of Charticulator will be the same as if you had made it by going to the Charticulator website and making it there.

Additional DAX Resources

The folks at SQLBI have generously donated both the DAX Guide and the DAX.do websites to the public domain. Business Ops offers direct access to these two excellent DAX resources. Every DAX function is listed in the DAX Guide along with information on its syntax, the values it returns, real-world coding examples created using DAX best practices, and, for many functions, a YouTube video in the upper-right corner that offers even more details in an easily navigable video format. We can select a specific category of DAX functions to examine on the DAX Guide site, or we can find out which DAX functions are the most recent to be published together with the dates they were made available. Being able to see, on the left, which products a certain DAX function would work with is incredibly beneficial to me as someone who uses DAX in settings other than Power BI. This is not just a Power BI feature.

On the other hand, **DAX.do** is a fully-featured DAX playground that gives you the ability to edit and reorganize some aspects to make them conform to the testing method that you want. You have access to two data models inside the playground; these are the Contoso and the DAX Guide models. They are interchangeable at any moment. Data can be dropped and dragged between columns in the DAX.do column list. After noting which functions you are trying to use, it will provide you with a drop-down list so you may visit the DAX Guide pages for those functions. You can view your results, and you will receive the appropriate error message if you make a mistake when submitting your query. We would concentrate on some of the most beneficial third-party tools because Business Ops gives us access to a wide range of them. We will specifically go over a DAX editor, a dataset editor, and an intuitive tool for assessing the health of datasets and producing measurements. To start, let's talk about DAX Studio, which is the most potent DAX querying tool out there.

DAX Studio

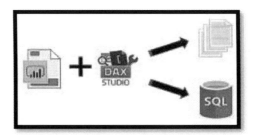

With the aid of DAX Studio, an open-source program that works with Power BI, you can create, execute, and review DAX queries. Data-centric analytical procedures can be performed using preconfigured codes, functions, and operators, together referred to by the abbreviation DAX. Concerning Data Analysis tasks, the Power BI DAX Library offers more than two hundred distinct functions, operators, and constants that provide a great deal of flexibility. Aside from this, DAX Studio is updated frequently with new features and functionalities to accommodate the inclusion of new capabilities. DAX Studio is pre-installed with an integrated query development and execution editor. This facilitates several functionalities, including object browsing, query editing and execution, formula and measure editing, integrated tracing, and query execution breakdowns. Stated differently, DAX Studio provides important details and information about the data model and your DAX queries.

What can you do with DAX Studio in Power BI?

- **Learn DAX Language:** DAX Studio not only assists you in authoring DAX queries and analyzing the performance of your data models, but it also aids you in becoming proficient in the DAX language. If you want to learn more about DAX, you can do so by navigating to the Home page and exploring the Query Builder there.
- **Optimize your Model Performance**: With the VertiPaq Analyzer, a DAX Studio-integrated tool, you can quickly and effectively enhance your model's performance. In addition to helping you solve the difficulties, it provides you with a brief overview of the data distribution and memory utilization. To gain insight into the way the formula is being handled, you may also run a measure in DAX studio and utilize the Server Timings tool.
- **Visualize DAX "table" Functions**: DAX Studio allows the results of DAX measures that contain a table function to be displayed. This enables you to examine the result table so you can make sure the right table is being generated. This capability is not available in the Power BI Desktop application.
- **Extract your measures into a Spreadsheet**: You can quickly extract a list of your measures from your DAX Studio data model into a Spreadsheet. This makes it simple for you to record and reuse the measures you've created.

Download, Install, and Setup DAX Studio Power BI

- Make sure you have downloaded the most recent version of DAX Studio to your computer before you start. This tool is available for free download at any time and is open-source. As soon as the file has been downloaded successfully, you can start the installation procedure.

- When the installation is running, you can choose either "**Current User" or "All Users**" to continue. It is highly suggested to make use of the **'All Users'** install option as the default since this option provides the user with the fullest possible experience.

- Enable Windows to access the application, and then accept the terms of the license agreement.
- Once you have chosen the target location, click the "**Next**" button.
- After selecting the components that you want to install, click the "**Next**" button.
- Proceed with the installation, and when it is finished, choose the "**Finish**" button at the bottom of the screen.
- On your system, the DAX Studio application has been installed successfully. Setting up a connection with Power BI is the next step. You can link DAX Studio to Power BI to use it by launching it directly from within the Program Files folder of Windows.
- The DAX Studio standalone application will ask you to select the type of connection you wish to utilize when you initially launch it. It can be linked to either a PBI file or a Tabular Server. You have the choice of both. Once a Power BI Desktop file has been opened, you can connect to any of them by selecting the relevant data model.

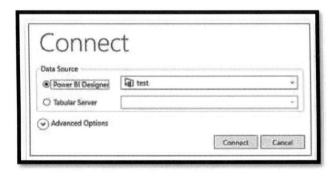

- Once you have chosen a kind of connection, click the "**Connect**" button;
- If you are attaching a PBI file, you can skip the "**Advanced Options**" step.

DAX Studio UI Basics

Now that DAX Studio and Power BI have been successfully linked, you can start interacting with the data models and making use of the fascinating features available in the DAX Studio User Interface (UI). DAX Studio is a vast tool, so let's start by going over some of the most important features of the user interface (UI).

1. Metadata Panel
2. The Ribbon
3. Query Pane
4. Output Pane

Metadata Panel

When you initially log into DAX Studio, the first thing you will see is the metadata of the tables in your data model. All of the tables, columns, and DAX measures that are a part of your data model are located in this panel, which is called the metadata panel. A symbol of a clock will be shown next to any table that has been marked as a "Date Table".

The Ribbon

The next part of DAX Studio is the ribbon, through which you can access all of the other functions. Let's talk about the many different significant options that are included inside this ribbon.

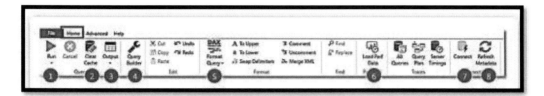

1. Choosing this "**Run**" button will cause your query to be carried out.
2. If you select the "**Clear Cache**" option, you will be able to erase the cache for the database that is now open.
3. Anytime you click the "**Output**" button, you will be able to choose the location to which you want the query results to be sent. From the Output Pane, you can also change the default output format to one of the other acceptable formats, such as Excel or a file (**CSV or TXT**).
4. Choosing this option brings up a drag-and-drop interface for the Query Builder.
5. The "**Format Query**" option makes use of the DAX Formatter service to produce a query that is properly structured and simpler to understand.
6. The performance data from Power BI Performance Analyzer will be imported by clicking "**Load Pref Data.**"
7. The connection to the Power BI Desktop files may be seen by clicking the "**Connect**" button. If you want to link DAX Studio to a different data model, you can do so by clicking this button.
8. Refreshing data is done manually when you click this button.

Query Pane

```
1 /* START QUERY BUILDER */
2 EVALUATE
3 SUMMARIZECOLUMNS(
4     'NBA Master Data'[NBA Season Year],
5     'NBA Master Data'[Player Team Name],
6     KEEPFILTERS( TREATAS( {"Miller"}, 'NBA Master Data'[Player Last Name] )),
7     KEEPFILTERS( TREATAS( {"Reggie"}, 'NBA Master Data'[Player First Name] )),
8     "Total Points Scored", [Total Points Scored],
9     "Count of Games Played", [Count of Games Played]
10 )
11 ORDER BY
12     'NBA Master Data'[NBA Season Year] ASC,
13     'NBA Master Data'[Player Team Name] ASC
14 /* END QUERY BUILDER */
```

You can write, modify, format, and view your queries in the Query Pane.

Output Pane

The results of your query are shown in this Output Pane, which is the default for the Output Pane. It has these three tabs:

- **Output:** You can get some basic information about the query's execution time in this section.
- **Results:** This is only a temporary storage place that is used to return the result table once the query has been executed.
- **Query History:** This shows a list of the queries that have been run in the past.

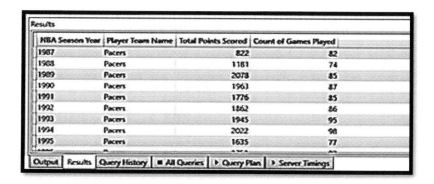

How to Write Queries in DAX Studio?

To write queries in DAX Studio, you can follow these steps:

1. **Connect to a data source:** Launch DAX Studio and establish a connection with the chosen data source. Numerous data sources, including Power BI Desktop, Analysis Services, Power Pivot, and Excel worksheets, are accessible through connections.
2. **Open the Query Editor:** After you have successfully connected, open the Query Editor by either clicking the "**New Query**" button that is located in the toolbar or by going to the "File" menu and selecting "**New Query**" from there.
3. **Write your DAX query:** When you're ready, open the Query Editor and begin creating your DAX query. Analysis Services, Power Pivot, and Power BI utilize the mathematical language known as DAX. While it contains some additional capabilities that may be useful when working with tabular data, it is essentially identical to the formulas present in Excel.

Here's an example of a simple DAX query to retrieve data from a table:

- *EVALUATE*
- *TableName*

Replace "TableName" with the name of the table you want to query.

4. **Execute the query**: After you have finished writing your DAX query, you can put it into action by either hitting the F5 key on your keyboard or choosing the "Run" button located in the toolbar.
5. **View the results**: After the query has been executed, the results will be shown in the bottom part of the Query Editor. You can review the data and conduct additional analysis if needed.
6. **Save the query:** If you wish to use the query in the future, you can go to the "File" menu and choose "**Save**" or "**Save As**" to save the DAX query file (.dax) to a specified place. This can be done if you want to store the query for future use.

And that's it! You have successfully created and executed a DAX query using DAX Studio. Best wishes! You can keep refining your query' precision, do computations, apply filters, and discover more about DAX's data analysis capabilities.

Tabular Editor

It is essential to be aware that Tabular Editor comes in not one but two unique versions, which are referred to respectively as Tabular Editor 2 and Tabular Editor 3. Tabular the initial solution developed is called Editor 2, and it is licensed under an open-source license. The same group that created Tabular Editor 2 also created Tabular Editor 3, which includes some more upgrades and improvements along with a more aesthetically pleasant user interface. The free, open-source version of Tabular Editor 2, version 2, will be covered. As of right now, Tabular Editor 2 can do all of the capabilities found in Tabular Editor 3 with the possible exception of greater effort. Tabular Editor will automatically connect to the Power BI data model that we currently have running when we open it from the External Tools list, just like it does when we visit DAX Studio. An easy-to-use editor for any SSAS tabular model is called Tabular Editor. It is comparable to the editor that serves as the foundation for Power BI data models. To get a sense of the interface's appearance, let's have a look at the image below.

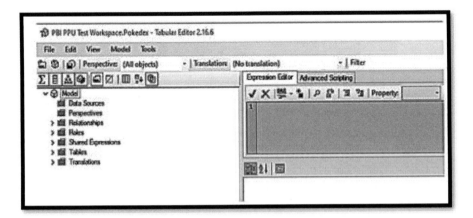

The File, Edit, View, Model, and Tools options are part of the standard Windows navigation, which is shown at the top of the screen. There are three distinct symbols after that. The first part is an open folder that opens whenever you save a copy of the model data in Tabular Editor, allowing you to access any BIM file created by the program. You can go to the files that Tabular Editor creates by opening this folder. Some businesses use BIM files, which are simply very large XML files, to fully manage their Power BI datasets in Tabular Editor. You may get BIM files here. In comparison to the PBIX equivalents, these files are of a far more manageable size, can be subjected to source control, and can be deposited in repositories. There's a picture of a translucent cube next to that. Any analytical services database that we have access to can be reflected in the Server section by changing the server URL. This includes datasets that are currently accessible through the Power BI service if you have enabled XMLA read capability. Remember that you will require at least the Premium per User licensing to accomplish this. The "Local instance" option allows you to select which of the Power BI datasets that is currently open in Power BI Desktop to connect to. If you need to pass a specific set of credentials, you can identify those credentials by selecting Username and Password and then providing the necessary information. Alternatively, you can use Windows or Azure single-sign-on credentials in either case. Azure can be accessed with a single click if you decide to use Windows single-sign-on credentials.

Lastly, inside that set, there is a symbol that resembles a disk save. If you make any changes in the Tabular Editor and then click this button, those changes will be sent to the database that the Tabular Editor is linked to. If that's the data model you're using for Power BI, any changes you make to the measures—whether they're additions, deletions, or edits—will be applied all at once. You developed some brand-new connections, right? These will also be added to the list. Have any new assignments been set? It is becoming clear to you. Once the button in question is pushed, Tabular Editor will return to the system it is now altering. Whether your data is stored locally or in the cloud, always make sure you have a backup of a Power BI dataset before making any changes to it. Just in case you make a mistake and need to go back to a previous state because you altered anything you hadn't intended to change, have a Power BI Template (PBIT) file or a BIM file handy. Nevertheless, there is an advantage associated with this. Assume for the moment that you wish to add a large number of distinct measurements to your data model. With Power BI Desktop, you have to create each one from scratch. There are moments when the user interface may seem a little slow. Although it is your responsibility to create the measure, you must go fix a mistake in the DAX. When the evaluation is complete, you will want to add it to your display folder for the sake of organization. However, you will need to accomplish this step one at a time. That's a real bother. You can submit many adjustments to the data model all at once using the Tabular Editor. And although you're working on things, the changes you make won't take effect on the data model until you save them. A few elements in Tabular Editor have a slightly higher learning curve than similar ones in Power BI Desktop. For this reason, I advise you to use Tabular Editor in a hybrid manner until you become more comfortable with the details needed to build many of these components outside of Power BI Desktop. You should employ a hybrid strategy up until then. The Model Navigation pane, on the left side of the screen, allows you to view every facet of your model.

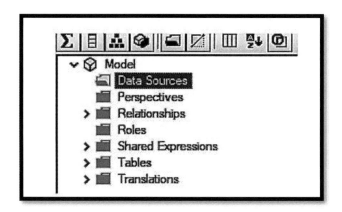

For each dataset created using Power BI Desktop, you will not be able to change or view the Data Sources. Seeing them is part of this. In Power BI, perspectives have a very particular use case: if the Personalize Visuals option is enabled, they can be applied to individual visuals. Perspectives are only relevant in this particular situation. Apart from that, they are inactive. They can be created with Power BI and included in the data model, but their functionality is limited to what was previously mentioned. When you want to create a new element related to a specific area of the data model, all you have to do is right-click on the element to bring up a contextual menu. This can be completed at any moment. I try to avoid managing connections via the Tabular Editor whenever feasible since I prefer a more visual way to comprehend how all the tables work together. However, this area also provides you with the opportunity to network if you so choose. This is something you will need to get used to if you are building a data model from scratch. We can also manage roles for RLS using Tabular Editor, and we can add measures, show folders, and other computed elements to our tables. The section under "**Shared Expressions**" provides a list of the parameters that may be found in the dataset, while the section titled "Translations" details the language (or languages) that can be used with the dataset.

Creating Roles

Step 1: Launch Tabular Editor

To get started, use Tabular Editor and load the project that contains your tabular models. The Tabular Editor offers a nice and intuitive user experience for the management of roles and other model components.

Step 2: Navigate to Roles

To expand the "Roles" folder, use the object tree view that is situated on the Tabular Editor window's left side. If any pre-existing roles are present in your model, you will be presented with a list of them. The folder will be empty if this doesn't happen.

Step 3: Create a New Role

Right-clicking the "Roles" folder will bring up a context menu; select "New Role" to create a new role. As a result, your model will have a new role to fulfill. To save the name, simply type in an informative name that accurately describes the role's function and hit the Enter key.

Step 4: Define Role Membership

The properties pane, which is situated on the right side of the window displaying the Tabular Editor, has the "Membership" tab. You can find out who the users or groups are that will be assigned this position in this section. Individuals or groups might be participants in the role. To add members to the role, click **the "..." button** next to the "Members" attribute. This will cause a member selection window to open. Here, you can choose Windows users or groups that you want to designate, or you can choose users or groups from your Active Directory. Make your desired selections and click the **OK button** to save the changes.

Step 5: Define Role Permissions

Select the **"Permissions" tab** from the properties pane. This is the section where you define the role's permissions, defining the items and information that the role's members can access. Permissions can be set at many various levels when using row-level security, including the model, table, column, and even individual row level. Expand your model's tree view inside the properties pane, then select the objects to which you wish to grant role members access or restrict it, to configure permissions. For every selected item, you can choose which permissions are accepted or rejected. These permissions can include Read, Write, or Process. In addition to this, you can specify permissions on a more detailed level for certain columns or measures.

Step 6: Save the Changes

Once you have defined the role membership and permissions, click the "**Save**" button in the toolbar or press **Ctrl+S** to save the changes to your tabular model.

Step 7: Test the Role

To assess the role, you will need to deploy your tabular model to a server (SQL Server Analysis Services, for example). Use a client tool such as Power BI to establish a connection to the deployed model. Use the login credentials of a user who already has access to the role you have defined when prompted. To confirm that the permissions are being used as expected, examine if the user can access the allowed objects and data but is blocked from accessing the banned ones.

Step 8: Maintain and Update Roles

It's possible that over time, roles will need to be updated in response to shifting user needs, adjusting permissions or access levels, or both. Utilize Tabular Editor to make any required adjustments to the role membership and permissions. To maintain data security and compliance, you should routinely examine and update your responsibilities.

Table and Measure Management

The development and administration of DAX-created items is the next area where Tabular Editor can save any Power BI developer time and effort. If your model has calculated tables, calculated columns, or measures, using Tabular Editor can almost immediately make your life easier. We can divide a table into numerous portions by right-clicking any table in my model and selecting "**Create New Measure, Calculated Column, Hierarchy, Data Column, or Data Partition**." We will be able to separate the table into several pieces as a result. If you have activated Incremental Refresh, you will notice that Power BI establishes the time-based divisions for you. This frees you from thinking about organizing the data and lets you concentrate on evaluating it. I have a lot of alternatives when it comes to the table; we can decide to hide it, copy it, or view its dependents. Right-clicking on a column allows us to link one column to another as well as build new display folders, measures, and calculated columns, hierarchies, and data columns. In addition, if you use the Tabular Editor to manage relationships, this can save you a great deal of time. You may also click and hold down the Control key to select many components at once. Let's say you create 10 new measures using the expression editor on the right. You may deploy them all at once with a single button click. You intend to move a collection of measurements into the newly created display folder, correct? That is something you can do. It is fascinating to watch how much quicker Power BI Desktop seems to adapt those adjustments when they are sent to it via Tabular Editor as compared to when you perform those things inside Power BI Desktop itself. Tabular Editor 2 does not provide version control on its own, nor does it maintain an accurate record of the changes you have made to the document. No matter how good you become at this, you will eventually make a mistake that needs to be fixed or reversed. This is the reason it is so crucial. You understand that the change might have been applied in a previous deployment.

The ALM Toolkit for Power BI

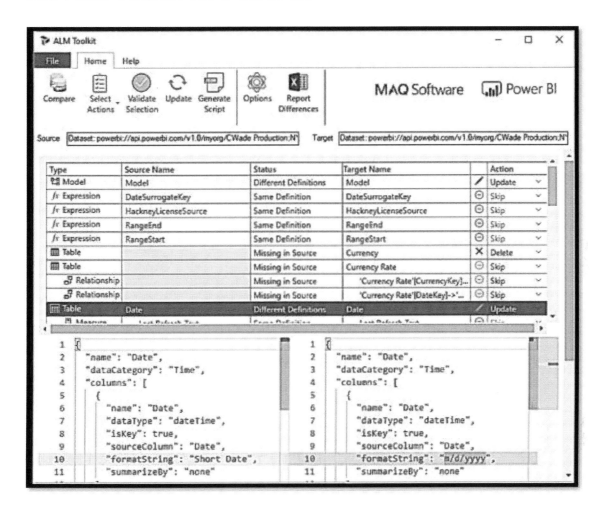

The **Application Lifecycle Management (ALM) Toolkit** for Power BI is a collection of tools and best practices that are intended to assist you in the management of the creation, deployment, and upkeep of Power BI applications in a way that is both regulated and effective. It offers features for controlling versions of Power BI assets, automating deployments, testing those assets, and documenting their use.

The following is an outline of the most important aspects and components of the ALM Toolkit:

- **Version Control Integration**: Through the integration of the ALM Toolkit with popular version control systems like Git, you can manage Power BI files (like. pbix and. pbit) and other pertinent artifacts (such as DAX scripts and data sources) in a version-controlled environment. Because the ALM Toolkit is integrated with various platforms, this is made possible. This furthers the controlled development process by enabling collaboration, change tracking, and rollbacks.

- **Automated Deployment**: The deployment of Power BI assets across development, testing, and production environments may be automated if you own the ALM Toolkit. It allows you to create deployment pipelines, specify target environments, and manage dependencies among the numerous components of your Power BI applications.
- **Testing and Validation**: The ALM Toolkit provides automated testing and validation of Power BI reports, datasets, and data models. This feature is part of the Testing and Validation module. During the process of creation and deployment of your Power BI assets, you can design test cases and scenarios to validate their correctness and dependability. This guarantees the quality of your BI solution and helps uncover problems or regressions that may have occurred.
- **Documentation Generation**: The process of creating documentation is an essential part of managing applications throughout their life cycles. The ALM Toolkit assists in the process of automatically creating documentation for your Power BI projects. This documentation may include report metadata, data lineage, and data dictionaries. This documentation helps gain a grasp of the Power BI solution as well as sustaining it over time.
- **Data Source Management:** One of the main purposes of the ALM Toolkit is to facilitate the management of data sources. Many data sources can be used in your Power BI projects, and you can create and maintain links to those data sources. This feature allows you to centrally manage the parameters of the data sources themselves and easily switch between numerous data sources throughout the deployment process.
- **Collaboration and Team Development**: Both of these tasks are supported by capabilities in the ALM Toolkit. Multiple developers can work on the same Power BI project at once, and the tools facilitate handling conflicts and combining modifications. It facilitates teamwork and improves the coordination of individual efforts within development teams.
- **CI/CD Integration**: The ALM Toolkit can be connected to CI/CD pipelines, which enables automation of build, test, and deployment procedures. The entire processes for development and release are streamlined as a result of this connection, which improves productivity and reduces the amount of human labor required.

The ALM Toolkit for Power BI improves the development lifecycle of Power BI projects by offering an organized approach to version control, deployment, testing, and documentation. This makes it easier to track changes and improve quality. It encourages cooperation, consistency, and dependability in the administration of Power BI assets, which eventually leads to solutions for business intelligence that are more effective and dependable.

Bravo

The Bravo software is an easy-to-use application that can help you instantly enhance the performance of your model. Bravo will open in the context of the Power BI Desktop file that is currently being used if you use it from Power BI Desktop. This conduct aligns with how every other external instrument we have employed functions. Information on datasets in Premium workspaces may be viewed by logging in to the Power BI service within the tool itself.

Analyze Model

When you launch Bravo, the Analyze Model window—which is displayed in the image below—will be the first thing you see. In a comparatively short time, we can utilize this to find out how big our dataset is, how many columns it includes, and—most importantly—how many columns are not mentioned within the model. It is important to note that Bravo is unable to ascertain whether any reports derived from the dataset might make use of one of these columns. Bravo, however, can give you some ideas about where to look for a solution if you wish to remove columns from your data model.

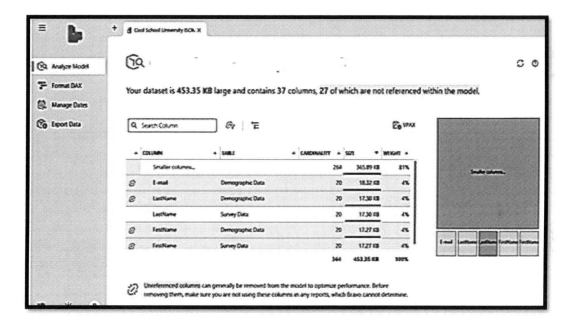

Another amazing graphic indicates the percentage of the model that is taken up by specific columns, or in my example, a group of smaller columns. If I choose the smaller columns collection in the columns list, the visual will also divide out those columns. Anything that has a yellow marker indicates that it is not currently being used in the model and could be a good candidate for removal. Using the search and filter functions—both of which are available—can be quite helpful if your model has a large number of columns. It is also possible to obtain a VPAX file, which is a file that is compatible with VertiPaq Analyzer, another program that was created by the people at SQLBI. My preference is to use Bravo to find columns that I may remove before committing my changes. Next, I'll deploy the modifications to an updated PBIT or BIM file by using the ALM Toolkit to create a record of the modifications made to the columns.

DAX Formatting

If you don't use Bravo for anything else, getting it only for the Format DAX page is worth it. You can see all of your measures, and the DAX Formatting service will read the script if you click **Analyze Now**. It will tell you how many of your measurements are incorrect and how many of your measurements are not formatted according to the DAX Formatting service's recommended guidelines. Measures can be chosen one at a time and prepared in bulk, or you can choose each one individually. A window displaying on the right side of the screen will appear when you click on a measure. You can see a preview of the formatted DAX and the format that is presently being applied in this window. If you have a strong reason to ignore a measure's formatting, you can do so; otherwise, you should concentrate on fixing the other formats. There is no need to have an unformatted DAX when you have something like Bravo; when your DAX is formatted and someone else's isn't, I guarantee that you will appear better than they do.

Manage Dates

Depending on the measurements that are already included in your model, you can ask Bravo to build a date table for you in addition to a multitude of time intelligence measures. By automatically producing hundreds of appropriately designed metrics, this application can help you save a great deal of time and accelerate the development of your program. That being stated, there's a catch. You are not allowed to have two things in your Power BI data model: one is another table that is already identified as your date table, and the other is the auto date/time function. Bravo will let you know whether the Manage Dates functionalities can be used with the data model that you currently have. If you can do so, you will be able to rapidly design a date table complete with predetermined time intervals, the language of your choosing, and even the option to choose which nation's holidays should be included in the model.

This device would already be considered amazing if that were all it was capable of. Things improve. You will be prompted to activate these measures in the time intelligence section. If so, you will be asked if you would like time intelligence to be built for all of your measures or just a subset of the ones you select. The following graphic should give you a general idea of how deep the measure rabbit hole in Bravo goes. It will also create display folders for you, which is a very useful tool. If you want to become better at DAX, there are some fantastic examples of how to create DAX utilizing time intelligence functions that you can use to help push you along in your DAX journey. If you want to get better at DAX, you can use these examples to help you get better at DAX.

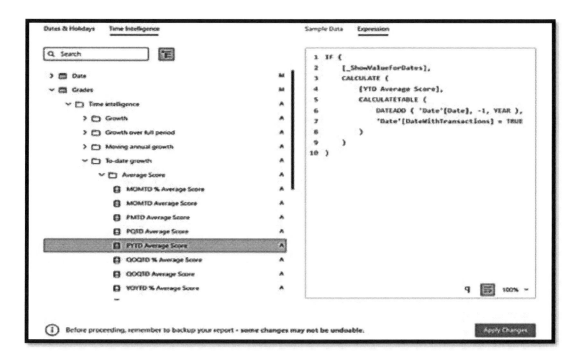

Export Data

Users can make use of the sophisticated visualization and analytical capabilities of Power BI with the data that is stored in Bravo by using a simple procedure that involves exporting data from Bravo to Power BI.

Understanding Bravo's Data Export Options

Before exporting data from Bravo, it is very necessary to have an understanding of the many export options that are at one's disposal and choose the format that is most compatible with Power BI. Exporting to **CSV (Comma-Separated Values), Excel, JSON (JavaScript Object Notation),** and maybe even other standard formats might be one of the many exporting features that Bravo provides. These formats offer flexibility and make data importation into Power BI easier and more compatible. Bravo can also provide you with an export summary page if you need more details about the data that was exported. Bravo will even present you with a visual link that you can click to access the file immediately once the export is complete and it has been saved. It can't export an infinite number of rows since as of right now, it can only export to Excel or CSV. If you have a procedure that requires you to get millions of entries from a table, you will almost certainly find that utilizing an Evaluate statement in DAX Studio and exporting the results from there is the most efficient course of action to take. On the other hand, if your table does not include millions of rows, using Export Data as a method to export data from a table in your data model can be an extremely useful option.

Preparing Data in Bravo

To ensure that everything goes smoothly throughout the export process, the data inside Bravo must be thoroughly prepared. For Power BI's reporting needs to be met, the data must be arranged and structured appropriately. Cleansing, formatting, and validating the data are all essential to maintaining its consistency and integrity. Bravo provides data preparation tools to help you enhance your data before exporting it. Filtering, sorting, and data aggregation techniques are some of these skills.

Exporting Data from Bravo

When the data is available, Bravo offers an export or downloads option that can be used to extract the data so that it can be used in Power BI. Find the export option inside the interface of Bravo. This option is often located in the menu or toolbar of the interface. Based on the needs you have for Power BI, choose the format you want to use (for example, **CSV, Excel, or JSON**). Follow the on-screen instructions to pick the particular data to export, such as the specific tables or queries, and then click "**Export**."

Conclusion

By using third-party apps, Power BI's functionality is increased and clients have better access to tools for data analysis and visualization. Apart from the features, customizations, and connectors that come with Power BI, these add-ons offer more features and functionalities. By adding third-party apps, users can increase Power BI's capabilities in a few areas, such as advanced analytics, data preparation, bespoke graphics, and access to a wide range of data sources. These technologies include advanced statistical analysis, predictive modeling, data profiling, and data cleansing capabilities, allowing users to gain deeper insights from their data. Custom visualizations created by outside parties offer unique visualization choices in addition to what Power BI's default visuals offer. These visualizations give users the ability to create more interesting and customized reports and dashboards by showcasing data in novel and visually appealing ways.

Commonly Used DAX Expressions

Aggregation Functions

Aggregation functions are used in DAX (Data Analysis Expressions) to perform calculations on a set of values within a column or table. These functions summarize or aggregate data based on specific criteria.

Here are some commonly used aggregation functions in Power BI:

1. **SUM:** Calculates the sum of a column or expression. Example: **Total Sales = SUM(Sales[Amount])**

2. **AVERAGE:** Calculates the average of a column or expression. Example: **Average Sales = AVERAGE(Sales[Amount])**

3. **MIN:** Returns the minimum value in a column or expression. Example: **Min Sales = MIN(Sales[Amount])**

4. **MAX:** Returns the maximum value in a column or expression. Example: **Max Sales = MAX(Sales[Amount])**

5. **COUNT:** Counts the number of rows in a table or column. Example: **Number of Orders = COUNT(Orders[OrderID])**

6. **DISTINCTCOUNT:** Counts the number of distinct values in a column or expression. Example: **Number of Customers = DISTINCTCOUNT(Sales[CustomerID])**

7. **COUNTROWS:** Returns the number of rows in a table or table expression. Example: **Total Rows = COUNTROWS(Sales)**

8. **MEDIAN:** Calculates the median value in a column or expression. Example: **Median Sales = MEDIAN(Sales[Amount])**

9. **VAR:** Calculates the variance of a column or expression. Example: **Variance = VAR(Sales[Amount])**

10. **STDDEV:** Calculates the standard deviation of a column or expression. Example: **Standard Deviation = STDDEV(Sales[Amount])**

11. **FIRSTNONBLANK:** Returns the first non-blank value in a column or expression. Example: **First Non-Blank Date = FIRSTNONBLANK(Sales[OrderDate])**

12. **LASTNONBLANK:** Returns the last non-blank value in a column or expression. Example: **Last Non-Blank Date = LASTNONBLANK(Sales[OrderDate])**

13. **DISTINCT:** Returns a one-column table with distinct values from a column or expression. Example: **Distinct Products = DISTINCT(Products[ProductID])**

14. **CONCATENATEX:** Concatenates values from a column or expression with a delimiter. Example: **Concatenated Names = CONCATENATEX(Customers, Customers[Name], ", ")**

15. **GROUPBY:** Groups rows based on a specified column or expression and apply an aggregation. Example: **Sales by Region = SUMMARIZE(Sales, Sales[Region], "Total Sales", SUM(Sales[Amount]))**

16. **RANKX:** Calculates the rank of a value within a specified column, optionally sorted by another column. Example: **Rank = RANKX(Sales, Sales[Amount], , DESC)**

17. **PERCENTILEX.INC:** Calculates the value at a given percentile within a column or expression. Example: **90th Percentile = PERCENTILEX.INC(Sales, Sales[Amount], 0.9)**

18. **TOPN:** Returns the top N rows based on a specified expression and ranking. Example: **Top 5 Customers = TOPN(5, Customers, Customers[TotalSales], DESC)**

19. **BOTTOMN:** Returns the bottom N rows based on a specified expression and ranking. Example: **Bottom 10 Products = BOTTOMN(10, Products, Products[Sales], ASC)**

20. **DISTINCTCOUNTNOBLANK:** Counts the number of distinct non-blank values in a column or expression. Example: **Number of Customers = DISTINCTCOUNTNOBLANK(Sales[CustomerID])**

21. **SUMX:** Calculates the sum of an expression for each row in a table, and then aggregates the results. Example: **Total Revenue = SUMX(Sales, Sales[Amount] * Sales[Quantity])**

22. **AVERAGEX:** Calculates the average of an expression for each row in a table, and then aggregates the results. Example: **Average Revenue per Customer = AVERAGEX(Customers, SUM(Sales[Amount]))**
23. **CALCULATE and ALLEXCEPT:** Modifies the filter context for an expression, removing all filters except those specified. Example: **Total Sales All Years = CALCULATE(SUM(Sales[Amount]), ALLEXCEPT(Sales, Sales[Product]))**
24. **FIRSTDATE and LASTDATE:** Retrieve the first or last date in a column or table, considering the filter context. Example: **First Sale Date = FIRSTDATE(Sales[OrderDate]) Last Sale Date = LASTDATE(Sales[OrderDate])**
25. **CONCATENATEX and VALUES:** Concatenates values from a column or expression, considering the filter context and returning distinct values. Example: **Concatenated Products = CONCATENATEX(VALUES(Products[Category]), Products[Category], ", ")**

Date and Time Functions

To work with and extract information from date and time values, utilize the date and time functions in DAX (Data Analysis Expressions). With Power BI, you can use these functions to calculate, compare, and transform date and time data.

Here are some commonly used date and time functions in Power BI:

1. **TODAY:** Returns the current date. Example: **Today = TODAY()**
2. **NOW:** Returns the current date and time. Example: **CurrentDateTime = NOW()**
3. **DATE:** Creates a date value based on specified year, month, and day. Example: **OrderDate = DATE(2023, 6, 14)**
4. **YEAR:** Extracts the year from a date value. Example: **Year = YEAR(Sales[OrderDate])**
5. **MONTH:** Extracts the month from a date value. Example: **Month = MONTH(Sales[OrderDate])**
6. **DAY:** Extracts the day from a date value. Example: **Day = DAY(Sales[OrderDate])**
7. **WEEKDAY:** Returns the day of the week as a number, where Sunday is 1 and Saturday is 7. Example: **Weekday = WEEKDAY(Sales[OrderDate])**
8. **EOMONTH:** Returns the last day of the month for a given date. Example: **EndOfMonth = EOMONTH(Sales[OrderDate], 0)**
9. **DATEDIFF:** Calculates the difference between two dates in specified units. Example: **DaysBetween = DATEDIFF(Sales[StartDate], Sales[EndDate], DAY)**
10. **TOTALYTD:** Calculates the year-to-date value for a specified expression. Example: **TotalSalesYTD = TOTALYTD(SUM(Sales[Amount]), Dates[Date])**
11. **SAMEPERIODLASTYEAR:** Returns a table that includes the same period as the current context, but in the previous year. Example: **SalesLastYear = CALCULATE(SUM(Sales[Amount]), SAMEPERIODLASTYEAR(Dates[Date]))**
12. **CALENDAR:** Generates a table with a continuous range of dates. Example: **DateTable = CALENDAR(DATE(2023, 1, 1), DATE(2023, 12, 31))**

13. **LASTDATE:** Returns the last date from the current context. Example: **LatestDate =** LASTDATE(Dates[Date])
14. **TODAY:** Returns the current date. Example: **Today = TODAY()**
15. **TIME:** Creates a time value based on specified hours, minutes, and seconds. Example: **OrderTime = TIME(9, 30, 0)**
16. **HOUR:** Extracts the hour from a time value. Example: **Hour = HOUR(Sales[OrderTime])**
17. **MINUTE:** Extracts the minute from a time value. Example: **Minute =** MINUTE(Sales[OrderTime])
18. **SECOND:** Extracts the second from a time value. Example: **Second =** SECOND(Sales[OrderTime])
19. **TIMEVALUE:** Converts a text string representing a time to a time value. Example: **OrderTime = TIMEVALUE("09:30 AM")**
20. **NOW:** Returns the current date and time. Example: **CurrentDateTime = NOW()**
21. **DATEVALUE:** Converts a text string representing a date to a date value. Example: **OrderDate = DATEVALUE("2023-06-14")**
22. **QUARTER:** Returns the quarter of the year for a date value. Example: **Quarter =** QUARTER(Sales[OrderDate])
23. **WEEKNUM:** Returns the week number for a date value. Example: **WeekNumber =** WEEKNUM(Sales[OrderDate])
24. **STARTOFYEAR:** Returns the first date of the year for a given date. Example: **YearStartDate = STARTOFYEAR(Sales[OrderDate])**
25. **ENDOFYEAR:** Returns the last date of the year for a given date. Example: **YearEndDate = ENDOFYEAR(Sales[OrderDate])**
26. **STARTOFQUARTER:** Returns the first date of the quarter for a given date. Example: **QuarterStartDate = STARTOFQUARTER(Sales[OrderDate])**
27. **ENDOFQUARTER:** Returns the last date of the quarter for a given date. Example: **QuarterEndDate = ENDOFQUARTER(Sales[OrderDate])**
28. **STARTOFMONTH:** Returns the first date of the month for a given date. Example: **MonthStartDate = STARTOFMONTH(Sales[OrderDate])**
29. **ENDOFMONTH:** Returns the last date of the month for a given date. Example: **MonthEndDate = ENDOFMONTH(Sales[OrderDate])**
30. **NEXTDAY:** Returns the next date after a given date. Example: **NextDay =** NEXTDAY(Sales[OrderDate])
31. **PREVIOUSDAY:** Returns the previous date before a given date. Example: **PreviousDay =** PREVIOUSDAY(Sales[OrderDate])
32. **ADDMONTHS:** Adds or subtracts a specified number of months to a date value. Example: **FutureDate = ADDMONTHS(Sales[OrderDate], 3)**
33. **ADDYEARS:** Adds or subtracts a specified number of years to a date value. Example: **FutureDate = ADDYEARS(Sales[OrderDate], 2)**
34. **DATESBETWEEN:** Returns a table of dates between two given dates. Example: **DateRange = DATESBETWEEN(Dates[Date], DATE(2021, 1, 1), DATE(2021, 12, 31))**

35. **TOTALMTD:** Calculates the month-to-date value for a specified expression. Example: TotalSalesMTD = TOTALMTD(SUM(Sales[Amount]), Dates[Date])

Time Intelligence Functions

Time Intelligence functions in DAX (Data Analysis Expressions) are specifically designed to perform calculations and analysis on time-based data in Power BI. These functions help in comparing, aggregating, and analyzing data over different periods. **Here are some commonly used Time Intelligence functions in Power BI:**

1. **TOTALYTD:** Calculates the year-to-date value for a specified expression. Example: **Total Sales YTD = TOTALYTD(SUM(Sales[Amount]), Dates[Date])**
2. **SAMEPERIODLASTYEAR:** Returns a table that includes the same period as the current context but in the previous year. Example: **Sales Last Year = CALCULATE(SUM(Sales[Amount]), SAMEPERIODLASTYEAR(Dates[Date]))**
3. **PREVIOUSYEAR:** Returns a table that includes the data for the previous year. Example: **Sales Previous Year = CALCULATE(SUM(Sales[Amount]), PREVIOUSYEAR(Dates[Date]))**
4. **PREVIOUSQUARTER:** Returns a table that includes the data for the previous quarter. Example: **Sales Previous Quarter = CALCULATE(SUM(Sales[Amount]), PREVIOUSQUARTER(Dates[Date]))**
5. **PREVIOUSMONTH:** Returns a table that includes the data for the previous month. Example: **Sales Previous Month = CALCULATE(SUM(Sales[Amount]), PREVIOUSMONTH(Dates[Date]))**
6. **DATESYTD:** Returns a table that includes all dates from the start of the year up to the given date. Example: **Sales Dates YTD = DATESYTD(Dates[Date])**
7. **DATESINPERIOD:** Returns a table that includes all dates in a specified period. Example: **Sales Dates in Q1 = DATESINPERIOD(Dates[Date], DATE(2023, 1, 1), DATE(2023, 3, 31))**
8. **FIRSTDATE:** Returns the earliest date from a given column or table expression. Example: **First Sale Date = FIRSTDATE(Sales[OrderDate])**
9. **LASTDATE:** Returns the latest date from a given column or table expression. Example: **Last Sale Date = LASTDATE(Sales[OrderDate])**
10. **OPENINGBALANCEYEAR:** Calculates the opening balance for a specified measure at the beginning of the year. Example: **Opening Balance Year = OPENINGBALANCEYEAR(SUM(Sales[Amount]), Dates[Date])**
11. **CLOSINGBALANCEYEAR:** Calculates the closing balance for a specified measure at the end of the year. Example: **Closing Balance Year = CLOSINGBALANCEYEAR(SUM(Sales[Amount]), Dates[Date])**
12. **TOTALMTD:** Calculates the month-to-date value for a specified expression. Example: **Total Sales MTD = TOTALMTD(SUM(Sales[Amount]), Dates[Date])**
13. **SAMEPERIODLASTMONTH:** Returns a table that includes the same period as the current context but in the previous month. Example: **Sales Last Month = CALCULATE(SUM(Sales[Amount]), SAMEPERIODLASTMONTH(Dates[Date]))**
14. **PARALLELPERIOD:** Returns a table that includes the data for the same period in a previous period. Example: **Sales Same Period Last Year = CALCULATE(SUM(Sales[Amount]), PARALLELPERIOD(Dates[Date], -1, YEAR))**

15. **DATESBETWEEN:** Returns a table of dates between two specified dates. Example: **Sales Dates Between = DATESBETWEEN(Dates[Date], DATE(2023, 1, 1), DATE(2023, 12, 31))**
16. **TOTALQTD:** Calculates the quarter-to-date value for a specified expression. Example: **Total Sales QTD = TOTALQTD(SUM(Sales[Amount]), Dates[Date])**
17. **SAMEPERIODLASTQUARTER:** Returns a table that includes the same period as the current context but in the previous quarter. Example: **Sales Last Quarter = CALCULATE(SUM(Sales[Amount]), SAMEPERIODLASTQUARTER(Dates[Date]))**
18. **PREVIOUSNMONTHS:** Returns a table that includes the data for the specified number of previous months. Example: **Sales Previous 3 Months = CALCULATE(SUM(Sales[Amount]), PREVIOUSNMONTHS(3, Dates[Date]))**
19. **STARTOFYEAR:** Returns the first date of the year for a given date. Example: **Year Start Date = STARTOFYEAR(Dates[Date])**
20. **ENDOFYEAR:** Returns the last date of the year for a given date. Example: **Year End Date = ENDOFYEAR(Dates[Date])**
21. **STARTOFQUARTER:** Returns the first date of the quarter for a given date. Example: **Quarter Start Date = STARTOFQUARTER(Dates[Date])**
22. **ENDOFQUARTER:** Returns the last date of the quarter for a given date. Example: **Quarter End Date = ENDOFQUARTER(Dates[Date])**
23. **STARTOFMONTH:** Returns the first date of the month for a given date. Example: **Month Start Date = STARTOFMONTH(Dates[Date])**
24. **ENDOFMONTH:** Returns the last date of the month for a given date. Example: **Month End Date = ENDOFMONTH(Dates[Date])**
25. **NEXTDAY:** Returns the next date after a given date. Example: **Next Day = NEXTDAY(Dates[Date])**
26. **PREVIOUSDAY:** Returns the previous date before a given date. Example: **Previous Day = PREVIOUSDAY(Dates[Date])**
27. **NEXTMONTH:** Returns the next month after a given date. Example: **Next Month = NEXTMONTH(Dates[Date])**
28. **PREVIOUSMONTH:** Returns the previous month before a given date. Example: **Previous Month = PREVIOUSMONTH(Dates[Date])**
29. **NEXTQUARTER:** Returns the next quarter after a given date. Example: **Next Quarter = NEXTQUARTER(Dates[Date])**
30. **PREVIOUSQUARTER:** Returns the previous quarter before a given date. Example: **Previous Quarter = PREVIOUSQUARTER(Dates[Date])**

Filter Functions

Filter functions in DAX (Data Analysis Expressions) allow you to apply specific filters to your data and calculate expressions based on those filters. These functions help you narrow down your data and perform calculations on specific subsets.

Here are some commonly used filter functions in Power BI:

1. **FILTER:** Returns a table that includes only the rows that meet specified criteria. Example: FilteredTable = FILTER(Sales, Sales[Amount] > 1000)
2. **CALCULATE:** Modifies the filter context by applying additional filters to the data. Example: TotalSales = CALCULATE(SUM(Sales[Amount]), Sales[Region] = "North")
3. **ALL:** Removes filters from a table or column, returning the entire table or column. Example: TotalSalesAll = CALCULATE(SUM(Sales[Amount]), ALL(Sales[Region]))
4. **ALLEXCEPT:** Removes filters from all columns except the specified columns. Example: TotalSalesAllexcept = CALCULATE(SUM(Sales[Amount]), ALLEXCEPT(Sales, Sales[Region]))
5. **RELATEDTABLE:** Returns a table that is related to the current table by a defined relationship. Example: RelatedProducts = RELATEDTABLE(Products)
6. **TOPN:** Returns the top or bottom n rows from a table based on a specified expression. Example: Top5Customers = TOPN(5, Sales, Sales[Amount])
7. **RANKX:** Calculates the rank of a value within a specified column. Example: Rank = RANKX(Sales, Sales[Amount])
8. **EARLIER:** Refers to a previous row context within an iteration of a calculation. Example: PreviousRowAmount = Sales[Amount] - EARLIER(Sales[Amount])
9. **USERELATIONSHIP:** Changes the active relationship between two tables for a specific calculation. Example: TotalSalesWithInactiveRelationship = CALCULATE(SUM(Sales[Amount]), USERELATIONSHIP(Sales[Date], Dates[CalendarDate]))
10. **SELECTEDVALUE:** Returns the value if there is only one distinct value in a column within the current filter context. Example: SelectedRegion = SELECTEDVALUE(Sales[Region])
11. **HASONEVALUE:** Checks if there is only one distinct value in a column within the current filter context. Example: HasOneRegion = HASONEVALUE(Sales[Region])
12. **SUMMARIZE:** Creates a summary table by grouping data based on specified columns and calculating aggregations. Example: SummaryTable = SUMMARIZE(Sales, Sales[Region], "Total Sales", SUM(Sales[Amount]))
13. **NATURALINNERJOIN:** Performs a natural inner join operation between two tables based on common columns. Example: JoinedTable = NATURALINNERJOIN(Table1, Table2)
14. **LOOKUPVALUE:** Returns the value from a column in a table that matches specified search criteria. Example: ProductCategory = LOOKUPVALUE(Products[Category], Products[ID], 123)
15. **VALUES:** Returns a one-column table that contains unique values from a specified column. Example: UniqueRegions = VALUES(Sales[Region])
16. **ISFILTERED:** Checks if a column or table is filtered. Example: IsRegionFiltered = ISFILTERED(Sales[Region])
17. **ISCROSSFILTERED:** Checks if a column or table is filtered by a specific column or table. Example: IsFilteredByRegion = ISCROSSFILTERED(Sales[Region], Dates[Date])
18. **CROSSFILTER:** Defines or modifies the cross-filter direction between two tables. Example: CrossFilterDirection = CROSSFILTER(Sales[ProductID], Products[ProductID], BOTH)
19. **RELATED:** Returns a single value from a related table based on a specified column. Example: ProductName = RELATED(Products[Name])

20. **KEEPFILTERS:** Retains the existing filter context while evaluating an expression. Example: **TotalSales = CALCULATE(SUM(Sales[Amount]), KEEPFILTERS(Sales[Region] = "North"))**

21. **FILTERS:** Returns a table containing all active filters in the current filter context. Example: **ActiveFilters = FILTERS(Sales)**

22. **REMOVEFILTERS:** Removes all filters from the specified table or column. Example: **FilteredTable = REMOVEFILTERS(Sales)**

23. **TREATAS:** Treats a table as if it were another table for evaluation purposes. Example: **FilteredSales = CALCULATE(SUM(Sales[Amount]), TREATAS({"ProductA", "ProductB"}, Sales[Product]))**

24. **ALLSELECTED:** Returns all the values that are currently selected in a column. Example: **SelectedRegions = ALLSELECTED(Sales[Region])**

25. **CALCULATETABLE:** Returns a table that is filtered by one or more expressions. Example: **FilteredTable = CALCULATETABLE(Sales, Sales[Amount] > 1000, Sales[Region] = "North")**

26. **ISEMPTY:** Checks if a table, column, or expression is empty. Example: **IsSalesEmpty = ISEMPTY(Sales)**

27. **USERNAME:** Returns the username of the current user accessing the data. Example: **CurrentUsername = USERNAME()**

28. **USERPRINCIPALNAME:** Returns the user principal name (UPN) of the current user accessing the data. Example: **CurrentUserUPN = USERPRINCIPALNAME()**

29. **USEROBJECTID:** Returns the object ID of the current user accessing the data. Example: **CurrentUserObjectID = USEROBJECTID()**

30. **USERROLE:** Returns the role of the current user accessing the data. Example: **CurrentUserRole = USERROLE()**

Logical Functions

Power BI uses logical functions in DAX (Data Analysis Expressions) to evaluate conditions and carry out logical operations. These routines provide decision-making, conditional expression creation, and data filtering using logical standards.

Here are some commonly used logical functions in Power BI:

1. **IF:** Evaluates a condition and returns different results based on whether the condition is true or false. Example: **Result = IF(Sales[Amount] > 1000, "High", "Low")**

2. **SWITCH:** Evaluates a series of conditions and returns a result based on the first true condition. Example: **Result = SWITCH(Sales[Region], "North", 1, "South", 2, "West", 3, "East", 4, 0)**

3. **AND:** Checks if all specified conditions are true and returns true or false. Example: **IsAllTrue = AND(Sales[Amount] > 1000, Sales[Region] = "North")**

4. **OR:** Checks if any of the specified conditions are true and returns true or false. Example: **IsAnyTrue = OR(Sales[Amount] > 1000, Sales[Region] = "North")**

5. **NOT:** Reverses the logical value of a condition or expression. Example: **IsFalse = NOT(Sales[Amount] > 1000)**

6. **TRUE:** Returns the logical value "true". Example: **IsTrue = TRUE()**
7. **FALSE:** Returns the logical value "false". Example: **IsFalse = FALSE()**
8. **XOR:** Checks if exactly one of the specified conditions is true and returns true or false. Example: **IsExclusive = XOR(Sales[Amount] > 1000, Sales[Region] = "North")**
9. **IFERROR:** Returns a specified value if an expression results in an error, otherwise returns the result of the expression. Example: **Result = IFERROR(1 / 0, 0)**
10. **BLANK:** Returns a blank value. Example: **Result = BLANK()**
11. **ISBLANK:** Checks if a value is blank and returns true or false. Example: **IsBlank = ISBLANK(Sales[Amount])**
12. **CONTAINSROW:** Checks if a table contains a specific row based on the specified condition. Example: **IsFound = CONTAINSROW(Products, Products[Category] = "Electronics")**
13. **ISFILTERED:** Checks if a column or table is filtered. Example: **IsFiltered = ISFILTERED(Sales[Region])**
14. **ISCROSSFILTERED:** Checks if a column or table is filtered by a specific column or table. Example: **IsFilteredByDate = ISCROSSFILTERED(Sales[Region], Dates[Date])**
15. **ISINSCOPE:** Checks if a column is in the current filter context and returns true or false. Example: **IsInScope = ISINSCOPE(Sales[Product])**
16. **ISERROR:** Checks if an expression results in an error and returns true or false. Example: **IsError = ISERROR(1 / 0)**
17. **ISNUMBER:** Checks if a value is a number and returns true or false. Example: **IsNumber = ISNUMBER(Sales[Amount])**
18. **ISTEXT:** Checks if a value is text and returns true or false. Example: **IsText = ISTEXT(Sales[Product])**
19. **ISLOGICAL:** Checks if a value is a logical value (true or false) and returns true or false. Example: **IsLogical = ISLOGICAL(Sales[IsApproved])**
20. **IFBLANK:** Returns a specified value if a value is blank, otherwise returns the value itself. Example: **Result = IFBLANK(Sales[Amount], 0)**
21. **COALESCE:** Returns the first non-blank value from a list of expressions. Example: **Result = COALESCE(Sales[Amount], Sales[Quantity], 0)**
22. **IN:** Checks if a value is found in a specified list of values and returns true or false. Example: **IsInList = IN(Sales[Region], {"North", "South", "West"})**
23. **INVERT:** Inverts the logical value of a condition or expression. Example: **IsFalse = INVERT(Sales[Amount] > 1000)**
24. **HASONEVALUE:** Checks if a column or expression has only one distinct value in the current filter context and returns true or false. Example: **HasOneValue = HASONEVALUE(Sales[Region])**
25. **RELATEDTABLEHASDATA:** Checks if a related table has data for the current row and returns true or false. Example: **HasData = RELATEDTABLEHASDATA(Orders)**
26. **AND/OR functions with multiple conditions:** You can use multiple AND or OR functions to combine multiple conditions. Example: **IsTrue = AND(Sales[Amount] > 1000, OR(Sales[Region] = "North", Sales[Region] = "South"))**

27. **SWITCH with multiple conditions:** You can use multiple conditions in the SWITCH function to evaluate different results. Example: **Result = SWITCH(TRUE(), Sales[Amount] > 1000, "High", Sales[Amount] > 500, "Medium", "Low")**
28. **&& (AND) and || (OR) operators:** DAX also supports the && (AND) and || (OR) operators for combining conditions. Example: **IsTrue = Sales[Amount] > 1000 && (Sales[Region] = "North" || Sales[Region] = "South")**

DAX Operators

You may execute a variety of operations on data in Power BI, including mathematical, comparison, logical, and text operations, by using DAX (Data Analysis Expressions). Within your DAX formulas, these operators facilitate the creation of expressions, calculations, and data manipulation.

Here are some commonly used operators in DAX:

1. Arithmetic Operators:
   - **Addition (+):** Performs addition between two values.
   - **Subtraction (-):** Performs subtraction between two values.
   - **Multiplication (*):** Performs multiplication between two values.
   - **Division (/):** Performs division between two values.
   - **Modulus (%):** Returns the remainder after division.
2. Comparison Operators:
   - **Equal to (=):** Compares two values for equality.
   - **Not equal to (<>):** Compares two values for inequality.
   - **Greater than (>):** Checks if one value is greater than another.
   - **Less than (<):** Checks if one value is less than another.
   - **Greater than or equal to (>=):** Checks if one value is greater than or equal to another.
   - **Less than or equal to (<=):** Checks if one value is less than or equal to another.
3. Logical Operators:
   - **AND:** Performs logical AND operation between two or more conditions.
   - **OR:** Performs logical OR operation between two or more conditions.
   - **NOT:** Negates a logical condition.
4. Text Operators:
   - Concatenation (&): Concatenates two or more text values.
   - Text Comparison Operators: DAX supports comparison operators for text values, such as =, <>, <, >, <=, >=.
5. Set Operators:
   - **UNION:** Combines two sets into a single set, removing duplicates.
   - **INTERSECT:** Returns the intersection of two sets.
   - **EXCEPT:** Returns the difference between two sets.

6. Membership Operators:

- **IN:** Checks if a value is a member of a set or a list of values.
- **NOT IN:** Checks if a value is not a member of a set or a list of values.

7. **Range Operators:**
   - **BETWEEN:** Checks if a value is within a specified range.
   - **NOT BETWEEN:** Checks if a value is not within a specified range.

8. **Parentheses:** You can use parentheses to group expressions and control the order of operations.

9. **Null-Coalescing Operator (??):** Returns the first non-null value from a list of expressions. Example: **Result = Sales[Amount] ?? 0**

10. **Unary Plus (+) and Minus (-) Operators:** Performs unary positive or negative operation on a value. Example: **PositiveValue = +Sales[Amount] NegativeValue = -Sales[Amount]**

11. **Power (^) Operator:** Raises a number to the power of another number. Example: **Result = Sales[Amount] ^ 2**

12. **Concatenation Operator (+):** Concatenates two or more text or numeric values. Example: **FullName = Customers[First Name] + " " + Customers[Last Name]**

13. Logical Operators in FILTER Function:
    - **&& (AND):** Performs logical AND operation within the FILTER function. Example: **FilteredTable = FILTER(Sales, Sales[Amount] > 1000 && Sales[Region] = "North")**
    - **|| (OR):** Performs logical OR operation within the FILTER function. Example: **FilteredTable = FILTER(Sales, Sales[Amount] > 1000 || Sales[Region] = "North")**

14. **IN Operator:** Checks if a value is in a specified list of values. Example: **IsInList = Sales[Region] IN {"North", "South", "West"}**

15. **CONTAINS Operator:** Checks if a text value contains a specified substring. Example: **ContainsSubstring = CONTAINS(Sales[Product], "ABC")**

16. **DISTINCT Operator:** Returns distinct values from a column or table. Example: **DistinctValues = DISTINCT(Sales[Region])**

17. **VALUES Operator:** Returns unique values from a column or table. Example: **UniqueValues = VALUES(Sales[Region])**

18. **SUMMARIZE Operator:** Creates a summary table by grouping data and calculating aggregations. Example: **SummaryTable = SUMMARIZE(Sales, Sales[Region], "Total Sales", SUM(Sales[Amount]))**

19. **TOPN Operator:** Returns the top N values based on a specified column or expression. Example: **Top5Customers = TOPN(5, Customers, Customers[Total Sales], DESC)**

20. **RANKX Operator:** Assigns a rank to each row in a table based on a specified column or expression. Example: **Rank = RANKX(Sales, Sales[Amount], , DESC)**

Some Favorite Custom Visuals

By using custom graphics in Power BI, you can increase the tool's functionality. Creating and adding your visualizations to your dashboards and reports is how you achieve this. This feature will allow you to display data in unique and imaginative ways, some of which may not be achievable with pre-installed visualizations. It's easy and quick to add a custom visual once you know where to look. In the Visualizations box, amidst all the fundamental Power BI visuals look for an ellipsis after the last image. When you click on this, a drop-down menu will appear, giving you the option to import an existing visual from a file, receive additional visuals, delete an existing visual, or restore the default visuals.

To use custom visuals in Power BI, you have a few options:

1. **AppSource Marketplace**: Users of Power BI can browse and download custom visualizations created by other users in the AppSource marketplace. The visualizations created by a wide range of companies and individuals satisfy the standards for this type of data visualization. You can download specific graphics that fit your requirements, search for them, and then utilize them in dashboards and reports that you design.
2. **Power BI Custom Visuals SDK**: Using the Power BI Custom Visuals SDK, you can construct your own custom visual if the custom visuals that are currently on the market don't meet your specific visualization needs. With this software development kit, you may create unique visuals using popular web technologies like HTML, CSS, and JavaScript. It also provides you with access to a number of tools, libraries, and sample code.

Using the SDK, you may produce graphics with unique capabilities for data processing, interaction, and display. Once a custom visual has been produced, you can use it in your dashboards and reports by saving it to your computer as a.pbiviz file and importing it into Power BI. Writing code to explain the behavior, rendering, and data interaction of a custom visual created using the Power BI Custom Visuals SDK will take up most of the time. You will receive documentation and APIs in the software development kit to assist you in the process. The specialized visuals that you design using the Software Development Kit (SDK) can be distributed to other people working for your company or uploaded to the AppSource marketplace to make them more widely available. A lot of unique images were created as PBVIZ files prior to AppSource becoming as commonplace as it is in the Microsoft ecosystem. You can choose that option to open an Explorer window, navigate to the file, and then choose it for import if you have a PBVIZ that you would like to import from a file, either from a custom visual that you have created using TypeScript or from an earlier version of a custom visual. You can use this option regardless of whether you used TypeScript to build the custom visual.

If you pick the "**Get more visuals**" option, an overlay will emerge that will lead you to a list of custom visuals that are accessible in AppSource as well as custom visuals that have been added to your organization. These custom visuals may be accessed by clicking on any of the options in the overlay. In the list of all visuals, things associated with your organization will always be shown in a more prominent position than those associated with other organizations.

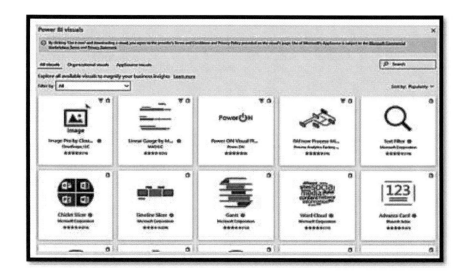

It is evident that all visuals, organizational visuals, and AppSource-only visuals have selection possibilities. It has the capacity to search. Furthermore, the ability to filter the images based on multiple categories is available. This category includes: Analytics, Advanced Analytics, and Change over Time, Filters, Infographics, Key Performance Indicators, and Maps. Frequently, the filter categories don't help you find what you're looking for. This is particularly the case in the Analytics domain, which is, in my view, too broad to be of any use. However, you can integrate search and filter into one action, which you may find more beneficial. Another benefit of using AppSource's custom graphics is that each one comes with an example PBIX that you can use to test out the functionality and discover more about its capabilities. This leads to an extremely low barrier to entry because you can see both the stated use case offered by the individual who generated the graphic and the image in its most effective form. After that, you can decide if it would be beneficial to you.

Here are some popular custom visuals that Power BI users often find valuable:

SandDance

With SandDance, a potent custom visual for Power BI, you can dynamically and visually explore your data. Navigating to the Custom Visuals section of the Power BI menu will get you access to SandDance. With its unique visualization toolbox, it can help you see patterns, trends, and insights that aren't always obvious when utilizing standard chart forms. After being developed independently by Microsoft Research, SandDance is now available as a custom visual in Power BI.

The following is a list of some of SandDance's most important features and capabilities:

1. **Multi-dimensional data exploration**: You can simultaneously analyze and visualize data across multiple dimensions with SandDance. It has interactive controls that let you associate

different properties of the data with visual elements like color, size, shape, location, and so on.

2. **Fluid and interactive visualizations**: SandDance is capable of supporting a wide variety of visualization formats, including scatter plots, bar charts, stacked charts, and many more. You can quickly switch between multiple visual representations and explore your data from a variety of viewpoints. The visualizations are quite interactive, enabling you to zoom in and out, filter the data, and sort it in a very fluid manner.

3. **Data transformations and grouping:** One major advantage of SandDance is that it allows you to perform grouping operations and data transformations from within the visual interface. This allows you to gather and condense the data based on a range of criteria, giving you a deeper knowledge of your data.

4. **Facets and insights**: The concept of "facets," or different viewpoints or slices of your data, is provided by SandDance. A more thorough analysis of your data is called an insight. By alternating between the aspects you've produced, you may compare and evaluate subsets of your data. You can create facets based on different features of your data. Furthermore, SandDance's analysis of your data allows it to automatically generate insights and recommendations based on the patterns it discovers.

You will find SandDance in the Visualizations pane of Power BI's report builder, which is where you employ it. After importing your data into Power BI, selecting it, and configuring it, you may alter the SandDance visual by mapping data qualities to visual properties. Upon completion of the configuration, you can interact with the visual to explore and analyze your data in a rich and user-friendly manner. SandDance is a powerful tool for data exploration and analysis, especially when working with complicated and multidimensional datasets. It can assist you in gaining fresh ideas and successfully communicating your results via the use of visualizations that are both aesthetically attractive and engaging.

Smart Filter Pro

A potent custom visual for Microsoft Power BI, Smart Filter Pro transforms how people interact with and filter data. Microsoft developed Smart Filter Pro. It enhances Power BI's built-in filtering capabilities and offers new features and functionalities to help customers get deeper understanding and extract valuable data from their datasets. The fact that it allows consumers to filter data makes these improvements possible. Smart Filter Pro is designed to simplify and streamline the filtering process in Power BI, making it more easily comprehensible and user-friendly. Users can quickly browse through vast datasets and zero in on the particular data subsets they want for analysis thanks to this visual. One of the standout features of Smart Filter Pro is its search functionality. Users can search for certain values or phrases inside the filter options, which speeds up data discovery and cuts down on the time spent laboriously going through lengthy lists of value possibilities by hand. This feature comes in quite handy when working with datasets that contain a lot of unique values or while searching for specific outliers or abnormalities. Smart Filter Pro has the ability to multiselect and search in addition to having hierarchical filtering. This functionality enables users to filter data based on hierarchical linkages, such as filtering data by region, country, and city. This feature allows users to analyze their data at many granularities and go deeper into the information. The ability to filter data hierarchically comes in particularly handy when dealing with complex data structures and when examining data from different organizational or geographical perspectives. Users can navigate through the data hierarchy and focus on certain subsets of data that are most pertinent to the study they are doing by expanding or collapsing hierarchical levels. Additionally, users of Smart Filter Pro can enjoy an aesthetically pleasing and easy-to-use user interface. The eye-catching design with its simple and modern layout ensures that the user experience won't be disrupted. Users can easily alter the visual's appearance to make it consistent with the overall theme and style of the reports they create using Power BI. A human resources solution called Smart Filter Pro can be used to filter employee data according to a variety of criteria, including tenure, job roles, and performance evaluations. This helps HR managers to learn more about the demographics of the workforce, spot talent gaps, and create efficient workforce planning plans.

Chiclet Slicer

One slicer that has choices for how many rows and columns of numbers you want to compress your options into is called the Chiclet Slicer. Since it has these controls, this slicer is one of my favorites. Another special feature of the Chiclet Slicer is that it allows you to connect photos with different "chiclets". A well-known example of this would be a report that covers multiple countries, maybe with a flag from each one included in each chiclet. I really enjoy how the Chiclet Slicer looks and works, even without the additional chiclet formatting. Microsoft first used car manufacturer logos as an example while announcing the Chiclet Slicer back in 2015. I like to keep my pictures for Chiclet Slicers on a SharePoint site or in a OneDrive folder. Subsequently, I like to include those links in my data model as Image URLs in a column. The visualization options and the Chiclet Slicer are shown below, as provided by Microsoft in the accompanying image.

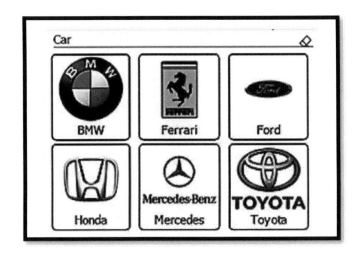

Timeline Storyteller

With the use of a timeline structure and a unique Power BI graphic, you can create engaging and interactive visual stories with the Timeline Storyteller. It gives you the ability to display information and occurrences in a sequential manner, giving your viewers a captivating and dynamic storytelling experience. Every data point and event in your data is shown at the appropriate moment on a horizontal timeline. You can customize a range of formatting settings, such as colors, fonts, labels, and scales, to build the timeline that you desire. It enables you to design transitions that are fluid and dynamic between various time intervals or periods that you have chosen. Within your timeline, you can establish numerous stages or phases, and then you can add animated transitions between them to create a smooth flow of information. You can construct a story with a Timeline Storyteller by including text, photographs, and notes at various points along the timeline. Because of this, you will have the ability to add context, explanations, and insights connected to the data points or events that are now being shown.

By engaging with the Timeline Storyteller graphic, users can explore individual data points or events, zoom in and out, and pan across different time periods. Depending on how they interact with the timeline, users will be able to filter or delve further into specific data. This may be achieved by connecting the visual to other visuals on the report page. Using Timeline Storyteller's many customization options can enhance both the overall narrative experience and the visual look. The layout, style, and interactivity may all be changed to suit your specific story needs. To utilize this Power BI capability, you must download and import the Timeline Storyteller as a custom visual into your report. Following the import of the data, you can add the Timeline Storyteller visual to your report canvas and personalize it by selecting the data fields that relate to the timeline and the associated information. The Timeline Storyteller is particularly useful when you want to present historical data, milestones, or a series of events as a narrative. It helps you effectively communicate the story that lies behind the numbers and engage your audience in an eye-catching manner.

Synoptic Panel

The Synoptic Panel is a specialized custom visual for Power BI that gives users the ability to present data on individualized floor layouts, maps, or any other individualized pictures. It gives you the ability to examine and analyze data in the context of certain places or layouts that you choose.

Here are some key features and capabilities of the Synoptic Panel:

1. **Custom mapping**: The Synoptic Panel gives you the ability to submit custom pictures to use as the backdrop for your visualizations. These images may be things like floor plans, maps, or diagrams. You can plot and show data points with the help of these photos by using them as a reference.
2. **Data mapping**: Once a custom image has been uploaded, you can choose areas or spots on the image where the data points you have supplied should be shown. Once the custom image

has been published, you can do this. Using the tools that come with the Synoptic Panel, these zones can be created and drawn in.

3. **Data binding:** Using the data binding functionality, you may connect your data to the specified regions on the personalized image. This means that specific sections or shapes displayed in the image can be associated with data values or metrics. At that moment, the Synoptic Panel will visualize the data by dynamically coloring or shading the areas based on the values of the data.

4. **Interactivity and drill-through**: Interactivity in the Synoptic Panel allows users to explore individual data points and engage with the visual. Drill-through makes this feature possible. You may configure actions and tooltips to display more information when a user clicks or moves their mouse over a data point.

5. **Customization and formatting**: The Synoptic Panel has some different customization options, which may be used to improve the data's readability and the way it appears visually. The colors, legends, labels, and tooltips can all be customized to meet the specifications of your design and to make the user experience more satisfying as a whole.

In order to utilize this Power BI capability, you must download and integrate the Synoptic Panel as a custom visual into your report. Once imported, you can edit the Synoptic Panel graphic by adding areas, binding data, and importing your own picture to your report canvas. Once the visual has been imported, you can proceed with this. The Synoptic Panel comes in particularly handy when you want to overlay data over personalized floor plans, maps, or images to gain perspective on certain locations or arrangements. It can be used in a variety of use cases, such as facility management, retail shop analysis, event planning, and many more, where it is essential to visualize data within the context of a particular layout.

Word Cloud

One type of data visualization that is being used for a growing variety of information types is the word cloud. The process of counting the frequency at which a word appears results in a word cloud. We are most likely to apply this image in the domain of marketing analytics where we are trying to gain some understanding of customer sentiment or identify the topics that are dominating a conversation. In the event that we were conducting a focus group and examining the participants' opinions regarding a product, we would be curious to see which terms were most frequently used to characterize my offering. Survey results also make reference to this as a good deal. Using a word cloud, for instance, it would not be difficult to generate a visual depiction of the selection count. You can choose which terms to remove from the word cloud using this graphic, and you can also choose to deactivate a predefined list to make the word cloud appear less crowded. By entering your own words to be deleted in the Formatting part of the Visualization window that comes with this visual, you may also choose which words are left out. Several more words might be added to the list by just placing commas between the items. Certain words may be given "weights" while examining emotion. You can do so by utilizing the values section of the Visualization pane. This will allow you to add the weights.

Card with States

One powerful tool in Microsoft Power BI is the "Card with States" custom graphic, which allows users to present critical metrics or figures in an engaging and interactive fashion. A thorough and simple way to communicate important information and track performance is the Card with States graphic. Its ability to display data utilizing a range of states or thresholds makes this possible. The Card with States visual's ability to highlight specific data points or values based on predetermined states or thresholds makes it particularly useful in these situations. Depending on their data, clients can declare multiple states or circumstances, such good, warning, and critical, among others. Users can easily and graphically depict a measure's performance or condition by selecting the color that best fits each potential state. Given that the graphic provides a quick and easy explanation of the data by using colors to signify separate states, users may quickly identify sections that require attention or further study. This allows users to quickly grasp the data. One of the most important features of the graphic representation called the Card with States is how easily custom states and thresholds can be defined. Users can set their own thresholds or ranges based on their data and business requirements. It is possible for users to set multiple revenue growth criteria, for example, low, moderate, and high growth rates in a sales scenario.

These growth rates can be as low as 0% or as high as 100%. By adjusting the states and thresholds, users can alter the visual to suit their needs and ensure that the information displayed adheres to their business context. There are numerous modification options available for the Card with States visual, which can be utilized to enhance the product's usefulness as well as its visual appeal. To make sure that the presentation of the card matches the general theme and style of their Power BI reports, users can change the card's appearance, including the font styles, colors, and backdrop designs. This customisation feature enhances the overall quality of the user experience by ensuring coherence in the report's visual presentation throughout. In project management, the visual depiction of a Card with States can be utilized to track significant project milestones, monitor project progress, and identify potential risks or delays. Project managers can utilize either the percentage of work performed on a project or specific milestones within a timetable to define states. The visual uses color-coded cards to visually depict the project stage, providing a concise and comprehensive overview of several projects. This makes it easier to effectively manage the projects and make decisions about them. In operational dashboards, where it can be used to track key performance indicators (KPIs) across several departments or processes, the Card with States graphic is very useful. It is also helpful when used in relation to financial dashboards. With the help of the visual, users may identify areas for improvement, track and evaluate key performance indicators (KPIs) in real-time, and take proactive measures to increase operational efficiency. The user's ability to alter the states based on performance standards makes this possible.

Radar Chart

With the help of a visual tool called a radar chart, you may see data from multiple variables at once and obtain a more complete picture that takes into account all of those variables. Since the scales of the axes that correspond to the various variables will differ from one another, the axes should not be thought of as comparable to one another in general. The example in the figure below contrasts the actual number of new hires made in each division versus the number of new hires predicted for each division for the purposes of demonstration. Although we do not necessarily know what the exact numbers are, we can easily compare how well each group fared with actuals to predict in a broad interpretative sense. The video game Street Fighter 5 is one of my favorite instances of the usage of the radar chart that does not include Power BI. In this game, each character has a radar chart that indicates their "stats" out of a rank of 5, which makes it easy to determine which characters have which kinds of overall advantages. Which kind of characters do you prefer: fast and possessing lots of special moves, or vibrant and powerful characters? The radar chart shows that it is a type of chart with numerous applications since it operates flawlessly in that context as well. Furthermore, it's easy to use with Power BI because all you need is a list of categories and numbers for the y-axis.

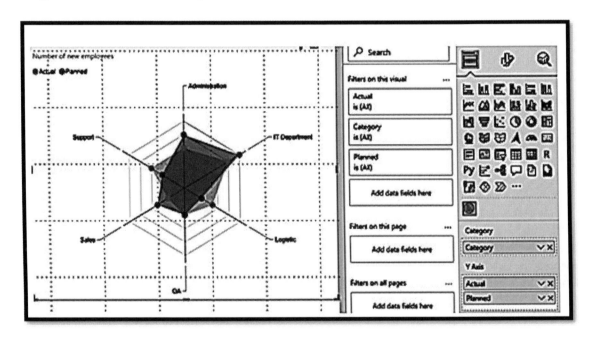

Hexbin Scatterplot

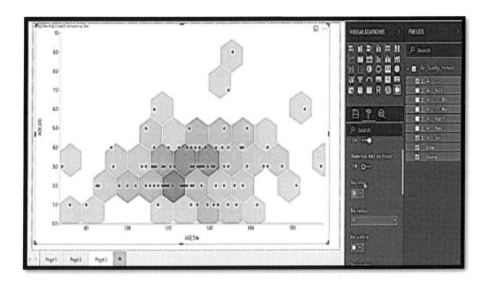

Within Microsoft Power BI, the Hexbin Scatterplot is a very effective and aesthetically pleasing custom visual that can be used for data analysis and visualization. It offers a novel and very efficient method for visualizing and analyzing huge datasets that include a significant number of data points that overlap one another. The Hexbin Scatterplot was developed to overcome the limitations of conventional scatter plots when working with datasets that have a high data density. In a scatter plot, it can be challenging to identify patterns, trends, and correlations when there are a lot of overlapping points. In a scatter plot, individual data points are represented by markers. The Hexbin Scatterplot classifies the data points into hexagonal bins in order to solve this issue. Each bin's size or color intensity indicates how many data points it contains. This kind of binning reduces clutter and provides a more accurate representation of the data distribution.

The Hexbin Scatterplot is an excellent tool in many areas, but its ability to handle large datasets is one of its most noteworthy features. When hundreds or even millions of data points are involved, traditional scatter plots can become visually bewildering and hard to interpret. On the other hand, because the Hexbin Scatterplot arranges data points into hexagonal bins, it can get around this problem. The underlying patterns and trends in the data are preserved along with the visible clutter by means of this data aggregation procedure. By combining data points, the Hexbin Scatterplot allows users to examine broad trends and pinpoint areas with high or low data density. This provides a more thorough perspective of the data. The Hexbin Scatterplot is created by grouping data points. The color scheme of the Hexbin Scatterplot is another crucial element. Because each hexagonal bin's color intensity correlates to the number of data points included inside it, users are able to discern between regions with high and low data densities with clarity. The use of color encoding facilitates the visualization of the distribution of the data and aids in the identification of concentration patterns, clusters, and outliers within the dataset. Users can select a color scheme that best suits their preferences for the data and how it is shown, resulting in a visually appealing and comprehensible representation of the data. There are interactive features in the Hexbin Scatterplot as well, which can help with data exploration and analysis. To engage with the visualization, the user can move over the plot, zoom in or out, and hover over certain hexagonal bins to view more details about the data points that are included within them. This interactive feature enables users to explore specific regions of interest and obtain targeted information from the presentation. By interacting with the Hexbin Scatterplot, users can find correlations, clusters, or outliers in the data, facilitating more thorough data analysis and wise decision-making.

Hierarchy Slicer

For Power BI, a unique visualization called the Hierarchy Slicer was created. It provides an easy-to-use and entertaining way to filter data according to hierarchical structures. The data displayed in other visualizations can be filtered by users by navigating through a hierarchy and selecting specific levels or nodes.

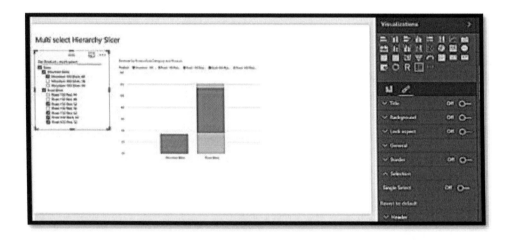

Hierarchical data structures, such as product categories, organizational hierarchies, geographical areas, or any other hierarchical data you have in your dataset, may be visualized with the help of the Hierarchy Slicer. It presents the hierarchy in the form of a tree view that can be collapsed, allowing users to traverse between various levels of the hierarchy by expanding or collapsing individual nodes. Users can select one or more nodes from the hierarchy to filter the data displayed in other report page visualizations. When a node is selected, the Hierarchy Slicer will send the selected values to other visualizations. This will make it possible for the other graphics to display and update data relevant to the chosen node or hierarchy level. Users can view many tree structures inside of a single visual representation by using the Hierarchy Slicer. This means that multiple tiers of hierarchies, including product categories, subcategories, and individual commodities, can exist within a single slicer. To develop complicated filtering combinations, users can traverse and choose nodes from several hierarchies. The Hierarchy Slicer comes with some different customization options, allowing users to alter both its look and its functionality. To fit the design and user experience needs of your report, you can adjust the font, colors, and icons, as well as the behavior of expand/collapse, and other visual characteristics. To utilize this Power BI capability, you will need to download the Hierarchy Slicer and import it as a custom visual into your report. You may add the Hierarchy Slicer graphic to your report canvas and configure it by selecting the field or fields that represent the hierarchical data in your dataset once it has been imported. By selecting the "Configure" button, you can accomplish this. After that, users can choose which levels or nodes within the hierarchy to expand or compress, as well as interact with the Hierarchy Slicer by doing so. The other report page visuals will alter in response to the selected hierarchy values, offering a dynamic and targeted perspective of the data. When working with datasets that have hierarchical relationships and need a versatile and easy-to-use method of filtering data based on these hierarchies, the Hierarchy Slicer comes in handy. This is so that you can slice data based on multiple hierarchical levels at once using the Hierarchy Slicer. By helping users explore and analyze data at various levels of granularity within a hierarchy, it allows them to gain deeper insights and analysis.

Gantt chart by MAQ Software

With its indefinite existence, the Gantt chart has grown to be an essential tool in the project management industry. A type of bar chart called a time series bar chart allows you to identify activities based on the number of steps involved and the estimated time needed to complete them. AppSource offers a variety of Gantt chart alternatives, but for the purposes of this discussion, I'll be using the Microsoft version. One of the things that people like best about this version is that you can make it as general or particular as you like. Ten distinct field options are available to you in this Gantt chart for data entry. The remaining fields are optional; just the task field needs to be filled out. Because the illustrations are not in project management very regularly, users frequently go to PBIX's easily readable help page when they need to recall which field performs what. This is a result of their infrequent use of project management. Some people wish that some of the basic visualizations could access some of the formatting options present in this chart. However, you can utilize the Gantt chart in "**off-label**" use cases to borrow some of that capability for more traditional bar chart use cases.

Bullet chart

A type of data visualization tool called a bullet chart is frequently used to show a metric's performance in relation to a target or threshold value in business dashboards and reports. It provides a concise and condensed representation of the data, making it easy to compare the actual values with the desired or expected values.

The Bullet Chart consists of the following elements:

1. **Target/Threshold Line**: This horizontal line depicts the value of the target or threshold against which you wish to evaluate the actual value. It helps determine if the actual number is lower than, on par with, or higher than the objective.

2. **Actual Value Bar**: This bar of a different color indicates the actual value or measure that you wish to see. The magnitude of the actual value is represented by the length of the bar in this graph.
3. **Qualitative Ranges**: The actual value bar is often separated into several colored ranges or zones that reflect qualitative levels. These ranges and zones are known as qualitative ranges. For instance, you can use color coding to signify poor, good, or great levels of performance.
4. **Performance Measures**: Additional indicators, such as the performance from the year before or benchmarks for the industry, can be added to the Bullet Chart to offer additional context and comparison.

A Bullet Chart can be used to quickly and readily evaluate performance, spot gaps, and determine whether the actual value matches or surpasses the goal or threshold. When tracking key performance indicators (KPIs) or advancing toward goals, it is quite beneficial. You can utilize Power BI's built-in Bullet Chart visualization, or you can experiment with custom visualizations from the marketplace that offer more customization possibilities and enhanced functionality.

Sunburst Chart

The Sunburst Chart is a captivating and informative custom visual in Microsoft Power BI that provides a unique and visually appealing way to represent hierarchical and categorical data. With its circular layout and interactive features, the Sunburst Chart enables users to explore and analyze complex data structures, identify patterns, and gain insights into the relationships between different levels of a category.

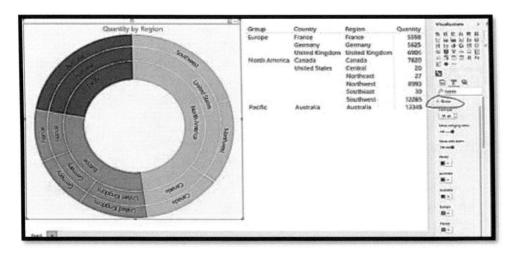

The Sunburst Chart was created to show hierarchical data in a radial style similar to a pie chart or sunburst. Both of those chart styles' structures are comparable to this one. It is made up of concentric rings, each of which is broken into sectors that reflect the values or subcategories that are included inside each level. These rings stand for the several levels of a category or dimension.

The size of the sectors itself indicates the proportion or amount of values that they reflect. The Sunburst Chart's circular design makes it easy for users to navigate the data structure and understand the hierarchical linkages. Tooltips and highlights give users an interactive experience with the Sunburst Chart. Tooltips are brief pop-up windows that show up when the mouse is over a data area. They enhance the user's understanding of the data by offering more details about the data piece, such as contextual information. Users can also select specific sectors or pathways within the picture to emphasize specific data points or compare different segments. Because of the interactivity that facilitates data exploration and analysis, users can interact with the chart to gain deeper insights from the data. The Sunburst Chart's color encoding is another important element that helps with a better understanding of the data. Users can assign various colors to the sectors based on specific categories or attributes of the data. This facilitates the process of distinguishing and recognizing the individual segments as distinct entities. Color encoding makes it easier for users to compare figures across multiple levels and subcategories, spot patterns, and identify irregularities. Users can select a color scheme that best suits their preferences for the data and how it is shown, resulting in a visually appealing and comprehensible representation of the data. The **Sunburst Chart** is a tool that can be used in the field of financial analysis to assess expenditure breakdowns. In this chart, each level represents a separate category of expenses. Financial analysts can find possibilities for cost optimization and budget allocation by visually representing the proportions of and linkages between different types of expenses. This diagram can be used in project management to analyze how resources are allocated and to show the hierarchy of the project visually. A comprehensive view of the project's development and resource utilization is offered by the ability to utilize each level to symbolize various project phases, tasks, or resources. Project managers can use the Sunburst Chart as a tool to identify bottlenecks, manage resources efficiently, and track project success at multiple levels.

Conclusion

Organizations can harness their data and obtain insights that are actionable with the help of Power BI, a flexible and potent business intelligence solution. With Power BI, users can turn unstructured data into insightful reports and dashboards that support data-driven cultures within organizations and promote informed decision-making. This is made possible by the software's user-friendly interface, wide range of connectivity options, strong data modeling capabilities, and rich visualization features. Power BI is a potent business intelligence tool created by Microsoft that has been thoroughly covered in this book. Throughout the guide, we have explored the key features, functionalities, and benefits of Power BI, as well as discussed various tips and best practices for effectively utilizing the platform. With the help of Power BI's extensive feature set, which includes data modeling, data analysis, and data visualization, organizations can convert unstructured data into meaningful insights. Because of its simple drag-and-drop interface, people with varying levels of experience may generate interactive reports and dashboards without needing to know a lot of coding.

We also talked about how crucial data visualization is to successfully communicating information and promoting better decision-making. With the extensive visualization possibilities offered by Power BI, users can show data in an engaging and interactive way using charts, graphs, maps, and tables. The guide has also emphasized a number of design best practices and concepts for producing powerful and intuitive dashboards and reports. Finally, we have discussed Power BI's collaboration and sharing features, which let users work together as a team, exchange ideas, and safely share reports both internally and outside the company. This fosters a data-driven culture and ensures that stakeholders have access to the right information at the right time. Users may easily combine data from multiple sources, including databases, cloud services, and spreadsheets, into a single, consolidated view by utilizing Power BI's connecting options. Organizations may obtain a comprehensive overview of their data and make well-informed decisions based on precise and current information thanks to this unified picture. Users may fully realize Power BI's potential in their company operations and optimize its value by adhering to the guidelines and best practices provided in this guide.

Best Practices for PowerBI

Limit the visuals in dashboards and reports

What is causing the report performance to slow down? The performance best practices for Microsoft Power BI emphasize that having a lot of visuals in one report is the cause of it.

You must take the following action to restrict the quantity of visuals in dashboards and reports:

- Keep the number of grids on each report page to a minimum of one, and keep the number of widget graphics to no more than eight per page.
- The maximum number of points on each page should be 30 (cards: 1, gauges: 2, charts: 3, maps: 3, grids: 5).
- Don't let a dashboard include more than ten tiles.

Remove various interactions between visuals that are not important

Are you curious about how to enhance the performance of Power BI reports? Here's a clue! That can be achieved by eliminating pointless visual encounters. This is made feasible by the fact that every visual in a report has the ability to automatically interact with each other. For best results, the interactivity should be adjusted and managed. Disabling unnecessary interactivity can also help to enhance report performance by lowering the quantity of queries that are executed at the backend.

Enable Row-Level Security (RLS)

RLS limits user access to certain rows in a database based on the attributes of the user running a query, while Power BI simply imports data that the user is permitted to view. However, how might significant performance gains be achieved? Combining roles from the backend with Power BI roles will enable this. Additionally, before releasing any roles to production, they must all be tested.

Make Use of Microsoft AppSource-certified custom visuals

Microsoft has confirmed that the custom visualizations with Power BI certification have reliable and efficient code. The only custom visuals that may be viewed in email subscribers and exported to PowerPoint are these AppSource images, which have undergone extensive quality testing.

Microsoft making hierarchical filters

Yes, in the event that you notice subpar Power BI performance, you should take that action. When you use hierarchical filters, are you disturbed by lengthy page loads? Give it a go! Take out the nested filters. Use several filters for the hierarchy in Power BI to get better performance.

Categorize the data for PowerBI reports

One of Power BI's best practices is providing data categorization for the Power BI reports (HBI, MBI, LBI). The Power BI data classification enables you to raise user awareness about the security level that is required to be used. This also helps you understand how reports should be shared inside and outside the organization.

The categories can be listed as follows:
- HBI or High Business Impact data needs users to obtain a policy exception to distribute the data eternally.
- LBI or Low Business Impact, as well as MBI or Medium Business Impact, have no need for any expectations.

Use the On-Premises data gateway

Since an on-premises data gateway can import data into Power BI, using one over a personal gateway is recommended and considered best practice. But why is the Enterprise Gateway needed? Because Enterprise Gateway imports nothing, it is more efficient when working with massive datasets.

Use different Power BI gateways for "Direct Query" and "Structured Refresh"

As you are aware, while Scheduled Data Refresh is in effect, using the same gateway for both Live Connection and Scheduled Data Refresh slows down Live Connection performance. To prevent such problems, you should set up distinct gateways for scheduled refresh and live connection.

Test each custom visual on a report to be sure of fast report load time

The custom visualizations that are not certified are not subjected to extensive testing by the Power BI team. Therefore, the custom graphics may not function well when managing massive datasets or sophisticated aggregations. When the selected graphic doesn't work well, what should you do? You can use a different viewpoint to get past the problem. Make sure that the report loads quickly by performing performance tests on each custom visual.

Reduce complicated measures and aggregations in data models

Whenever feasible, move calculated columns and measurements as close to the source as possible to increase the chance of better performance. Additionally, while designing data models with star schema, calculated measures must be created rather than calculated columns.

Import what is needed

When you can keep the model as lean and tight as feasible by importing only the fields that are relevant, why is it necessary to import full datasets? Leaner and longer indexes are desirable when using Power BI on columnar indexes.

Limit the Amount of Data Loaded on the Page

Enhance performance by lowering unnecessary data loads. Use dynamic loading or pagination to handle large data sets efficiently. Putting into practice efficient data loading techniques gets rid of slow report performance and makes sure users have a good experience—especially when working with large datasets. One of the most crucial recommended practices for using Power BI effectively is this one. Applying the necessary filters to the edit query and loading only the necessary data will speed up refresh times and lighten the burden on data platforms like Snowflake, MySQL, and so forth.

Making use of version control systems (VCS) in Power BI

Developers can work with Power BI more effectively by using version control; just follow the instructions. To use version control with Power BI, create a Git repository, a.gitignore file, and stage/commit changes. To work together, push and pull changes, create branches for features and bug fixes, and tag releases, connect to a remote repository. Improve Power BI Service's development and collaboration workflows by including version-controlled assets. VCS falls within the category of power BI design best practices, which enhance developer cooperation and change tracking by offering more control and history management.

Select Storage Mode for Tables Appropriately

You can improve query performance greatly by choosing the appropriate storage mode. To increase efficiency, consider utilizing the "Import" option for large fact tables. The Composite Data Model in Power BI makes connecting to many data sources simple. This makes it possible to easily construct large-scale data models by combining imported and DirectQuery tables. When working with large data sets, choosing the optimal storage method aids in optimizing data retrieval, enhancing query performance and general effectiveness. One of the most important Power BI best practices that must be adhered to is storage selection. I have found that when working with huge models that I use to quickly calculate an item's availability for commerce, we import multiple tables as composite data sources into Power BI and establish links between them. Power BI would crash and become unusable if a massive table containing more than two million records was loaded.

Check well for Referential Integrity for Relationships

Accurate analysis is made possible by establishing clearly defined relationships. Referential integrity tests guarantee the consistency and dependability of the data. Referential integrity checks guarantee the reliability and correctness of table relationships, as well as the integrity of your analysis's output. For instance, in an Ecom configuration, it is possible to have a foreign key connecting the "Orders" and "Customers" tables. By ensuring that every order is linked to an actual client, a referential integrity check helps to avoid data inconsistencies.

Make sure reports and data sources are in the same location

Delay can be reduced by synchronizing reports and data sources. By optimizing data retrieval, hosting both in the same Azure region speeds up the entire report. Co-locating data sources and reports reduces transmission latency, resulting in a faster and more efficient reporting ecosystem. Although many analysts tend to ignore Power BI best practices for datetime variables, it is evident that they can enhance the report's overall stability and reliability.

Make use of hierarchy to drill down and up the chart

Given that Power BI uses hierarchies for both drill-down and drill-up tasks, the user experience is enhanced. Users can drill down from yearly to quarterly or monthly facts in a time-based hierarchy, such as **Year > Quarter > Month,** to gain more in-depth understanding. Conversely, drill-up enables users to return up the hierarchy. Because it makes navigating and analyzing data easier, this hierarchical structure enhances data exploration skills. In companies similar to Instamart, Blinkit, and Zepto, it is crucial to examine the present stock levels of campaign items at the city > store level at various times of the day, such as before 12 PM, after 4 PM, and 10 PM closing stock. A drill down chart can be very helpful in this regard, allowing stakeholders to promptly identify stock outs and make appropriate plans.

Avoid Bi-Directional and Many-to-Many Relationships against High Cardinality Columns

Improve performance by making good use of relationships. In order to avoid processing too much information, take into account many options in complex circumstances. Extensive exploration of many types of linkages and possibilities facilitates more efficient information processing in complex analytical contexts. Relationship management is within the category of Microsoft Power Bi performance best practices, where report performance is examined. Bidirectional and many-to-many relationships (such as countries to state names) can slightly affect the model depending on the cardinality of the dataset, but single-to-one relationships are ideal for indexers to work faster in the backend (e.g., capital city to country mapping). More many-to-many relationships result in more queries processing, which leads to overload in scenarios with high cardinality.

Avoids Making Use of Floating Point Data Types

To prevent precision problems, use data types for whole numbers or decimals. Reliable computations are ensured by using the appropriate data types. Reliability and precision are increased when calculation errors are reduced through the use of precision-appropriate data formats. In order to achieve accuracy in computations, data must be stored in a specific manner. In SQL, many precision point data types, such as NUMBER(38,0), NUMBER(38,5), DECIMAL, INTEGER, etc., are available for optimal computation. You can change the dataset to only use INTEGER or NUMBER(38,0) types if you are certain that the value you are looking for is just a number without a decimal point. Improved memory consumption and hence improved query performance are associated with more appropriate data types. When it comes to better visual and pertinent points, one of the simplest ways I leverage Power BI best practices is efficient floating point number utilization.

Replace the Auto-Generated Date Table with a Custom Date Table in Your Model

You have more control over date-related activities when you use a custom date table. In order to comply with reporting requirements, add extra columns for fiscal quarters and holidays. In most circumstances, as an analyst, you will have to perform calendar-related computations. However, you can increase your flexibility and accuracy by modifying a date table to suit specific reporting requirements. Gaining an awareness of PowerBI best practices opens the door to very simple and successful data analytics. By carefully limiting data visualizations, simplifying data models, and guaranteeing security with Row-Level Security (RLS), I've learned the art of producing powerful reports. Power BI is significantly more stable and efficient when region-specific hosting and Microsoft AppSource-certified visuals are used. These techniques, in conjunction with prudent gateway management and careful assessment of premium images, improve user experience while strengthening the basis for precise and prompt decision-making. If you're a beginner or intermediate professional looking to learn these, your best bet may be to enroll in courses similar to KnowledgeHut Power BI training. One of the keystones that guide professionals toward excellence in Power BI usage, value creation for customers, and cost efficiencies for the business is the implementation of Microsoft Power Bi best practices.

INDEX

E

K

L

S

T

U

Y

Made in the USA
Coppell, TX
13 September 2024

37268178R00151